65-24881 (10-24-66) (2-3-67)

CAMBRIDGE CLASSICAL STUDIES

General Editors

D. L. PAGE   W. K. C. GUTHRIE   A. H. M. JONES

THE
FRONTIER PEOPLE OF
ROMAN BRITAIN

THE
FRONTIER PEOPLE OF
ROMAN BRITAIN

BY

PETER SALWAY

*formerly Fellow of Sidney Sussex College,
Cambridge*

CAMBRIDGE
AT THE UNIVERSITY PRESS
1965

PUBLISHED BY

THE SYNDICS OF THE CAMBRIDGE UNIVERSITY PRESS

Bentley House, 200 Euston Road, London, N.W.1
American Branch: 32 East 57th Street, New York 22, N.Y.
West African Office: P.O. Box 33, Ibadan, Nigeria

©

PETER SALWAY

1965

Printed in Great Britain by The Broadwater Press Ltd
Welwyn Garden City, Hertfordshire

To

GILLIAN, ANNE *and* JANE

... we drank a bottle of wine, to the memory of the founders; then poured some of the red juice into the fountainhead, to the Nymph of the place.

STUKELEY

CONTENTS

CONTENTS

LIST OF ILLUSTRATIONS
TEXT FIGURES

PLATES
At end of book
(Where no acknowledgement is made, photographs are by the author)

PREFACE

To evoke the spirit of the past is as much the function of the archaeologist as of the historian: indeed it is not so much that the functions
of the two are complementary as that they cannot be separated.
The material background is the essential framework without which
an age cannot be understood. In this study of the frontier region of
Roman Britain the frame and canvas are inevitably more complete
than the picture itself. Yet the broken utterances of epigraphy, the
mould of the law and the dim traces of religion are touches of the
brush that build up an impressionistic if faded and cracked picture
which, if viewed too closely, will seem out of focus and incomplete
in detail, but which conveys at least an atmosphere. Moreover, a
knowledge of the Roman style allows us to understand much of
the design. Nor is this metaphor from art inapposite, for we are
dealing with the work of men with the power, knowledge and will
to shape a state according to a definite pattern.

For the most part we can only guess at the thoughts and feelings
of the people who are my subject, but every now and then, in the
wording of a tombstone perhaps, we catch a glimpse of personal
and individual humanity. I shall have cause to go into detail, to
enumerate statistics and to analyse the material remains in the
archaeological manner, yet I hope that it will be clear throughout
that human beings are the essential subject of the inquiry. Indeed it
would be pointless were it otherwise.

That is the ultimate justification for studying any society in the
past. Yet there are other reasons also for investigating this particular
field. Admittedly the civilians of the frontier region can hardly be
considered the highest products of their age. Their art was largely
lamentable, their architecture undistinguished, their culture measured by the standards of their time fairly low, their output of anything above the needs of daily life mostly lost if indeed much ever
existed. Yet it was behind the screen formed by the Roman army
and its dependent civilians that the mighty culture of the Roman
world existed. The perpetuation of the Roman imperial ideal, the

creation of Roman imperial architecture, the development of Roman law into an oecumenical force, the survival of classical art and literature and the spread of the Christian faith could not have happened but for the existence of these people on the perimeter of the empire. Moreover, in themselves they represent for Britain something new: nearly four centuries of a cosmopolitan society with the basic elements of true civilization—an altogether greater magnitude of security, personal freedom, justice, literacy and prosperity than at any previous time or for many centuries to come.

Nor were they people without character. Here were the homes and families of that tough, proud and sometimes turbulent army of Britain that from time to time erupted on to the stage of world politics. In contemplating the relative poverty of their culture and their relative obscurity in the literary picture of the ancient world, we must not underestimate the importance of these formidable people.

Every author with a spark of conscience must make the usual acknowledgements to his mentors and colleagues at this point. I propose to take the rather unusual course of acknowledging first my debt of gratitude to the antiquaries of the past. So much of what they saw and recorded has now disappeared that it is not an exaggeration to say that their observations are a primary source for this book. But their work has more than an informative value. It has been a considerable personal pleasure to visit sites for the same object as these men who so obviously enjoyed what they were doing. Stukeley and Gale who 'laboured hard at the inscriptions [at Housesteads], and made out what we could of them under all disadvantages', or Horsley who interrogated his landlord at Greta Bridge (or, more likely, dutifully listened to the favourite local theory on the ruins) are sympathetic characters to the modern field-archaeologist. I am left in wonder at the prodigious amount these men managed to see before the days of car and aircraft or even of railway. It is easy to dismiss their books as of no importance in the light of modern archaeological advances or to treat them merely as matters of antiquarian interest. Yet not only their observation but also their interpretation is worth serious attention, and on the civil settlements much of their work is exceedingly sound.

Remarkably little has been done in Britain to investigate the civilian population of the frontier. One short but important paper written a quarter of a century ago,[1] notes in a recent paper[2] and an unpublished undergraduate thesis on a fraction of the sites,[3] that is substantially the total. I have, of course, to acknowledge my debt to numerous foreign scholars for their patient work on the frontiers, notably Mommsen, Bohn and Mócsy. Their detailed work was on the continental material, and it has been a considerable part of my task to examine their discussions and to apply the results to the problems of Britain. In the process, it has become clear that this province has much to offer the continental student in return, especially in material securely dated by reliable excavation and from aerial photography. Much is derived from the published reports which here, as in any archaeological study, must be treated as primary sources. Sometimes it has been necessary to re-interpret these in the light of more recent knowledge, a technique which can have useful results if the original work was well done and well reported, though no substitute for re-excavation. In certain instances I have used unpublished reports, notes and verbal information and I am especially grateful to the Archaeology Division of the Ordnance Survey and to Professor Birley for assistance in gaining access to these sources.

Since a main purpose of the book is to assemble the reliable evidence for civilians, particular attention has been paid to eliminating doubtful instances. This has inevitably led to the omission of many sites and inscriptions where the presence of civilians may legitimately be suspected but where the evidence is insufficient for reasonable certainty. The criteria for accepting or rejecting material purporting to represent civilian activity will appear in the course of the inquiry.

Wherever possible I have inspected the site, monument, small

---

[1] Birley, *AA* (4), XII, 205 ff.
[2] Richmond, *Roman and Native in North Britain*, 112 ff.
[3] Merrix, B.A. dissertation, Durham.

find or written source myself and made my own records of it. The illustrations form an important part of the evidence. Two plans (Figs. 5, 8) devised from oblique aerial photographs by a method suggested by Dr J. K. S. St Joseph are included both for their direct relevance and as an indication of a technique which has possibilities outside the immediate subject. Aerial photographs are also reproduced in the plates, and are derived from the collections of the University of Cambridge and of King's College, Newcastle upon Tyne (now the University of Newcastle upon Tyne). Those from Cambridge were taken by Dr J. K. S. St Joseph, Director in Aerial Photography (to whom I am grateful for permission to use them) and are subject to Crown copyright; those from Newcastle were taken by myself, the negatives being the property of the University.

The comparative material from other provinces was largely collected during fieldwork and reading in 1955 and 1956 under the kindly auspices of the Römisch-Germanische Kommission, to whose lately retired Director Professor Gerhard Bersu and his staff I am much indebted. The full co-operation of the majority of the museums and other institutions visited is also much appreciated. It is probably inevitable that many ideas, suggestions and references should emerge in conversation, and wherever possible I have given credit where it is due (though it is often difficult to decide who was responsible for a particular point). To those I have forgotten, I would apologize and recognise my debt.

For detailed help and criticism I owe special thanks to Professors E. Birley, A. H. M. Jones, I. A. Richmond and J. M. C. Toynbee, to Dr J. K. S. St Joseph and Mr J. P. Gillam and, for making the index, to my wife.

The work for this book was carried out with the generous aid of fellowships, studentships and grants from Sidney Sussex College, Cambridge, the University of Cambridge (Sandys, Henry Arthur Thomas and Craven Funds) and King's College, Newcastle upon Tyne (Sir James Knott Fellowship).

CAMBRIDGE *December, 1960*   P. S.

Note. From the necessity of restricting the geographical area dealt with in this book I have not taken into account the central Pennines south of the Stainmore Pass. There can be no doubt that, as with Wales, there is need for a separate study of the civil settlements of that area. A cursory examination suggests that conditions may be found to be rather different from those closer to the frontier line.

The typescript of this book was delivered to the publisher in October 1961. Such modification of the text as has been possible in the proof stages in 1964 and 1965 is signified by the use of square brackets. The proofs of the line drawings were corrected in the course of 1963 and the figures therefore do not take account of additions made to the text in the final stages.

January, 1965   P. S.

ACKNOWLEDGEMENTS

For permission to reproduce illustrations I am grateful to the following: the Air Ministry and the Director in Aerial Photography for plates I, VI, VII, VIII; Alec Tiranti Ltd for plate II (from *Furniture in Roman Britain* by Joan Liversidge); the Editor of the *Journal of Roman Studies* for plate IV(a) and figure 11; the Editor of *Archaeologia Aeliana* for plates III, IV(b), V and figures 5, 8, 10.

I am also grateful to the Controller of H.M. Stationery Office for permission to base figures 1 and 4 on the Ordnance Survey Map of Roman Britain (3rd ed.) and the Ordnance Survey 1,625,000 Physical Map of Great Britain respectively; and to Alec Tiranti Ltd and the Editors of the *Journal of Roman Studies* and *Archaeologia Aeliana* for generously loaning blocks. Kind assistance over illustrations was provided by Dr John Mann, Mr Wilfred Dodds, Dr David Smith, Dr Robert Hogg and Mr David R. Wilson, which I am glad to acknowledge.

LIST OF ABBREVIATIONS

AA *Archaeologia Aeliana*, ser. 1–4, Newcastle upon Tyne.

Acta Arch. Acad. Scient. Hung. *Acta Archaeologica Academiae Scientiarum Hungaricae*, Budapest.

AE *l'Année Epigraphique*, Paris.

Ant. J. *Antiquaries Journal*, London.

Anz. öst. Akad. Wiss. *Anzeiger d. österreich. Akad. d. Wissenschaft: phil.-hist. Klasse*, Vienna.

Arch. Camb. *Archaeologia Cambrensis*, Cardiff.

Arch. Ért. *Archaeologiai Értesitö*, Budapest.

BGU *Aegyptische Urkunden aus den Museen zu Berlin. Griechische Urkunden.*

Black Gate cat. (see Bibliography to Part II, under Collingwood, R. G.)

BM Cotton Iulius F.VI (Camden papers, British Museum, published by F. Haverfield, *CW* (2) XI, 1911, 343 ff.)

Bonn. Jhb. *Bonner Jahrbücher*. Bonn.

Caerleon cat. (see Bibliography to Part I, under Nash-Williams, V. E. and A. H.)

Chesters cat. (see Bibliography to Part II, under Budge, E. A. W.)

CIG *Corpus Inscriptionum Graecarum*, Berlin, 1828–77.

CIL *Corpus Inscriptionum Latinarum*, Berlin, 1863, in progress.

Cod. Just. *The Code* of Justinian.

Cod. Theod. *The Code* of Theodosius.

CW *Transactions of the Cumberland and Westmorland Antiquarian and Archaeological Society*, ser. 1, 2, Kendal.

Dig. *The Digest* of Justinian.

DN *Transactions of the Architectural and Archaeological Society of Durham and Northumberland*, Durham.

Dumfr. & Gall. *Dumfriesshire and Galloway Natural History and Antiquarian Society: Transactions and Journal of Proceedings*, Dumfries.

EE *Ephemeris Epigraphica*, Berlin, 1872–1913.

Gent. Mag. *Gentleman's Magazine*, London, 1732–1922.

Germania *Germania: Anzeiger d. röm.-germ. Kommission d. deutsch. archäol. Inst.* (formerly *Korrespondenzblatt* . . .), Bamberg, Frankfurt a. M.

ILS Dessau, H. *Inscriptiones Latinae Selectae*, Berlin, 1892–1916.

JBAA *Journal of the British Archaeological Association*, London.

JRS *Journal of Roman Studies*, London.

xvii

Lancs. & Ches. *Transactions of the Historical Society of Lancashire and Cheshire*, Liverpool.

LS Bruce, J. C. *Lapidarium Septentrionale, or a Description of the Monuments of Roman Rule in the North of England*, London and Newcastle upon Tyne, 1875.

Latomus Collection *Latomus—Revue d'Études Latines*, Brussels.

Mz. Zeitschr. *Mainzer Zeitschrift: Zeitschrift des Röm.-Germ. Zentralmuseums und des Vereins zur Erforschung der rheinischen Geschichte und Altertümer*, Mainz.

Nat. Hist. Trans. *Natural History Transactions of Northumberland, Durham and Newcastle-on-Tyne*, Newcastle upon Tyne.

NCH *A History of Northumberland* (Northumberland County History), Newcastle upon Tyne, 1893–1940.

Netherhall cat. (see Bibliography to Part II, under Bailey, J. B. and Haverfield, F.)

ORL *Der obergermanisch-rätische Limes des Römerreiches*, Heidelberg, Berlin and Leipzig, 1894–1936.

Philos. Trans. *Philosophical Transactions of the Royal Society*, London.

Philos. Trans, Abridg'd Lowthorp, J. (a series) *The Philosophical Transactions and Collections. . . Abridg'd . . .* , London.

PSAL *Proceedings of the Society of Antiquaries of London*, London.

PSAN *Proceedings of the Society of Antiquaries of Newcastle upon Tyne*, ser. 1–4, Newcastle upon Tyne.

PSAS *Proceedings of the Society of Antiquaries of Scotland*, Edinburgh.

Rav. Ravenna Cosmography (cf. Bibliography to Part I, under Richmond, I. A. and Crawford, O. G. S.).

RCHM Royal Commission on Historical Monuments.

RW (1–3) Bruce, J. C. *Handbook to the Roman Wall*, Newcastle upon Tyne, (1) 1863 (Wallet-book. . .); (2) 1884; (3) 1885.

RW (6) Blair, R. (ed.) Bruce, *Handbook*, (6), Newcastle upon Tyne, 1909.

RW (9) Collingwood, R. G. (ed.) Bruce, *Handbook*, (9), Newcastle upon Tyne, 1933.

RW (11) Richmond, I. A. (ed.) Bruce, *Handbook*, (11), Newcastle upon Tyne, 1957.

RWS (2) Macdonald, Sir George, *The Roman Wall in Scotland*, (2), Oxford, 1934.

Saalb.-Jhb. *Saalburg-Jahrbuch: Bericht des Saalburgmuseums*, Frankfurt a. M.

Tullie House cat. (see Bibliography to Part II, under Haverfield, F.)

YC *Y Cymmrodor*, London.

The inscriptions and sculptured stones are collected in the Appendix. References to these throughout the book are in the form e.g. (15). Aerial photographs in the collection of the Cambridge Committee for Aerial Photography are referred to by their serial numbers with the prefix 'Cambridge'. The detailed site-descriptions (which the general reader will probably wish to skip) assume their reader to have access to the relevant Ordnance Survey six-inch maps.

CHAPTER I

INTRODUCTORY

I. BRITAIN AND ROME

When the Emperor Claudius landed a Roman army on the south coast in A.D. 43 a process was begun which was to transform the face of Britain and give a new direction to its history. For four hundred years Britain was to be a significant part of an empire that embraced most of the known world, transformed from a land of warring, primitive and almost entirely illiterate tribes into a united realm under an administration based on the rule of law, sharing however partially in the universal Greco-Roman culture. I do not wish to derogate the magnificent achievements of the pre-Roman kingdoms of south and east England in the field of art, nor to deny that they achieved a measure of political stability (which the Roman government found useful in the early stages of the conquest), but the difference is fundamental. However chaotic the state of Britain in the post-Roman Dark Ages these facts were never forgotten.

By the seventies of the first century the Roman army had broken the power of the last great tribe in England and was tentatively probing into Scotland. The early policy of employing friendly chieftains as client kings had failed—indeed it had probably never been intended to be more than a temporary expedient—and the process of absorbing the British tribes into the normal framework of Roman provincial administration was well advanced. In the next decade the energetic Governor Gnaeus Julius Agricola not only greatly encouraged the adoption of Roman ways by the Britons but also defeated the Caledonians in battle and made an ambitious attempt to complete the subjection of these islands. The Emperor Domitian, however, decreed otherwise. Probably on considerations of manpower and expense, he decided to hold that part of Britain which was reasonably easy to control and profitable, and to watch but not occupy the Highlands of Scotland. Ireland was left outside the empire. With a few exceptions and some changes in detail future Roman governments endorsed this decision throughout the period of their sway over Britain.

This policy created the frontier region in north Britain which is the scene for this book. The first system of control was based on the two great roads from the south, one through Carlisle, the other through Corbridge, linked by the Stanegate through the Tyne–Solway gap, and on legionary fortresses at York and Inchtuthil. Trajan, in need of troops for his campaigns in other parts of the empire, withdrew the Scottish garrisons and strengthened the Tyne–Solway line. Variations on these two themes form the basis for future policy in the region.

Hadrian and his governor in Britain, Aulus Platorius Nepos, replanned the Tyne–Solway system. Their first scheme envisaged a continuous barrier as a screen to the Stanegate and its forts, the second transferred the whole weight of defence to the Wall itself. Twenty years later the Antonine government, pursuing a general policy of shortening and simplifying frontier lines, re-occupied the Forth–Clyde isthmus and garrisoned southern Scotland. Mounting external and internal trouble in the late second century forced the abandonment of this scheme and a return was made to the Hadrianic line. Then came the first of a number of disasters caused by over-ambitious governors and the pride of the army in Britain. In A.D. 197 Clodius Albinus, pretender to the imperial throne, drew off the frontier garrisons to fight on his behalf in Gaul. The barbarians swept through the deserted frontier posts and destroyed every Roman installation in their way.[1] The victorious claimant for the throne, Septimius Severus, was obliged to buy them off to gain time to prepare a crushing retaliation. The frontier was restored with the addition of a deep protective zone ahead of the old line. This comprised new forts constructed for the employment of the spring-driven artillery coming more and more into use and a new system of patrols. A series of successful campaigns

---

[1] [Some doubts about the date of the late second-century destruction layers have been recently expressed.]

launched by the emperor himself brought the northern tribes to their knees and only his death at York in A.D. 211 saved them from annexation. Peace was established for nearly a hundred years in an age notable elsewhere in the empire for invasion and internal strife.

The difference between the predominantly military north and the largely civil south in the Roman period was emphasized by the Severan division of the country into Upper and Lower Britain— London, Chester and Caerleon falling into the Upper Province, Lincoln, York and all the frontier region into the Lower. The motive was largely political—to secure the loyalty of provincial governors to the central power by making their commands too small to encourage rebellion. Nevertheless, Britain continued to play her part in the cycle of military usurpations. In the second half of the third century the country fell successively into the hands of the separatist 'Gallic Empire' and the independent realm of the renegade admiral Carausius and his lieutenant, murderer and successor Allectus. The latter repeated the action of Albinus in withdrawing the frontier garrisons with the same result, and Constantius Chlorus had both to restore the links with the central administration and to repair the frontier once more. At this period raiding by Saxon and Irish pirates became serious for the first time and a new system of coastal defence had to be evolved to deal with the threat. Yet neither this nor the basic re-organization of the Roman army under the Tetrarchy and its immediate successors greatly altered the character of the northern frontier, for the chief enemy and his tactics remained the same.

Considerable trouble occurred in the region before the middle of the fourth century but it pales into insignificance before the tremendous destruction wrought by the *barbarica conspiratio* of 367 when in unnatural alliance the Picts, Scots and Saxons attacked simultaneously. For the first time the Wall fell when fully garrisoned but it was not in fair fight. The sinister feature of the affair was the treachery of the auxiliary scouts, a symptom of that fatal disaffection in the Roman imperial system which, unlike the internal dynastic struggles, struck at the heart of the empire by destroying the essential cohesive force of loyalty to the imperial idea. Nevertheless, the Roman military machine, still surprisingly resilient, once more drove out the enemy and restored the frontier under Count Theodosius. He seems to have done his work well, for in A.D. 383 Magnus Maximus, plotting an attempt on the throne, was able to make an arrangement with the tribes beyond the frontier to ensure the peace of Britain when for the last time the frontier garrisons were withdrawn. Stripped of its regular troops the life of the region was drastically impoverished, but even so civilized life survived in some places. Further troubles in the north were checked by Stilicho and it is probable that in an attenuated form Roman civilization remained alive in the region until the final withdrawal of imperial authority from Britain at the end of the first decade of the fifth century. This closed the career of Britain as part of the Roman empire and at this point the history of the region, which was now *ipso facto* no longer an imperial frontier, passes out of the sphere of this book and into the province of the Dark-Age historian.

2. THE FRONTIER REGION

The districts with which this study is concerned are those which comprise the area of permanent frontier defence to the provinces of Britain. This is the northern area of Roman Britain (to call it the 'military zone' begs too many questions) which formed a block of territory broadly homogeneous both in the nature of its terrain and in the character of its occupation. Its limits may be defined in Roman terms by the Antonine Wall and its outliers in the north, and by the southern points in the system of communications marked by Scotch Corner, the Stainmore Pass and Overborough (Burrow-in-Lonsdale). This includes southern and central Scotland, Northumberland, County Durham, Cumberland, Westmorland and adjacent parts of Lancashire and Yorkshire. The whole area may conveniently be termed the frontier region.

This definition requires some explanation. The Roman frontier in north Britain had more than one purpose; and its purposes changed in the course of its history; but though the line and form of

4

of agricultural development. Later, the North itself became an important agricultural region, and by the third century the local surplus of produce was sufficient to support a city at York. This process went so far that eventually York itself lay at the centre of an essentially civil region, and the true frontier region lay well to the north.

A glance at the military map of Britain will immediately reveal the fact that for the Roman army Lower Britain fell into the regions I am postulating. This is clearest on the east. Here Catterick is the last town north in the predominantly civil region, and henceforth there are more important military sites than civil. South of Scotch Corner there is not a permanent fort for fifty miles; north of Scotch Corner a fort, fortlet or signal station appears every few miles. That so much military activity should occur so far from the actual line may seem strange, but is explained by the dual nature of the system. Though its primary purpose was the prevention of invasion from the north, it was also involved with a very serious problem of internal security. The Pennines and the Lake District held the defeated and discontented remnants of the Brigantes, as dangerous to the peace of Britain as the enemy outside. Nor was it even possible to hold a secure frontier against the northern barbarians without tackling the problem of these dangerous regions behind. The answer was the normal Roman method, a cordon of forts, signal stations and roads around the dangerous areas to control the inhabitants of each and prevent them combining in revolt. This system had the effects of securing the peace of the frontier region itself and of providing a defence in depth behind the forward line.

The dual nature of the system explains too the boundary chosen for this book in the centre and on the west. In the Stainmore area the forts both guard the trunk route and form part of the ring round the northern Pennines. This ring also protected the agricultural lowlands of the Eden valley on the west and County Durham on the east, essential to the support of the military and civilian population of the region. The functions of this ring were basic to the internal security of the frontier zone.

the defence altered, the essential object at all times was the protection of the lowland zone of Britain and its outliers from incursions from the north. It was considered impracticable to conquer and hold the whole of Scotland, though it is indeed a question whether an all-out attempt to defeat and absorb the Highland tribes might not in the long run have proved cheaper and more efficient—a thought which probably occurred to the perspicacious Emperor Septimius Severus. Domitian represented the regular attitude of Roman governments when he recalled Agricola from his ambitious attempt to complete the total conquest of the British Isles.

Until the late third century the main threat to Roman Britain was always from the north, and at least till the end of the fourth it remained substantial. We are therefore justified in seeing the military organization of the North as the main frontier defence of the country. The northern part of Roman Britain, which became in the third century the separate province of Britannia Inferior, falls into two regions, militarily, topographically and, as will later appear, politically. The headquarters of the army in the area and the capital of the Lower Province lay at Eburacum, at the heart of the peaceful Vale of York, a hundred miles south of the nearest point on the actual frontier line. At first sight this may seem odd, for it is unusual in Roman military practice, but the reasons are sound and in part historical. In the early days of the conquest the major problem was the control of the Brigantes who occupied most of northern England, but whose centre lay in the Vale of York. From York both the central Pennines and the hills of the East Riding could be controlled, while any large-scale movement southwards across the Humber or east into the territory of the civilized tribe of the Parisi could be checked. Moreover there were important reasons of supply. The 5,000–6,000 men of a Roman legion in themselves constituted a serious problem for the commissariat, while the auxiliaries in the outlying forts vastly complicated the problem. York was a particularly suitable centre for two reasons. In the early stages of the scheme it was possible to supply it by water via the Car Dyke canal system, the Trent and Ouse from the Fens, which were taken in hand in the second century as a vast new area

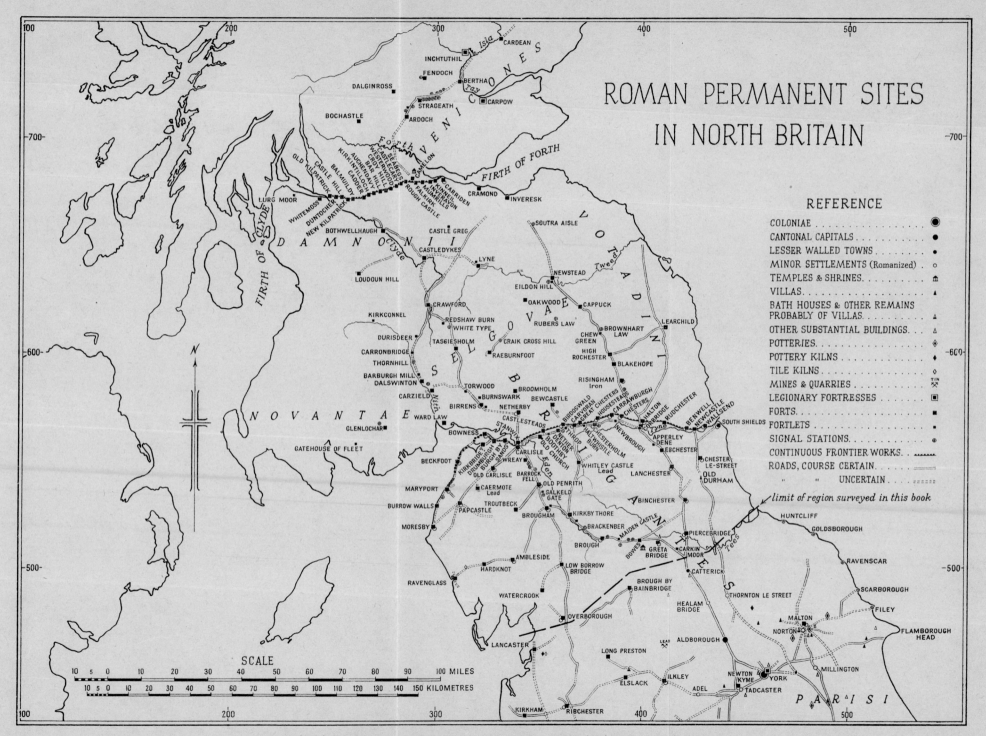

ROMAN PERMANENT SITES IN NORTH BRITAIN

REFERENCE

COLONIAE	◉
CANTONAL CAPITALS	●
LESSER WALLED TOWNS	●
MINOR SETTLEMENTS (Romanized)	○
TEMPLES & SHRINES	⏛
VILLAS	▲
BATH HOUSES & OTHER REMAINS PROBABLY OF VILLAS	◬
OTHER SUBSTANTIAL BUILDINGS	△
POTTERIES	◈
POTTERY KILNS	◆
TILE KILNS	◇
MINES & QUARRIES	⛏
LEGIONARY FORTRESSES	▣
FORTS	■
FORTLETS	▪
SIGNAL STATIONS	⊕
CONTINUOUS FRONTIER WORKS	▪▪▪▪▪
ROADS, COURSE CERTAIN	═══
" " UNCERTAIN	═══

limit of region surveyed in this book

SCALE

10 5 0   10   20   30   40   50   60   70   80   90   100 MILES

10 5 0   10   20 30 40 50 60 70 80 90 100 110 120 130 140 150 KILOMETRES

Fig 1 *(after the Ordnance Survey Map of Roman Britain (Third Edition), with modifications)*

Further south is another set of forts—Brough-by-Bainbridge, Long Preston, Elslack, Ilkley, Ribchester and others—but their problem is the different one of control of a district difficult but not directly threatening the frontier of Britain as a whole. Their communications are with York and Chester and not with the frontier: even Brough-by-Bainbridge has not yet been proved to be linked by road with the Stainmore Pass. It seems reasonable to surmise that these forts formed a separate subdivision in the Northern Command, even as those of East Yorkshire must have done.

West of the Stainmore–Carlisle road the Lakes posed a problem similar to the northern Pennines and the answer was the same. There were complications in that the dangerous area threatened areas of lowland both in the north (the Cumberland Plain) and on the southern fringe of the region around the rim of Morecambe Bay and, in course of time, further difficulty occurred in the vulnerability of this bay to seaborne raiders from Ireland. This coast was from the first a source of worry to the Romans and, unlike the eastern seaboard, was protected by an extension of Hadrian's Wall. In the late-Roman period intensification of the threat from the sea led to strengthening of this soft underbelly of the frontier region by a new base at Lancaster. The defence of this district— Lancaster, Overborough, Low Borrow Bridge and Watercrook— hangs together as a southern outlier of the frontier system, but south of the Lune and into the Forest of Bowland we are in a region essentially concerned with the internal security of the province rather than the holding of its northern frontier.

3. THE PEOPLE AND THEIR SETTLEMENTS

This is intended to be a study of the processes and products of Romanization, of the impact of Rome on the British frontier region and the place of the civilian in the Roman system in that area. I shall therefore be chiefly concerned with those people who were recognizably Roman. The criterion must be of culture, not race, for there is neither cause to believe that the tribesmen consciously rejected Roman culture from nationalistic motives nor possibility of considering the civilian population in the Roman period as a simple mass of subjected Britons. Indeed, it will appear later that it was an amalgam of people drawn from all over the Roman world. An awareness of the region as part of the empire must lie behind all investigation of its problems if they are fully to be understood. The local features of the region are particularly interesting, but they are often unintelligible without reference to other provinces or the empire as a whole, or, if intelligible in their local context, their full significance is nevertheless lost.

In most of the frontier provinces it is difficult or impossible to draw clear distinctions between the various types of settlement, for they show an infinite number of shades from the humblest homestead or village to the *municipium* and the *colonia*. It is fortunate for the present purposes that on the British frontier it is possible to make a practical division on the basis of Romanization and prosperity between the native homesteads derived from pre-existing patterns and the new and essentially urban (if sometimes miniature) settlements which developed under Roman rule.

It is true that the influence of Roman culture is to be seen in a few of the native settlements. In the one as yet unique instance of Old Durham such a place acquired some of the luxuries common in the countryside further south, and it is clear that the presence of the army and a growing urban population stimulated the multiplication of the native settlements, permitted a very limited degree of Romanization in the form of cheap goods and possibly stimulated some improvements in building technique and design. The exclusion of detailed examination of these sites in this study is due partly to practical considerations. The urban settlements themselves are a type which deserves comprehensive treatment, which can only be given within the limits of this book by sacrificing some of the other aspects of civil life.

The 'Roman' civil occupation of this region falls naturally into three divisions—the official, semi-official and purely private. Under the first heading come the non-military activities of the imperial government and the operations of such local administrations as had received a limited autonomy from Rome. The semi-official category includes the civil people officially attached to the army and its officers. All other civilian activity can be classed as private. This study, however, will be especially concerned with a slightly different distinction: between on the one hand those civilians resident or carrying on business in towns and the urban agglomerations round forts and on the other such persons as were permitted to live in official buildings inside or attached to military establishments. The latter group included the *familiae* of fort commandants, visiting agents of the imperial government and other suitably accredited persons, the presence of whom at a military site does not prove the existence of a civil village, as distinct from the normal extra-mural buildings of the fort. Such official extra-mural buildings, it must be emphasized, are an integral part of the establishment and are placed outside the defences as a matter of convenience. Nor can the private activities of the army, such as the religious monuments dedicated by soldiers or their cemeteries, be classed as civil, except when they involve civilians—wives, children, servants and friends.

On the purely civil and private side of the division lie the traders, craftsmen, their workpeople, servants and families, gatherings of civilians for commercial or religious purposes and all manifestations of civil local government. Ex-servicemen and their families are clearly civil, and it seems reasonable to class with them the dependants of 'other ranks', for these, even when recognized by the government, continued to live in private houses outside the forts. The presence of any of these classes can be taken as evidence of a civil town or village, however impermanent it may have been. For any particular site we must therefore ask two questions: were there any civilians there, and, if so, did any of them live in an extra-mural settlement?

4. 'VICUS', 'CANABAE' AND 'CONSISTENTES'

The greater part of the considerable literature on such settlements has concentrated upon those civil communities which gathered around the legionary fortresses, for they are both larger and better-documented than those groups that lived alongside the smaller forts of auxiliaries and legionary vexillations. This concentration of interest has obscured one important point, that despite frequent modern use of the term *canabae* when referring to the smaller settlements it cannot be shown that the Romans themselves employed it in the same manner. Ten, or possibly twelve, places are known to me to possess civil settlements epigraphically recorded as *canabae*.[1] All the located sites had legionary fortresses except for Lyon, and there it has recently been suggested that the reference is to a civil settlement attached to the special unit of urban troops whose status was comparable to that of legionaries.[2]

In many cases the settlements are specifically entitled *canabae legionis*,[3] while others are often mentioned with variations on the phrase *cives Romani consistentes ad legionem*. . . . One stone contains the phrase *c.R. leg. XIII* which can only refer to the *canabenses*.[4] The term *canabenses* itself is used on several occasions and at different sites.[5]

Since the Romans themselves apparently confined the use of *canabae* as a name for extra-mural settlements to those alongside legionary fortresses or special stations, it is clear that we should not apply it to those outside the normal small forts. Moreover, since the Romans drew this distinction between the two types of settlement, we should not expect necessarily to find the same organization and development in each. Caution is therefore required in using the evidence of legionary civil settlements to understand the smaller settlements.

In the British frontier region only four inscriptions provide evidence of what the inhabitants of the civil settlements collectively

[1] Mainz, CIL, XIII, 6730; Strasbourg, CIL, XIII, 5967; Bonn, ILS, 9450; Aquincum, CIL, III, 10548; Troesmis, CIL, III, 6166; Durostorum, CIL, III, 7474; Viminacium, CIL, III, 14509; Apulum, CIL, III, 1100; Lyon, ILS, 7030; Regensburg, ILS, 7111 (interpretation disputed) and two referring to unknown sites—CIL, III, 4850 (from Virunum) and Bonn. Jhb. 154, 137 (from Gelduba).

[2] *Acta. Arch Acad. Scient. Hung.* III, 179, n. 5. Alternatively, it can be argued that the inscriptions (which refer to the *negotiatores vinarii Lugduni in canabis consistentes* (ILS, 7030, 7490) and a civilian *qui gessit in canabis*) have no reference to an extra-mural settlement but refer solely to the warehouses (*canabae*) of merchants.

[3] Troesmis, Durostorum, Apulum, Viminacium and both the unknown sites.

[4] CIL, III, 1158, Apulum.   [5] E.g. CIL, III, 10336.

called themselves. The *vicani Vindolandesses* appear at Chesterholm
(32), the *vik(anorum) mag(istri)* at Old Carlisle (80), the *vicani con-
si(s)tentes Castel(lo) Veluniate(nsi)* at Carriden (26) and an act done
d(ecreto) vica(norum) at Housesteads (65).

Vicus is a general term for a small settlement, *vicani* for its inhabitants. The words occur both in purely civil contexts[1] and as
above in the settlements outside forts. The terms sometimes refer
to the whole settlement, as at Vindonissa in A.D. 79,[2] sometimes to
sections or wards of larger settlements.[3] The Mainz example is of
particular interest since it shows that (though *canabae* is not used of
the small settlements) *vicus* can be used outside legionary fortresses
to refer to wards of *canabae*. The dates of these two inscriptions
prove that the terms in use in the first century persisted in the third.
In essence a *vicus* is a much smaller settlement than the *canabae*.
Where we find *vicani* applied in general at a fortress site it may just
mean vaguely the people who live in the *vici* of the *canabae* but perhaps implies more precisely that the settlement was still small.

The precision of the Carriden inscription is most welcome. The
nearest approach to a parallel that I can find is an inscription referring to Mainz-Kastel (where a small fort guarded the bridge
across the river to Mainz), dedicated by *vicanis veteribus consistenti-
bus Castel(lo) Mattiac(orum)*.[4] These are the inhabitants of the normal
extra-mural settlement (and reappear as *vicani vici veteris* on ILS,
7094, after A.D. 238), and as such are distinct from the *hastiferii* (sic)
sive pastor(es) consistentes kastello Mattiacorum or *hastiferi civitatis
Mattiacor(um)*, an unusual cantonal levy[5] recorded in 224 and 236.

The term *consistere* occurs frequently and is of considerable interest. It is used sometimes with reference to Roman citizens living
away from their places of origin, whether within the empire as
incolae or on foreign soil. This is clearly the sense of ILS, 1362a
on which the dedicators give themselves as *cives Romani (e)x Italia
et aliis provinciis in Raetia consistentes*. Such societies of Roman

---

[1] As at Brough-on-Humber, under Antoninus Pius, *JBAA* (3), VII, 1 ff.
[2] CIL, XIII, 5195.
[3] E.g. in A.D. 230 at Heddernheim, the centre of a *civitas* (CIL, XIII, 7335) or in the
canabae at Mainz ten years earlier (CIL, XIII, 6688).
[4] ILS, 7085: *Mz. Zeitschr.* 48/9, 70 ff.   [5] ILS, 7095.

citizens abroad, chiefly merchants, existed long before the Principate. It was doubtless the mercantile associations of the term *consistere* which caused it to be applied to the inhabitants of the extramural settlements (compare the *negotiatores vinarii* of Lugdunum). It came to have a general sense, as at Aquincum: *vet(erani) et (cives) Romani consistentes*[1] (Trajanic); *c.R. et consisstentibus in canabis Aelis leg. XI Cl.*[2] (A.D. 138/161). CIL, III, 10548, from the same settlement, is a legal curiosity but is of interest in demonstrating an attitude of mind which thought of the civil settlement as the exact opposite of a place of temporary residence. It is a tombstone recording the death of a Roman citizen whose place of origin is given as *cana(bis)*. Taking this with his tribe (probably *Po(llia)* rather than *Po(mptina)*) it seems that he was enfranchized but illegitimate. There is no reason to think that his father was a soldier, for the sons of such often give their place of birth as *castris*. He was therefore a pure *canabensis*. It is important to note that for practical purposes the distinction between such local products and *incolae* like the *cives Agrip(p)inenses Transalpini* who assisted this citizen's wife and brother in the erection of his tomb was disappearing. Such a feeling encouraged the tendency for the communal organization to take root, for the expatriate merchant *conventus*, the ancient equivalent of the Hanseatic Steelyard, to admit others dwelling in the settlement and, by basing itself on the qualification of residence rather than profession, take on the appearance and functions, if not the authority, of a sub-division of the Roman state.

The formal distinction between the local and the resident foreigner is not the only one found in the settlement. Indeed, the inscriptions show that several different types of people could *consistere*. This is demonstrated quite plainly in the Antonine epigraphy of the Dobrudja: *c(ives) R(omani) et Bessi consistentes vico* . . .[3]; *veterani et c.R. et Bessi consistentes*. . . .[4] Sometimes peregrines are included in such assemblages.[5] There is no reason to think that the phrases in these inscriptions in fact describe a single set of people, who were, for example, veterans, Roman citizens (which they would be, any-

---

[1] CIL, III, 3505.   [2] ILS, 2475.   [3] ILS, 7180.   [4] *AÉ*, 1924, nos. 142–6.
[5] As Sherwin-White has pointed out (*The Roman Citizenship*, 211).

how) and Bessi all at once—though some may well have been. The numerous references to *veterani et cives Romani* might mean just this, were there not the clear evidence of the reverse contained in ILS, 2475: *c.R. et consisstentibus in canabis.* . . .[1]

Having demonstrated how there can be a number of groups in a settlement, I must hasten to add that this does not mean that the verb *consistere* can only occur where there are such distinct groups. This is made absolutely certain by ILS, 6885, where an additional phrase was required when it was desired to emphasize that there were two distinct groups: *veterani et pagani consistentes aput Rapidum* who were . . . *intra . . . eundem m(u)rum inhabitantes.* Thus the basic meaning of *consistere* is simply 'to live together', *vicani consistentes* means individuals living together in a *vicus*, and if the verb develops any technical sense it is of living together in this (to a Roman) rather peculiar fashion in a community that exists in a practical sense as a civil settlement but has no very certain place in the hierarchy of municipal institutions.

5. THE DATING OF THE CIVIL SETTLEMENTS

The evidence for dating individual settlements in the British frontier region is presented below but it will be convenient here to summarize the results, since these provide a chronological framework within which the discussion of the civil life of the region may be conducted and a basis of observed fact to which the more theoretical aspects of the study may be referred.

A comparison of the numbers of civil settlements which can be definitely allotted to particular periods immediately creates the impression that they first appeared in the second century, increased considerably in quantity in the third century and continued strong in the fourth. [There seems no doubt that along the Wall the Severan obliteration of the Vallum,[2] allowing civil development

---

[1] Such cases as the three brothers *c.R et Taunenses* (CIL, XIII, 7335) are irrelevant, for they merely record the desire of Roman citizens, when *incolae*, to specify their family homes. Indeed, these men go on to emphasize the point, for they explain how they come to be Taunenses *ex origine patris.*

[2] [For the Vallum and its problems see the important unpublished Durham thesis by Dr B. Swinbank.]

13

right up to the Wall-forts and reflecting that emperor's readiness to go as far as possible to retain his popularity with his troops characteristic of this new age, was a major factor in the growth of the substantial stone-built *vici* which are a prominent feature on the air photographs of the Wall and are extensively recorded by the antiquaries. But Mr R. E. Birley's recent excavations at Housesteads remind us that we may expect to find at other Wall-sites timber and stone buildings of the second century, south of the Vallum and outside the prohibited zone. Away from Hadrian's Wall at forts where there was no physically delimited prohibited zone there are clear signs of *vici* beginning in the second century, for example at Chesterholm, Brough-under-Stainmore and Old Carlisle. First-century inscriptions at Ilkley, not far south of our region, emphasize that the later Roman period did not monopolize such settlements. If in our present very imperfect state of knowledge the greater amount of civil occupation seems to come in the later period, the answer is likely to have something to do with the fact that the measures taken in late Antonine and Severan times to suppress opposition and strengthen the military system in the region seem to have been successful in securing internal peace as well as protection against attack from without.]

After the *barbarica conspiratio* there is at present only one extramural settlement in which there is even a hint of occupation—Piercebridge—and the position of this station on the southern edge of the region, as well as its unusual military features, suggest that it may not be typical. The apparent general absence of post-367 occupation has long been held to support the view that after that war the civil population moved into the forts, now garrisoned with a wholly peasant-like militia, and that the stations took on the appearance of the fortified towns of the late Rhine–Danube *limes*. Behind this theory is the occurrence of additional buildings in certain forts at the time of the Theodosian reconstruction.[1] Nevertheless, it is abundantly clear that a demand for extra accommodation

---

[1] Housesteads (*AA* (2), xxv, 241 ff.; *AA* (4), IX, 223 ff.); Chesterholm (*AA* (4), VIII, 195 ff.; IX, 217); Chesters (*RW* (11), 94); and alterations in function of some buildings (e.g. *AA* (4), XIII, 225 ff.; *AA* (2), xxv, 223 ff.).

within a fort could be the result of purely military needs caused by the introduction of a different type of unit (for example, the Constantian conversion of storehouses at South Shields into quarters for N.C.O's.).[1] It will clearly be necessary to learn more about the form and requirements of the Theodosian units on the Wall before any certainty can be reached in the interpretation of these changes in the fort.[2]

On the other side, there is practically no evidence to judge whether any considerable part of the Romanized civil population in the region survived the war. Professor Richmond has recently underlined the fact that nothing is known of the origins of the Theodosian garrisons,[3] and the families that doubtless accompanied them may have had no connexion with the pre-367 *vicani*. Negative evidence is notoriously unsafe, but I am inclined to suspect that the shopkeepers and craftsmen were not attracted back by the new garrisons, whose lower standard of life cannot have been promising for trade. At Piercebridge and Corbridge, however, there may still have been regular troops, and the former probably remained an agricultural centre on the fringe of a rich area. Moreover, I shall show later that there is good legal reason for thinking that the private citizen without military connexions would be excluded from military property, even at this period, and in that uncertain age few civilians are likely to have risked life on the frontier except in the two walled towns of Corbridge and Carlisle, or well back and under a strong garrison at such places as Piercebridge.

There is therefore some reason to believe that the civil population of the Theodosian period was different both in composition and in habitat from the preceding periods, but it cannot be too much emphasized that the evidence is inconclusive. Too few *vici* have

[1] *AA* (4), XI, 94 ff.

[2] The building blocking the south gate at Housesteads, which seems to have been the origin of the theory (*AA* (2), xxv, 241 f.) was later proved modern (*PSAN* (4), VIII, 191 ff.). One piece of a type of evidence suggesting, but not proving, women in barracks (infant burials) comes from outside the frontier region and was dated by the excavator *before* 367, at a period when it is not suggested that this was a general practice. It probably represents some quite exceptional occurrence (Corder, *The Defences of the Roman Fort at Malton*, 67). [Infant burials were also found in an interval tower at Chesters.]

[3] *Roman and Native in North Britain*, 125.

yet been excavated on sufficient scale to be sure that the lack of post-war occupation is regular and the investigation is likely to be hampered by the inevitably fragmentary condition of the topmost levels of sites and the probability that late *vicus* buildings would be at least as insubstantial as those in the forts.[1]

The last period of all, that following the withdrawal of troops by Magnus Maximus in A.D. 383, is if possible even more obscure. The civil populations attached to the forts are hardly likely to have remained when both the family and economic motives for their presence were withdrawn. Nor is there any evidence to suggest that they did. Of course, there are signs of sub-Roman occupation —Dark-Age princelings at Netherby and Old Carlisle, a church to St Martin at Old Brampton, the tombstone of Brigomaglos at Chesterholm—but the most likely explanation is that some of the rulers of the sub-Roman North had the good sense to make use of existing fortifications. It is not suggested that the region was de-nuded of population: the native sites continued in their old ways and the area was to provide a rich field for the missionaries of the insular church. But that the essentially urban life of the *vici* sur-vived, even if it had recovered after 369, is both unproven and unlikely. Only at Corbridge, where the civil settlement had the rare distinction of its own substantial defences and where the civil population had perhaps grown big enough in proportion to the troops to stand economically on its own, is there any indication of civil activity after 383. How long the troops remained is uncertain, but the occupation of Corbridge as a town can be carried down to the end of the century.[2] Yet even Corbridge cannot be shown to have survived the final withdrawal of the Roman army from Brit-ain, and it may well be that the collapse of administration and de-fensive power behind, combined with the moving of the friendly Votadini from in front, dealt the last blow to the crumbling fabric of Roman civilization in the North.

[1] *AA* (4), XI, 97; *CW* (2), XXX, 171.
[2] Carlisle, the other walled town, may have had a similar history, but there is no direct evidence and it is impossible to know whether its existence as a living city in the seventh century is a matter of survival or revival.

CHAPTER II

THE PEOPLE: AN ANALYSIS

1. THE ORIGINS OF THE POPULATION

The civil settlements of the British frontier display no such simple composition as in the well-known *vici* of the Dobrudja: *cives Romani et Bessi*. Information on the original nationality of the *vicani* can only be based on analysis of the inscriptions. Unfortunately this limits the inquiry to the more prosperous members of the community able to afford a tombstone or a dedication. Yet the range between the memorial of Regina (107) and that of, say, Sudrenus (45) or Tancorix (83) is practically as great as between the best and worst houses in a settlement such as Housesteads, so it is reasonable to infer that the epigraphic habit went fairly far down in the social scale.

Of the *vicani* proper, approximately 50 per cent are Celtic or people whose nationality is not disguised by the adoption of purely Roman names. This does not necessarily imply a very large local element. Some certainly were from Celtic provinces overseas, e.g. (10) or the south of Britain (107). Rather more than a third of the names are from the western provinces or Italy, the remainder being from the eastern parts of the empire. Persons of specifically Germanic origin make up about one-fifth of the people with identifiable nationality.

Perhaps the most interesting feature is that the known *vicani* are almost equally divided between those whose names are purely Roman, those possessing some Roman elements and those wholly non-Roman. Of the last group less than a half are Celtic (less than a sixth of the total). Some non-Romans added Latin elements on receiving the citizenship—for example L. Novellius Lanuccus (49) or his ancestor. Even in families without the franchise the same conscious Romanization can be traced. At Old Penrith the Celtic Avo erected a monument on the death of his Romanized son

17

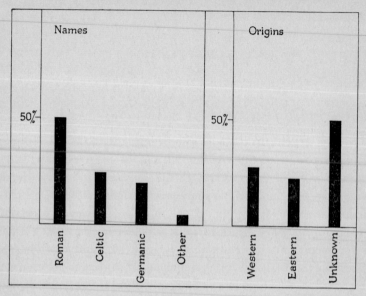

Fig. 2

Aurelius (92)—and in doing so incidentally displayed a surprising grasp of Latin idiom. Not a word of the Celtic language is written anywhere in these settlements. These people consider themselves Roman and strive to follow Roman manners, and even so British and peregrine a couple as Annamoris and Ressona at Brougham produced a creditable if simple Latin memorial for their child (14). Only those who are away from their homeland make any reference to it (e.g. 20, 78, 107). There is in fact absolutely no evidence for anything but the most wholehearted desire on the part of the heterogeneous population of the *vici* to be considered Roman, at least in public.

2. RELIGION

The cosmopolitan and Romanized nature of the civilian population is well illustrated by its religious monuments, though to analyse the religious beliefs and practices is made difficult by the same factors that have complicated those other aspects of this study which are chiefly based on epigraphy—the facts that only the more prosperous are likely to record their beliefs in concrete form, and that where no status is given for the erector of a particular monument it is often impossible (in the case of men) to be sure that a civilian is involved. Dedications by persons demonstrably civilian are far fewer than those of the military, and religious buildings are all but non-existent. The operation of chance in discovery of religious monuments is thus far more likely to result in a distorted picture than if the total body of material were larger. It will be hazardous to draw general conclusions, but it seems worth while to present some analysis of the material at present available.

The appendix of civil inscribed and sculptured stones includes twenty-four religious dedications.[1] Purely Roman deities are represented by Fortuna (including herself in the guises of Fortuna Servatrix, Sancta Fortuna and Fortuna Augusta), Iuppiter Optimus Maximus (thrice), Vulcan (twice), Hercules, Silvanus Pantheus and Isis.[2] The imperial cult appears not only in the form of Fortuna Augusta but also as the Numina Augustorum and Virtus Augusta, though never as a direct dedication to a living or dead emperor. Eastern deities are twice recorded—Iuppiter Dolichenus and Heracles Tyrios.[3] The western provincial area is not unnaturally better represented, thrice by local nymphs, once by a curious conflation of Celtic and classical in the Matres Parcae, and by the wholly un-Roman Sattada, the Veteres (Huitris), the Genii Cucullati and Belatucadrus.

Some further information emerges on examining the dedicators. These include four communal associations of civilians, six men and fifteen women. Persons with Roman names made five dedications to Roman deities, four to western non-Roman and one to an eastern god. East Mediterranean people were responsible for two to

---

[1] 4, 9, 11, 16, 23, 26, 29, 32, 39, 46, 47, 54, 60, 66, 68, 70, 71, 79, 80, 81, 82, 95, 96, 97. (The appendix omits dedications by people of uncertain status, many of whom were probably civilians.)

[2] A Roman goddess since her official reception by Caligula on the basis of a decision of the Second Triumvirate.

[3] Also Astarte, dedicated by a *probable* civilian, CIL, VII, p. 97.

Roman deities, one to an eastern and one to an unknown. Western provincials, however, kept rigidly to Celtic or Romano-Celtic cults. Nor is it surprising that those with Roman names should be the most catholic in their religious tastes, easterners second and westerners least of all. The Roman-named group must include many of provincial or barbaric origin or descent, but neither of the other groups is likely to have possessed any of origin alien to itself. The eastern people are naturally second, for every one was *ipso facto* an expatriate living in a new cultural atmosphere and more likely to be emancipated by education and the breaking of local ties from his ancestral religion. A similiar list compiled in an eastern province should produce the same relation in reverse between eastern and western people.

The western group must have included a considerable proportion of locals and people from provinces of similar cultural background. Possibly a matter of chance, but perhaps indicative of comparatively greater wealth among the immigrants than among the locals, is the total absence of dedications by civilians to the local deities Maponus, Cocidius and Brigantia.[1] Purely native religion is hardly represented, and the explanation is perhaps to be found in the fact that the epigraphic form of dedication is Mediterranean, only likely to be common in the Roman-type settlements where the inhabitants were no longer purely native in culture. Only the strange altar to Sattada by the curia Textoverdorum (4) seems to represent a genuine example of local tribal religion, a communal dedication by a clan gathered in the Celtic *tuath*. Yet even there the form is Roman, the language is Roman and the altar is of normal Roman type. There is every reason to suspect that the leaders of the tribe were Romanized and their religion already taking a Roman tinge. It may be that, if there were any natives Romanized in other respects who retained their native religion pure, there can be no way of detecting them, since they would not have employed Roman forms for their religious expression; but it is perhaps more likely that those natives who become recognizably Romanized adopted Roman religious forms as an integral part of their Roman-

[1] [The exception seems to be Belatucadrus.]

ization, while retaining a preference for deities of Romano-Celtic origin.

In a few cases the dedications shed some light on the occupations of the dedicators. The relative frequency of Vulcan among the deities popular with the communal organizations of *vici* will later be noted in connexion with the industrial activities of the *vicani*. Similarly the altar of the archpriestess Diodora (39) and its twin to Astarte has suggested a considerable eastern element in the town of Corbridge, probably merchants like the Palmyrene Barates (43). Dedications by citizen women of Mediterranean origin to deities normally associated with military and official circles (70, 71, 79, 95) arouse suspicion of association with the household of a fort commandant. These households are also represented by the dedications of freedmen (9, 60 and probably 97) and were probably, like the private relationships of the lower ranks with natives, a significant factor in the import of religious forms and ideas from overseas.

It would be improper to leave the subject of religion without mentioning the great goddess of the region, Brigantia herself.[1] The reason for leaving her to the end is that there are no absolutely attested civilian dedications to her, but there can be little doubt that she represented the personified spirit of the greater part of the frontier region. The political background for the surprising upsurge in her worship in the third century will be matter for later discussion but it is pertinent to our present business to note here the very Roman nature of her cult. The fact that its main flowering did not come till the third century is significant, and her manifestations as a mural-crowned, Minerva-like figure identified first with Victory and later possessing African and Syrian attributes underlines her imperial and cosmic character. At least one of her worshippers was a Celt and some seem to have been persons recently enfranchised, but the dedicators are largely Roman and reach as far up the social scale as a legionary centurion and even a procurator. All the evidence points to the purely Roman creation of a cantonal deity and none to a survival from Celtic religion.

[1] *AJ*, xcvii, 36 ff.

3. OFFICERS' FAMILIES

The civilian population has so far been presented as a whole, but we can now subdivide it. The wives, children and servants of officers form a small but important class. These families fall into two groups, divided by the fact that legates, auxiliary commanders, legionary tribunes and other fairly senior officers were allotted houses of considerable size within the military establishments.[1] Centurions and equivalent ranks, however, were given quarters sufficient only for themselves. Their families when they accompanied them on a posting must have lived outside the fort, and, unlike the families of more senior officers, their presence attested at a site is reliable evidence for the existence of a *vicus*. Yet very few are known in the region[2] and it is probable that this last group was not a major factor in the growth of *vici*.[3]

4. THE POSITION OF WOMEN

Women, *ipso facto* civilian, are well represented in the region. They are no less cosmopolitan than the men and include such persons as the Raetian Titullinia Pussitta (78) and the Greek Aurelia Achaice (40). The former lady (or her heir) proudly recorded her overseas origin, as did the soldier Aurelius Marcus that of his citizen wife (27). The women recorded range from the aristocratic Iulia Lucilla (61), through the middle classes (e.g. 94), to freedwomen (107) and slaves like that of M. Cocceius Firmus.[4]

Soldiers' wives received official cognizance of their existence as early as the reign of Domitian (ILS, 9059). Their position was much improved when under Septimius Severus full legal marriage was allowed. It seems clear that the wives even of private soldiers

---

[1] *Familiae* in this class are recorded with certainty at Birrens, Risingham, High Rochester, Old Penrith, Birdoswald, [Westerwood, *JRS*, LIV, 178.—add. note Jan. 1965], probably at Chesters, and Maryport. [2] Birrens, Piercebridge.

[3] The husband of Aurelia Afra (50) may have commanded a legionary vexillation garrisoning the fort, and she cannot therefore be included under this head. [Professor Birley thinks that centurions' wives were allowed to live in the centurions' quarters in the barrack blocks, citing weaving combs from pre-Hadrianic Corbridge and similar finds from Newstead. More evidence on this point would be welcome.]

[4] Birley, *Roman Britain and the Roman Army*, 51 f.

accompanied them on transfer to another province (53). Other
unions with troops were less permanent, and a soldier in Egypt
refers to the mother of his child as his *hospita*.[1] There must, too,
have been plenty of prostitutes in the British settlements as near any
army, though there is not surprisingly no epigraphic record.

Life cannot have been easy for most women on the frontier.
Their tombstones reveal that even those who survived the perils of
childhood could not on the average expect to live beyond the age
of thirty. However, there were compensations in the fluidity of
the social structure which permitted a slave like Regina to achieve
both her freedom and the wealthy marriage which her magnificent
memorial records (pl. III, a). Very considerable respect and affec-
tion is demonstrated for these women, the *coniuges carissimae* of the
funerary inscriptions.

Independence in their personal affairs is implied by the monuments they commissioned. Typical is the altar dedicated to the
Nymphs (29) by two ladies at Carvoran, more unusual the dedications to Iuppiter Optimus Maximus and Virtus Augusta by Hispana
Hermione (70, 71); while at Corbridge a lady of eastern origin rose
to a senior office in the cult of the Tyrian Hercules (39). This digni-
fied position of women is not surprising in view of their influence
and personal independence both at Rome under the empire and
in Iron-Age Britain.

5. FREEDMEN AND SLAVES IN THE SERVICE OF SOLDIERS

Two special classes of people resident not in the fort but in the civil
settlement were the slaves and freedmen of serving soldiers. As
early as the first century it is clear that the troops had their *familiae*
resident in some provinces near their stations.[2] These must often
have formed part of the population of extra-mural settlements. In
the second century M. Cocceius Firmus, a centurion, seems to have
possessed a slave-woman in the province in which he was serving.
Birley has convincingly identified Cocceius Firmus with one of the

[1] *BGU*, VII, 1690.   [2] Tacitus, *Hist.*, II, 80.

23

same name who served at Auchendavy in the mid-second century.[1] While it is not certain that she was resident near her master's station, the fact that a few civilians are attested on the Antonine frontier makes it just possible.

As early as the mid-first century a freedman appears on a tombstone from a cemetery used also for the burial of legionary veterans.[2] In the early third century troops were legally entitled *domum comparare*,[3] which must include the settling of slaves and freedmen in the civil settlement. Soldiers might engage in business other than agriculture, especially through agents since leave was not granted to troops for the purpose of *negotia privata*.[4] Richmond's suggestion that the freedman Victor (108) (pl. III, b) was managing a business at South Shields for his master, a trooper stationed at Benwell,[5] seems in accordance with the state of the law in the third century.

6. TRADE AND INDUSTRY

There can be no doubt that traders and craftsmen formed an important element in the civil settlements.[6] Some were resident in the *vicus*, supplying the civilian population and the off-duty soldier from small, open-fronted shops like those of Housesteads and Benwell, equipped with such tools of trade as the steelyard whose weight was found at Old Carlisle (pl. IV a).[7] Some were probably middlemen, exchanging for the products from the farms which grouped round the forts the goods required by the local farmers— pottery, nails, salt and similar commodities—like the *negotiatores salsari* (?) *leguminari* (?) *cives Romani* of Vindonissa.[8] Others were more interested in trade with the barbarian beyond the frontier, who might cross to do business in the *vicus*, passing the customs control at such points as the Knag Burn gate or the post of the *beneficiarius consularis*, as at Stockstadt[9] in Germany, or he might be reached by merchant adventurers penetrating into his own lands.

[1] *PSAS*, LXX, 363 ff.   [2] *Acta Arch. Acad. Scient. Hung.* III, 182.
[3] *Dig.* XLIX, xvi, 13.   [4] Vegetius, II, 19.
[5] *The Roman Fort at South Shields*, 13.
[6] Cf. CIL, XIII, 5195, A.D. 79 and 7222, A.D. 198.
[7] *JRS*, XLVII, 203.   [8] CIL, XIII, 5221.   [9] CIL, XIII, 6635, etc.

Just such a project, the dispatch of an argosy perhaps, is the subject of a vow at Bowness (11). Vast quantities of goods passed across the Roman frontiers in this way, into such areas as Scotland[1] and unoccupied Germany.[2]

Some of these men may have been native. Others, like Barates of Palmyra (43, 107) and perhaps Salmanes (2), Flavius Antigonus Papias (20) and the father of the boy at Brough under Stainmore (13), came in search of wealth from the eastern parts of the Roman world. Many of the traders and craftsmen were probably itinerant, like the metal-workers of the later prehistoric ages or the peddlers of mediaeval England. Some men of business primarily served the army. Barates, for example, supplied standards. Performing a public service, these men must have been officially encouraged, and soldiers sometimes took up such work on retirement.[3] At least once the army bought tiles from a civilian factory situated in legionary *canabae* for use in an auxiliary fort, a transaction which probably occurred in the first half of the third century.[4]

The merchants, shopkeepers and craftsmen who supplied the rank and file of the army off duty with its luxuries and entertainment had been considered a nuisance under the republic.[5] With the settling of units into regular stations under the empire they became both more necessary and more tolerated. Monumental masons like the artists of the two South Shields civilian tombstones come into this category, as well as the bronze-smith of the same place who seems to have been making a special type of cross-bow brooch in the fourth century.

The possibility that the army had some of its metal-working done in the *canabae* and *vici* may explain a curious feature of the communal dedications by *vicani*. Frequently (including Chesterholm and Old Carlisle) these are to Vulcan, occurring both in legionary *canabae*[6] and in *vici*.[7] The one from Aquincum is the

---

[1] *PSAS*, LXVI, 277 ff.; *Roman and Native in North Britain*, 69.
[2] Eggers, *Der römische Import im freien Germanien, passim*.
[3] E.g. CIL, XIII, 6677.   [4] *Bonn. Jhb.* 154, 137 ff.
[5] Val. Max. II, 7, 1; Sallust, *Jug.* 45; Caesar, *Bell. Gall.* VI, 37.
[6] E.g. Aquincum, CIL, III, 3505; Regensburg, ILS, 7111.
[7] E.g. Benningen, CIL, XIII, 6454.

earliest reference to the *canabae* there. Egger, commenting on this inscription, suggested that it may have something to do with fire risks among the timber buildings of the *canabae* in the early period, but the persistence of these dedications in civil settlements indicates that they may rather be associated with industry. Vulcan would be particularly appropriate as a communal subject for dedication where smiths and perhaps armourers were important. Admittedly, the half-timbered buildings of Old Carlisle are now known to have been burnt twice, but this was a fate that overcame the stone forts of the North as well. The industrial explanation is the more convincing. On the British frontier metal-working by civil workshops is known from the mid-second century to the fourth.[1] Iron slag is reported from Chester-le-Street, Lanchester and (with coal) from Maryport.

Lime kilns, as at Piercebridge, probably represent military building activity rather than civilian industry, but it is clear that some at least of the kilns, ovens and furnaces recorded in extra-mural buildings must have been used by civil craftsmen (e.g. Buildings A + and F, Benwell; Site XII, Corbridge). The manufacture of pottery in the region is not satisfactorily located, nor is it certain whether the comparatively small amount produced was made by independent civilian potters or by the army,[2] but its existence as an industry is certain.

Many sculptors and epigraphic masons worked in the region and much of their work survives. There is no direct evidence for their identity or status but we may imagine that, though the makers of official inscriptions and statuary and perhaps the votive and funerary monuments of officers were specialist soldiers, the artists responsible for the multitude of civil tombstones and dedications were normally themselves civilians. Not a single work is signed,

---

[1] In the second-century bronze at Stanwix and Brough-under-Stainmore, both apparently supplying military and civil markets, and Kirkby Thore (cf. *Archaeologia*, LXXX, 37 ff.) and South Shields in the third or fourth century.

[2] A probable kiln was noted at Wallsend, two pots with pre-fired dedications to the local goddess at Carrawburgh, apparently unfired pots at Papcastle, and a waster at Carvoran (Bruce, *Roman Wall* (3), 248)—none of this is conclusive evidence. Even at Corbridge the details and status of the potteries are unknown, though the mortar-makers seem to have been civilian.

so the pieces themselves afford the only indications of the nature of their makers. Their quality and character vary enormously. Few need necessarily have been made by a craftsman trained outside Britain, but there are pieces that challenge comparison with the best products of the province. The Lady with a Fan at Carlisle is probably by a British sculptor, but the tombstones of Victor and Regina from South Shields were almost certainly designed if not executed by a Palmyrene, perhaps a relative of the commissioner of the latter piece.[1] In contrast the tombstones of Sudrenus and Ahtehe from Corbridge are so incompetently made that they arouse suspicion of amateur workmanship.

Most of the artists tried to produce purely classical work, though the result is occasionally the pathetic comedy of the funerary banquet relief from Kirkby Thore. A very few works suggest a lingering influence from Celtic traditions in art—mostly small votive heads such as the three with lentoid eyes in the Corbridge Museum. Yet the very fact that the artists were working in stone as their pre-Roman forebears had never done is sufficient proof of the weight of Roman fashion. In such pieces as the Lady with a Fan whose purpose and overall design are wholly Roman it seems fanciful to see in the artist's preference for flowing curves and a certain flatness anything more than a certain Celtic element natural in the northern provinces. Like a very great deal of Roman provincial art this doubtless has some traces of the amalgam of local traditions and tastes with classical fashion, but it would be very surprising if these artists, who were using a new medium in which their masters and models were classical and who were working for a public consisting partly of Romans from other parts of the empire and partly of Britons striving to appear Roman, should have deliberately tried to retain the fashions of a past and discredited age.

7. VETERANS

In the inscriptions from *canabae* and *vici* in the empire as a whole the prominence of military veterans is very notable. It is probable

[1] *AA* (4), xxxvii, 203 ff.

that in some of the smaller settlements they were the *only* Roman citizens before the franchise decree of A.D. 212. Domitian granted the veterans exemption from certain taxes,[1] and from the Severan period they were classed as *honestiores*. They are in general more likely to have been prominent in public life than some of their fellow *vicani*. Their importance in the legionary *canabae* noted by Bohn[2] is true not only of former legionaries[3] but also of ex-auxiliaries. T. Flavius Longinus,[4] a former officer of *ala II Pannoniorum*, was elected (probably under Trajan) not only to the council of the *canabae* of *legio XIII Gemina* but also to those of a colony and a municipality—a truly remarkable achievement which serves to emphasize that the former regular was not the pathetic figure of some ages, but a solid citizen of means recruited into the upper level of society in the civil settlements. In the fourth century he sometimes received special favours at the hands of the government.[5] Even in the field of commerce the veteran sometimes appeared,[6] and Arrian mentions them (τῶν πεπαυμένων τῆς στρατιᾶς) as living in a settlement together with traders.[7]

Although the veterans were regarded in one sense as a military force, a reserve which could release troops for service in the field by its presence in rearward but politically unsafe areas,[8] nevertheless it would be incorrect to see them as more military than civil. They were indeed often banded together in an organization headed by a *curator* as early as the first quarter of the first century A.D., but that does not make them part of the army. These associations seem to have been formed mainly in the chartered towns,[9] or the large legionary *canabae*,[10] and civilians could equally well form similar organizations with a *curator*. Such an association existed at Mainz, where we find the *c.c.R.M.neg.Mog.* It is often not certain whether such an organization contains veterans or not. In the case of this particular inscription (from Finthen near Mainz)[11] the dedicator, L. Senilius Decmanus *q(uaestor) c(urator) c(ivium) R(omanorum)*

---

[1] ILS, 9059.   [2] *Germania*, 10, 32.   [3] E.g. CIL, III, 1008, 1093, 1158.
[4] CIL, III, 1100.   [5] E.g. *AE*, 1937, 232.   [6] E.g. CIL, XIII, 6677—Commodus.
[7] *Periplus*, IX.   [8] Tacitus, *Ann.* XII, 32.   [9] E.g. Turin, ILS, 2464.
[10] CIL, XIII, 6676—if *c.v.* is correctly interpreted as *curator veteranorum*.
[11] CIL, XIII, 7222.

M(ogontiacensium) neg(otiator) Mog(ontiacensis), was probably purely civilian. Yet rather more than a century earlier[1] there is a record of a *veteranus leg. XVI curator civium Roman(orum) Mogontiaci*. The only explanation can be that, although the veterans could form their own ex-service organization, they could also take part in and even lead the normal civilian associations with whose other members they were also associated in business and private life.

Ex-service clubs were not normally formed in the auxiliary settlements. As the veterans were among the most prominent and sometimes the only citizens there, such clubs would be superfluous —indeed any communal organization of citizens would automatically be largely an ex-service club. Only in a very few special cases does there seem to be a variation. Such is the case of the Sarmatians of Ribchester,[2] who seem to have been an unusual group, settled *en bloc* under a special officer. Richmond indicates that there is considerable evidence for the view that these semi-barbarians did not receive the citizenship on discharge and were quite unlike ordinary veterans. On the latter there was normally no compulsion to settle in a particular place, and the occasional attempts on the part of the government to place them in spots not of their own choice failed dismally. They often preferred to live close to the places where they had served their time and where they had strong ties of sentiment.[3] Inevitably they drifted back to their provinces,[4] doubtless to the *canabae* and *vici*.

It is perhaps strange that comparatively few veterans are recorded on the British frontier.[5] It may be merely the operation of chance in the discovery of inscriptions. Or were the conditions (and the climate) too grim to encourage residence in retirement, despite the draws of friendship and familiarity? A tendency to move south in old age is still noticeable in Britain. Certainly those veterans who are mentioned chose some of the most sheltered places to settle, and the size of the *vici* at the first three sites listed in footnote 5 suggests that their fellow civilians agreed with them.

[1] Julio-Claudian (ILS, 2465); CIL, XIII, 7222.   [2] *JRS*, XXXV, 15 ff.
[3] Tacitus, *Hist.* II, 80.   [4] Tacitus, *Ann.* XIV, 27.
[5] (38), Chesters (and the Chesters Diploma); (87), Old Penrith; (81) and (82), Old Carlisle; (57), near Greta Bridge.

The veteran gained another freedom by his honourable discharge, a freedom normal to a civilian. In his inscription cited above, Flavius Longinus demonstrates that not only was he able to take part in the public life of a civilian citizen but also was not barred from a normal private life. Marriage and the raising of children were permitted him. Sometimes it is impossible to be sure of the legality of the marriages mentioned on these inscriptions, but here in Longinus' case, on a dedication for the health of the emperor, on a monument erected on land donated by the local council, it is inconceivable that the wife and three children would all be named were the union irregular and the children bastards.

Longinus was a former auxiliary, but we do not know whether he was enfranchised on discharge from the army or whether he was already a citizen during his term of service (as one may infer in the case of the man from Vetera at Old Penrith mentioned above). Many of his fellow auxiliaries had to await their release before achieving the citizenship. The diplomas (certificates of honourable discharge and citizenship) throw considerable light both on the condition of the veterans and the life of the *vici*. Auxiliary troops *missi honesta missione* received not only the Roman citizenship *qui eorum non haberent*,[1] but also *conubium cum uxoribus quas tunc habuissent cum est civitas iis data aut siqui caelibes essent cum iis quas postea duxissent dumtaxat singuli singulas*. Since there is no evidence either of a grant of citizenship to the wives or that they must be *cives Romanae* in their own right, this is in effect *conubium cum peregrinis mulieribus*,[2] permission to marry non-citizens. It is intended to prevent the occurrence of a ridiculous consequence to the grant of citizenship, for without this provision the men would have been rewarded for their honourable service by a permanent ban on legal marriage in Roman form with a considerable proportion of the women in their community—all those who were peregrine. With these some of them already had formed unofficial unions before leaving the army. The diploma extends the right to wives acquired

---

[1] E.g. the diploma from Chesters of the reign of Antoninus Pius.
[2] Cf. Gaius, I, 76.

after discharge from the army. This affirms that it is a full *conubium cum peregrinis*. Since they had become civilians as well as Roman citizens it would be unnecessary to give them specific permission to marry citizen women.

8. THE SEVERAN REFORM

Previous to the reign of Septimius Severus troops other than officers were denied legal marriage and a married man joining the army was apparently automatically divorced.[1] Dio, within whose active lifetime the Severan changes occurred, mentions that Claudius granted to soldiers as a special case the concessions allowed to married men because the military were forbidden by law to marry.[2] Yet it is quite clear that for all practical purposes soldiers took wives, both from the terms of the discharge papers—*uxores quas tunc habuissent*—and from the papyrus references to wives and children, the birth certificates and the numerous tombstones. When units were stationed in cities the soldiers must often have resided permanently with their families, and the growth of civil settlements round many of the greater Roman military establishments well before Severus suggests most strongly that even where barrack accommodation was provided many soldiers were permitted to live outside the fort walls.[3]

Severus' action seems to have been the simple reform of a legal anomaly. Herodian states that he gave the troops permission γυναιξὶ συνοικεῖν. This must mean that they were allowed legal[4] marriage rather than mere cohabitation since they were already doing that. Indeed the women to whom the soldiers had attachments would not have considered themselves wives at any time if their husbands had been prevented from regular cohabitation. By the fourth century troops were certainly able to contract a legal

---

[1] *Fontes Iuris Romani Antejustiniani*, III, 19; [if this is the real implication of this passage: it is possible that the woman had been deceived by one who was already a soldier]. Perhaps this was an inducement to recruitment.

[2] Dio, LX, 24, 3.

[3] For the solemn argument that this formula cannot mean official permission to have intercourse, see Schulten, *Hermes*, XXIX, 509.

[4] Herodian, III, 8.

marriage and there seems no reason to doubt that this is what Severus' reform effected.[1]

9. THE STATUS OF SOLDIERS' CHILDREN

Tombstones recording the children of serving soldiers are not uncommon, though in this province it is seldom so certain that the father is in the army as it is in the case of the stone from Kirkby Thore (69). The status of these children varies both with the status of the parents and with the period in the history of the empire at which they were born.

Important evidence for the position in law of the children of soldiers is contained in the several surviving birth certificates.[2] From the reign of Augustus the regulations on the registration of births (*lex Aelia Sentia, lex Papia Poppaea*) ruled that all legitimate citizen children must be registered within thirty days of birth by the parent (or an agent) at Rome or the tabularium of the provincial governor.[3] At first, illegitimate children of Roman citizens could not be registered but frequently had their birth recorded by their parents in a private document prepared before witnesses (*testatio*) as an aid to future claims. Marcus Aurelius extended the compulsory registration (*professio*), to all children of citizen parents, whether or not legitimate, but peregrines were never included. Finally, from the practical end of peregrine status in A.D. 212 almost all children had to be registered.

Under the early empire children born during the military service of their father were illegitimate, and therefore followed the status of their mothers. The Severan reform reversed both these consequences. Finally, from A.D. 212 they were all citizens under the *Constitutio Antoniniana*. Children born to the couples whose marriages were permitted under the grants of *honesta missio*, of course, were both legitimate and citizen irrespective of the mother's status,

---

[1] In view of this argument I am obliged to reject my own former opinion in *AA* (4), XXXVI, 238 f.

[2] Schulz, *JRS*, XXXII, 78 ff.; XXXIII, 55 ff.

[3] The distance of many settlements from the provincial capital must have created a great demand for agents.

since the child of a lawful Roman marriage took after the condition of his father.[1]

10. ALLOTMENTS OF LAND TO TROOPS

The *Vita Severi Alexandri* has sometimes suggested that under the Severi a second important change came in the condition of the troops,[2] the introduction of a general system by which lands were allotted to soldiers and to their heirs provided that these were prepared to serve in their turn. With this has been associated an inscription of the reign of Septimius Severus,[3] mentioning a *conductor*. This suggested that, as well as being allowed marriage, soldiers were also permitted to till the soil—in fact becoming the peasant militia. Egger,[4] however, has shown that the *conductores* occur on military papyri from Egypt in the first and second centuries and had nothing to do with leasing lands to soldiers. Their duty seems to have lain in the supplying of food to the army, probably from the *prata legionis*. Alföldi has moreover thrown considerable doubt[5] on the reliability of the passage in the *Vita*. It is, in fact, a clear fiction. Again, Aemilius Macer, a jurist writing after 217 and very probably under Alexander Severus himself, is cited in the *Digest*[6] as stating that troops were forbidden to hold land either themselves or under another name in the province in which they were on active service, lest in farming they should lose their military preparedness. Alföldi's preference for Macer against the *Vita* is wholly reasonable, nor is there any cause to doubt the *Digest's* rendering of the jurist, since it is highly improbable that the Byzantine compilers should have altered a passage to make it *conflict* with more recent practice.

It is, of course, just possible that Alexander introduced the system shortly after Macer wrote, but it is at least clear that the system was not part of Septimius Severus' army reforms. I myself do not believe that the *hastiferi sive pastores* who are recorded at the beginning of Alexander's reign at Mainz-Kastel indicate the presence of

---

[1] Gaius, I, 76. [2] S.H.A. *Vita Severi Alexandri*, 58.
[3] CIL, III, 14356.3.a (= Vorbeck, 38).
[4] *Anz. Ost. Akad. Wiss.* 18 (1951), 231 ff.
[5] *Arch. Ért.* (1940), 214 ff. [6] XLIX, xvi, 13.

any such system in the northern provinces, for they seem not a normal unit but a special levy of the *civitas Mattiacorum*.

The changes in the family arrangements of the troops have often been linked with these supposed land allotments and presented as a change from a mobile professional army to a peasant militia. Nothing could be further from the truth on the British frontier. The Severan reforms introduced regular marriage and followed up with a general extension of the franchise which incidentally put the soldier, his family and his neighbours on the same level in private law. The army remained a wholly professional force. It improved its conditions of service, dealt with a situation detrimental to discipline and encouraged good relations with the local population, its chief source of recruitment. The changes were of detail, aimed at efficiency and loyalty. The army was still the army of Hadrian and the Antonines.

So far from the introduction of a farmer-soldier system being a matter of the Severan age, there is in Britain no positive evidence for it at any period. If such a system was ever introduced it seems unlikely that it was employed here before the changes in type of unit that seem to have accompanied the Theodosian reconstruction of the frontier. Those changes and their civilian implications will be discussed below.[1]

[1] The Theodosian Code refers to the allotment of land to troops, but it is not clear whether it was a universal system or not. The Code is, moreover, remarkably vague about the date of introduction, for it says that these allotments were made 'by antiquity'. Since the passages in question are dated to A.D. 409 and 423 respectively, the allotment may not be much before, say, the mid-fourth century (*Cod. Theod.* VII, xv, I and 2). Moreover, whatever the truth of this matter, it is clear that the *limitanei* were not just a peasant militia, for in the time of Aetius they were being incorporated into the field army.

CHAPTER III

THE CIVILIAN IN HIS SETTING

antiqua urbecula cadaver iacet. LELAND

In the last chapter we saw something of the people who made up the Romanized civil population of the region. In this and the next I shall try to present the detailed evidence for their existence and date, to fill in the material background to those people's lives and to examine the factors that led them to settle in particular places. First, a few words on the general principles governing the selection of sites by civilians. It is obvious that the degree of freedom of choice and the extent to which natural and economic factors could operate varied according to the occupation of the person concerned. Civil officials and officers' families were ruled by the commands of higher authorities and, since their material needs were supplied, no economic factors operated. The families of other ranks in the army were equally bound by the whims of posting officers, but whether or not they accompanied the troops was controlled to some extent by the suitability of the area for civil settlement. In some places it is probable that an extra-mural settlement would have been unsafe from enemy attack. On the other hand, inclemency of climate or situation seem seldom entirely to have deterred civilians, a fact which so many of the sites on Hadrian's Wall underline for the modern visitor, even in mid-summer. In winter they are unbearable for the Southerner if not for the modern Northumbrian.

Traders, craftsmen, shopkeepers, and to some extent farmers, were in a different position. The farmer was, of course, limited by his land, and in many cases must have been tied to the place of his origin where he is most likely to have come into possession of his property. Nevertheless, the introduction of a money economy, the breaking down of tribal barriers and the emergence of a codified and Romanized system of land law must have made the trans-

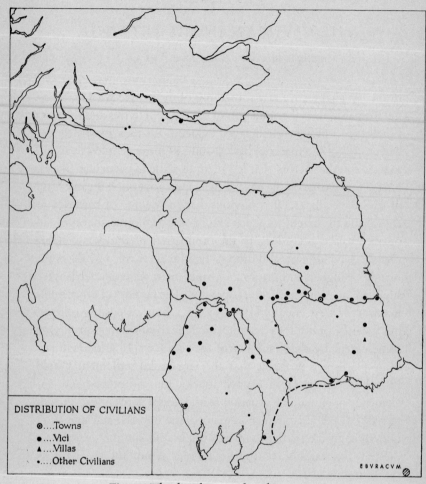

DISTRIBUTION OF CIVILIANS
⊙....Towns
●....Vici
▲....Villas
•....Other Civilians

EBVRACVM

Fig. 3 *The distribution of civil occupation*

ference of property immensely easier. In the main it is probably true to say that the producers and middlemen were free to choose where they plied their trade having regard to economic advantage. The Roman army provided a security never before known and hardly seen again until recent times. Purely economic factors were thus able to operate with unusual freedom. The largest civil settlements naturally grew up where good communications and busy traffic, a source of raw materials or fertile land were added to the perennial attraction of the military market, official and private. To some extent the buying policy of the military authorities must have determined the position and prosperity of trading centres. There is no doubt that the Severan base at Corbridge vastly stimulated civil development there, and good reason to believe that the probable adoption of local supply for the army in the third century in place of shipments from the Fens greatly encouraged the process throughout the region. Nevertheless, the presence at all the larger stations of considerable numbers of men in receipt of that comparative rarity in the ancient world, a regular wage in cash, acted at all times as a honey-pot to the swarms of civilians eager to make money out of the troops and their families.

Two classes of people had exceptional freedom of choice. The wealthy could choose their places of residence at will and it is therefore particularly significant that the region is almost without villas. It is of course possible that it was too unsafe to build an unprotected house in the countryside and that the wealthy were forced to keep to the towns. In face of the lack of the signs of cultured opulence in private houses—mosaics, painted plaster, expensive furniture and fittings—this is improbable. The conclusion must be that there was no considerable class of private gentry in the region. Nor is this particularly surprising. The area is physically not particularly suitable for agricultural estates, except around Carlisle, and the presence of the army and the dangerous nature of the countryside must have discouraged such development. Nor do the local notables seem to have been pro-Roman, for the government had to deal with one uprising after another from the days of Venutius to the end of the second century.

This situation has important consequences. It helps to explain the failure of the region to develop any lasting structure of local government on any considerable scale—the people to man such an organization were simply not available. Moreover, it implies that the prosperity of the towns, such as it was, rested essentially on commerce. This is corroborated by the material evidence—for example the vow of a trader at Bowness that was to be lettered in gold (11). Nor were these merchants particularly rich, for it might be expected that they would have adopted some of the luxuries of the south if they had been—or, if they were, they had their permanent homes out of the region. It is interesting that the one really costly object that can be proved to have been paid for by a civilian, the monument of Regina (107), was at the expense of a trader—and one who, to judge from his own tombstone, speculated and lost.

If the rich merchant moved south, the same may have been true of the veteran,[1] the other class normally free to choose where he would live. When he had an *origo* elsewhere, he doubtless preferred to go where he could exercise his rights and enjoy the pleasures of office. Even if he had not, nevertheless the attractions of a better climate, better land and the civilized amenities of the cities probably proved too strong a draw. Certainly if he remained in the frontier region, he seems to have preferred the pleasanter spots.

This brings us to the more general point of the settlements in their topographical setting. John Horsley two hundred years ago was clearly aware from his own observation that the civilians settled outside a fort tended to prefer certain positions. He noted that they were often settled on a slope between a fort and river[2] and were not always deterred by steep ground.[3] To some extent the choice of situation was controlled by the principles of selection employed by army engineers laying out forts. These officers very frequently chose a promontory in a bend of a river, often at a good crossing, for tactical and strategic reasons. The position of the main roads also affected the situation of the *vicus*, and the placing of the official extra-mural buildings and restricted areas, such as parade

[1] See p. 29, above.   [2] *Britannia Romana*, 399.   [3] *Ibid.* 112.

grounds and wagon parks, shrines and cemeteries, clearly had their effect. Nevertheless the civilians clearly preferred a protected, sunny and well-drained slope, and tended to avoid the north side even at sites where, unlike the Wall stations, there was no military reason for such an avoidance.

It would be interesting to study in detail the wider problem of the general distribution of the settlements over the area in relation to its physical geography. Unfortunately the present lack of soil maps for the area makes it difficult to form an accurate picture of the probable appearance of the countryside in Roman times and its potentialities for settlement. Nevertheless, it will be worth examining the distribution in relation to the natural features of relief and water and the man-made systems of communication.

Two points become immediately apparent on examining the distribution of settlements and comparing it with the general map of the north in the Roman period.[1] The first is the contrast between the heavy concentration of settlements in the region of Hadrian's Wall and south of it and their extreme sparseness further north. The reasons for this will be discussed later, since certain of the details depend on first studying the general picture of the settlements as shown in the area where they are more common and can be studied in more detail. The second point is the paramount importance of the army and its communication system in attracting settlements. The concentration of settlements was densest along the major routes, both as a result of the normal factors of trade in a civilized community and the fact that the roads and sea routes were themselves part of the military system, linking forts and harbours where the presence of garrisons attracted civilian settlement. Trade with the barbarian in regulated markets[2] also acted as a magnet to draw civilians into the region, and opportunities of doing business with the native farms that grew up in the districts around forts[3] swelled the influx. The majority of settlements were in places where the military activity and general traffic may be supposed to have been heaviest, the densest concentration lying near Hadrian's Wall

---

[1] [Fig. 4 does not include information received since 1960.]
[2] Cf. Dio, LXXII, 15.   [3] Cf. Fig. 9, p. 115.

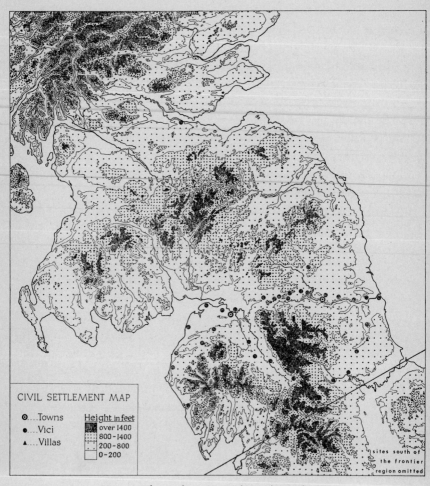

CIVIL SETTLEMENT MAP

⊙....Towns
●....Vici
▲....Villas

Height in feet
over 1400
800-1400
200-800
0-200

sites south of
the frontier
region omitted

Fig. 4 *The settlements in their physical setting*

and the two most important settlements developing at Corbridge
and Carlisle, where river crossings coincided with the intersections
of the east–west road-system with the major routes to the north and
south.

The most convenient and at the same time profitable way to
study the sites in detail is undoubtedly by area, except for special
types of site. I therefore propose first to examine the towns, and
then to proceed to the main subdivisions of the region: Hadrian's
Wall and its outliers, Scotland and the Antonine Wall, the area
west of the Pennines and the Stainmore Pass and, finally, the north-
east.

1. THE TOWNS

In complete contrast to the simple *vici* are the two towns, Corbridge
and Carlisle. In this chapter I am using the word 'town' to denote
size rather than status. The latter I shall discuss later. For the moment the distinction I am making is between the *vici* clustering
around a fort and normally not exceeding ten acres and Corbridge
with twenty acres and Carlisle whose limits are not yet exactly defined but cannot contain less than about seventy acres. There are
other vital differences, too. *Vici* in the frontier region are unwalled
and dependent on a fort. Corbridge and Carlisle seem both to be
walled, while the latter is purely civil in its developed form, and the
former as a civil town encloses not a fort of normal type and size
but a military ordnance depot. Corbridge in fact defies classification, for it seems unparalleled in the empire, but it is more like a
town in dimensions than anything else. [It now seems likely that
Kirkby Thore, an anomaly in the fort-*vicus* class at thirty acres, will
have to be transferred to the town class, since Miss Charlesworth
has discovered that the civil settlement was walled. It is interesting
to remember in this context that Ilkley seems, on evidence produced by Mr Brian Hartley, to have been walled in the first half of
the fourth century.]

Carlisle (LVGVVALIVM)

(a) Anonymous, *Vita Sancti Cuthberti*, IV. (698/705):

. . . sanctus episcopus noster ad civitatem Luel pergens visitavit

reginam, illic rei effectum exspectantem. Sabbato ergo die, sicut pres-
byteri et diaconi, ex quibus multi adhuc supersunt, affirmaverunt, hora
nona, considerantibus illis murum civitatis et fontem in ea a Romanis
mire olim constructum, secundum id quod Paga civitatis praepositus
ducens eos revelavit. . . .[1]

(*b*) William of Malmesbury, *Gesta Pontificum Anglorum*, III, prologue
(first half of the twelfth century):

. . . videas mira Romanorum artifitia; ut est in Lugubalia civitate tri-
clinium lapideis fornicibus concameratum, quod nulla umquam tem-
pestatum contumelia, quin etiam nec appositis ex industria lignis et
succensis, valuit labefactari . . . scripturaque legitur in fronte triclinii:
'Marii Victoriae'.[2]

(*c*) Leland, *Itinerary*, Hearne (2), VII, 54. (1539):

In diggyng to make new Building yn the Towne often tymes hath
bene, and now a late, fownd diverse Fundations of the old Cite, as Pavi-
ments of Streates, old Arches of Dores, Coyne Stones squared, paynted
Pottes, Mony hid yn Pottes so hold and muldid that when yt was stronly
towchid went almost to mowlder. . . .

The hole Site of the Towne is sore chaungid. For wher as the Streates
where and great Edifices now be vacant and Garden Plottes.

(*d*) Camden, *Britannia* (6), 641. (1607):

Romanis temporibus hanc floruisse varia antiquitatis indicia subinde
eruta, & celebris eius tunc temporibus memoria satis affirmate loquun-
tur.

(*e*) Hodgson, *Northumberland*, II, iii, 219. (1840):

That it was fortified in the Roman age is plain, from the fact that much
of the city wall was built upon old ramparts, as appeared not many years
since, by several centurial stones still remaining in them, in their original
position.

---

[1] This tour of Carlisle took place on the day of the battle of Nechtansmere, A.D. 685.
The account of the anonymous writer is closely followed by Bede (*Vita Sancti Cuthberti*,
XXVII), except for an implied rebuke on the name of the town: 'Lugubaliam civitatem
(quae a populis Anglorum corrupte Luel vocatur)'. There seems to be some doubt about
the name of the *praepositus* (Stevenson, translation, 115 f.).

[2] William of Malmesbury is describing the desolate condition of the north under
William I—among more recent ruins those of the Romans might still be seen. The inscription presumably read MARTI (et) VICTORIAE.

The city of Carlisle has long been renowned for its Roman anti-quities—indeed since the seventh century—and scattered finds in many quarters have been reported from the days of Leland and Camden. Many of these finds were plotted by R. C. Shaw in 1924,[1] and I propose not to recount the details easily obtainable from that article but to make use of more recent discoveries and to examine some of the major problems of the site.

It is now clear that a first-century fort[2] was evacuated by the army early in the second century, perhaps on the establishment of the Wall-fort at Stanwix across the river. No further military occupation is known, but the cemeteries show continuous activity down to the end of the Roman period and prove a large and prosperous civilian population (16–22).

Knowledge of substantial structures is slight. William of Malmesbury records a building containing stone arches, apparently a temple or shrine to Mars and Victory, presumably of official origin. Another structure, the fountain seen by St Cuthbert, was still standing in A.D. 685 but cannot be the tank in a polygonal portico found at Tullie House,[3] since the latter was superseded by another building within the Roman period. Other waterworks, in the shape of timber tanks, have been recorded on the site of the old gaol-yard,[4] on the south side of Bank Street at several points, and under the Crown and Mitre. The only other structures known are the hypocaust on the site of Carrick's Café and a column, base and concrete floor from a point just north of the junction of English Street and Victoria Viaduct.[5]

The framework of the town is provided by the roads: the main road from the south, now represented by A6; a bridge across the Eden to Stanwix and the north; and a road from Old Carlisle, presumably on the line of the present Wigton Road. A short section of metalling in Tullie House garden must represent an internal town-street roughly parallel to Castle Street. It appears to be a projection of the road from the south, though this leaves a problem of how the main route reached the bridge. It is interesting that the

[1] *CW* (2), XXIV, 94 ff.   [2] *CW* (1), XII, 344 ff.   [3] *JRS*, XLVII, 202.
[4] *AA* (1), II, 313 f.   [5] *CW* (2), XXIV, 94.

Roman predecessor of A6 appears to be heading for the early fort rather than the river crossing.

Leland's statement (c) makes nonsense of the theory that Roman Carlisle was substantially smaller than its medieval successor. The plentiful finds in the centre of the city prove Roman occupation there, while Leland is definite that considerable buildings once stood where there was open ground in the late-medieval town. The limits of Luguvalium are suggested by the cemeteries located by Chancellor Ferguson.[1] The heaviest concentration of burials was along the east side of the road from the south, from Gallow's Hill almost to the English Gate, a distance of a little under a mile. An extension lay north-west of the present Courthouse. Further north, along the West Walls, burials found included a cremation associated with stone (17). West of the town (22) came from Murrell Hill, some way east of the road to Old Carlisle. On the opposite side of the town inhumations were recorded in Spring Gardens, from which area (21) came, and a mile further east two further inhumations were found at Botcherby.

These limits prompt the more difficult question of defences. Corbridge, in the corresponding position on the eastern route to the north, possessed its town defences. It has long been said that civil Carlisle was bounded by a stockade, the timber-work found by Ferguson in English Street and Bank Street, and reported to him by 'old inhabitants' as seen in Citadel Road and crossing Castle Street.[3] The purpose of this triple row of stakes (showing signs of burning) is obscure, but Ferguson pointed out that it was early, since it was overlaid by a thick stratum of Roman material. If indeed it is a Roman defensive work, the general probability is that it represents an annexe to the fort rather than town-defences.

There is, however, other and quite different evidence for walls. The anonymous biographer of St Cuthbert, writing within the lifetime of some who had witnessed the incident, states that the saint's tour included the *murus civitatis*. If this means a stone wall, it poses the question of whether it is likely that at so early a date in the Anglo-Saxon period and so far north a town possessed walls

[1] CW (1), XII, 365 ff.   [2] CW (1), III, 134 ff.; Cumberland, 99 f., etc.

not of Roman origin. The answer must be no. Ferguson noted stones in the medieval walls which he presumed to come from Hadrian's Wall,[1] but Hodgson (e) suggested something rather different—'centurial stones' *in situ*.

For the dating of phases in the life of the civil town it will be necessary to await the full publication of Mr Robert Hogg's work. Mr Gillam's analysis of the pottery from Scotch Street[2] attests occupation from the end of the first century into the third on that site. The tombstone of the Lady with a Fan (22) (pl. II) is probably to be put into the second century, but others seem to be later, and (20) must surely date from the fourth century. The re-use of this last stone within the cemetery takes the occupation very late in the Roman period, but not necessarily beyond. Within the Roman period, reconstructions are indicated by a late building superseding the Tullie House tank and by the multiple re-surfacings and raising of kerb level on the road at the same site.[3] By A.D. 685 the town had recovered sufficiently to have a *praepositus civitatis*, a monastery fit to receive a queen[4] and a proper pride in its public architecture. Yet there is little evidence to show continuity of town life in the intervening three centuries.

Corbridge (CORSTOPITVM)

(a) Gordon, *Itinerarium Septentrionale*, 176. (1726):
Scarce three miles eastward of Hexham are the ruins of a Roman city now called Corchester. The circuit of the walls is still very conspicuous.

(b) Bruce, *Roman Wall*, (3), 342. (1867):
. . . a bason, weighing twenty ounces, ornamented with foliage, and bearing the Christian monogram; this valuable relic seems to have been speedily committed to the melting-pot.

In 1934 G. S. Keeney read a paper to the Society of Antiquaries of Newcastle upon Tyne entitled 'Corstopitum as a civil centre', the intention of which was to redress some of the balance of study

---

[1] *Cumberland*, 99.   [2] *CW* (2), LV, 73 ff.   [3] *JRS*, XLVII, Fig. 12.
[4] Bede, *Vita Sancti Cuthberti*, XXVII.

which then, as now, concentrated on the military aspects of the site.[1] Subsequent work has corrected much in that paper and justified the general emphasis by northern archaeologists on the military importance of Corbridge, which Keeney was inclined to discount, but his main point that Corbridge in its later days possessed an important civil element remains true. The discoveries of the twenty-five years since Keeney wrote his paper have produced a revolution in the understanding of the chronology and successive layouts of the military site and it is now possible to reinterpret the evidence for civil occupation in the light of this knowledge.

Early civil occupation

The finding of early timber structures outside the then presumed southern limits of the fort of the *ala Petriana* ('Flavian I')[2] suggested the existence of a pre-Wall civil settlement.[3] The situation has been radically altered, however, by the discovery of a fort dated between the departure of the first unit and the building of the Wall ('Flavian II and III'), on entirely different lines from that of Flavian I and apparently close in size and position to that of the first Antonine period. The consequence is that unless it can be proved that the timber structures mentioned definitely date from the first Flavian period, either by discovering the requisite number of layers above or by establishing a clear distinction between the pottery from these points and that from Flavian II and III levels elsewhere on the site,[4] it will remain in doubt whether these traces lie outside the first fort or inside its immediate successors. Moreover, now the limits of the Flavian I fort are themselves no longer so strongly asserted as they once were. The existence of a Flavian civil settlement remains unproven.[5]

Antonine civil occupation is both more likely and slightly better attested. In a recent paper Gillam suggests that the considerable

---

[1] *AA* (4), XI, 158 ff.

[2] *AA* (4), XV, 258; XVII, 111; XXI, 215 f., 217. [The terminology is now changing to 'Roman I', etc.]

[3] *AA* (4), XV, 265, etc.   [4] E.g. *AA* (4), XXXI, 205 ff.; cf. *AA* (4), XXI, 219.

[5] It may also be noted that the structure under the Headquarters of the West Compound was remarkably solid for a civil building of that early date, unless it were an official structure (*AA* (4), XVII, 111).

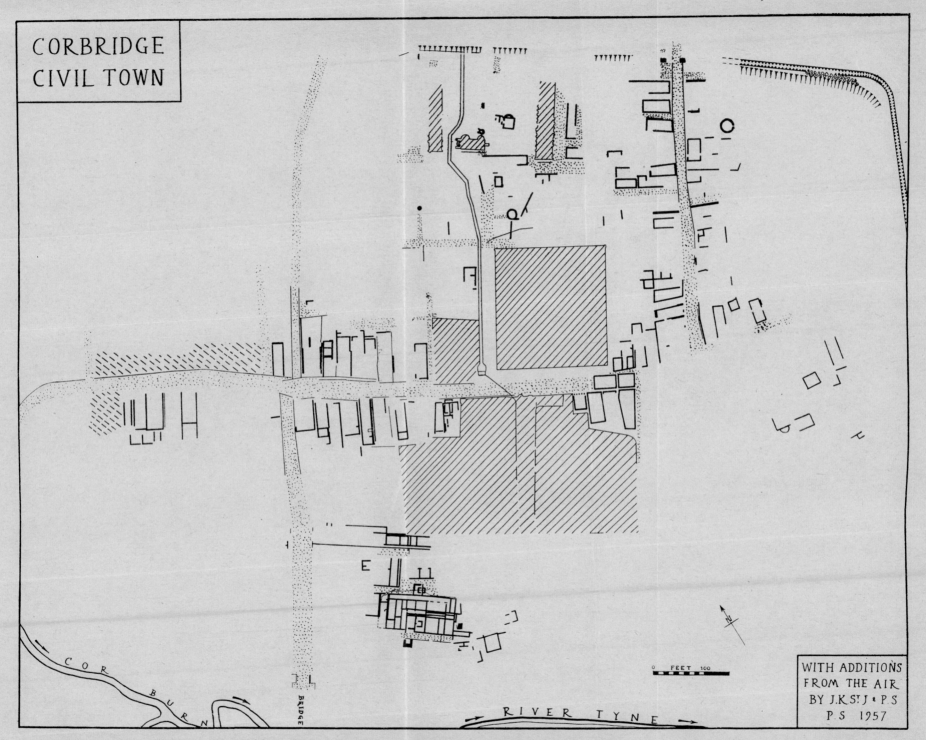

CORBRIDGE CIVIL TOWN

WITH ADDITIONS FROM THE AIR BY J.K.St J & P.S P.S 1957

COR BURN

BRIDGE

RIVER TYNE

0 FEET 100

Fig. 5 *Solid hatching: main military installations; broken hatching: faint traces of buildings visible from the air (for site numbers see reports cited in footnotes)*

quantities of Antonine pottery reported from early excavations of sites outside the known area of Antonine military occupation may well represent such civil activity.[1] Indeed, the existence of Antonine strip-houses along the east–west road would not be surprising. [It is clear now (1964) that the military station was already ceasing to be an ordinary fort in the later Antonine period, and it seems very likely that the development of the civil town was beginning then.]

The third century

The details of the supply depot that the Severi constructed do not concern this study, but the general planning of the site had direct influence on the civil development. The framework is provided by the roads and it will be vital to establish their chronology before any sure picture of the town can be established in the future. Some preliminary notes based on the fragmentary information at present available may be in order here. The road north from the bridge provides a start. There seems no reason for doubting that it represents Agricola's road and can be regarded as original and properly called Dere Street. However, it is almost certain that the route to the north did not originally describe the double bend through the centre of the site now so prominent a feature of the plan. The road in the eastern part of the town commonly called Dere Street is later than the filling of the outer fort-ditch which it overlies, whether that ditch be Trajanic or Antonine.[2] South of this is another road, which perhaps acted as a by-pass around the south of the compounds, and was constructed on top of the demolished Antonine defences. There is no sign of any earlier north–south road east of the military area. By contrast in the west a continuation northwards of the road from the bridge has been observed from the air to bend towards the north-east as it approaches the present Beaufront road,[3] as if skirting the angle of a ditch found in 1909 and clearly belonging to an early fort.[4]

The early date of this western route has important consequences.

[1] *Roman and Native in North Britain*, 86.   [2] *AA* (3), VII, 144; cf. *AA* (4), XXI, 143.
[3] See Fig. 5.   [4] *AA* (3), VI, 244 ff.

Where it crosses the main east–west street its course is not quite straight. The inference must be that the east–west street was already planned at the time Dere Street was projected north from Corbridge. This makes it very difficult to accept R. P. Wright's theory that the east–west street is comparatively late.[1] It is indeed unfortunate that no complete section of the road west of the military area has yet been published.

The associated problem of whether the Stanegate reached eastwards from Corbridge remains unsettled. Neither that road nor any fort has been detected to the east, prompting the suspicion that the Stanegate was never intended to go beyond Corbridge, but that its function was to link the two great roads into Scotland, its terminals lying at Corbridge and Carlisle. The street sometimes labelled Stanegate in the eastern part of the Roman town may be no more than an internal street, perhaps issuing into a minor country road beyond the built-up area and probably following the line of a similar road from the east gates of the earlier forts. If this is true, the Severan planners were presented not with a cross-roads of major highways round which to fit their new depot, but a site east of the cross-bar of a T-junction.

The detailed chronology of the central layout is still only partially known. The granaries, retained from the Antonine plan and the courtyard-storehouse (site XI)[2] are original features.[3] The compounds are probably a little later, dating from the Caracallan consolidation of the Hadrianic frontier system. Temples I, II, III, VI, VII, however, were either built or their plots already irretrievably consecrated before the compounds were laid out.[4]

The final effect of the Severan central area is thus the result of additions and alterations, at each stage of which the planners made use of features already standing. In this they showed on a small scale the same ingenuity displayed in the Severan beautifying of Lepcis Magna, the home of the dynasty. The same factor is apparent also in the planning of the outer sectors of Corbridge. The plan

---

[1] *AA* (4), XIX, 207 f.   [2] Site numbers as in reports in *Archaeologia Aeliana*.

[3] Together with the two long storehouses, XVII West and LVI, these almost certainly form part of Septimius' campaigning base, the first phase of Severan Corbridge.

[4] Their cults are discussed in detail by Richmond, *AA* (4), XXI, 149 ff.

(Fig. 3) reveals that some attempt was made to achieve a grid-pattern of streets. This grid, whose *insulae* are of varying size but approximately rectangular, extends not only among the civil houses but also appears in the area north of site XI where the storehouses, industrial sites and baths probably formed part of the military depot. Here the difficulties faced by the town-planners are emphasized by a curious kink introduced into the aqueduct to avoid a pre-existing bath-house which it was evidently desired to retain in use.

Further modifications were not long in coming. The development of new quarters outside the central area produced a demand for new access roads from one to another, by-passing the centre, doubtless crowded with official activity, and perhaps denied to private traffic.[1] The construction of the road along the east side of the east compound was perhaps the first remedy—and it is in any case clear from the siting of temples on sites XX, XXI S and XXXI N that a through road to the north was not at first intended on this side of the town.

The next stage is rather surprising in view of the care with which the temples had so far been respected. Convenience overcame piety, and the structure on site XX was demolished within the third century[2] and replaced by a road or gravelled yard. Unfortunately, like the precise dating of the erection of the temples south of the east–west road, the occasion of the demolition of this structure is uncertain, emphasizing how much still remains to be learnt of the chronology of the third century.

Temples IV and V, if they existed,[3] probably came down with that on site XX. Their disappearance may have been a contributory factor in the growth of a new route to the north, whose primary cause was most probably the increasing importance of the civil development in this part of the town. The importance as a through route, if not the original construction, of the third-century road

---

[1] Cf. the bollards preventing the entry of wheeled traffic into the forum of Pompeii, and the restrictions on the movement of vehicles in the city of Rome.

[2] *AA* (4), XXXIII, 242 ff.

[3] [*AA* (4), XXI, 143 f.: but their existence is highly problematical and they should probably be deleted from Fig. 5.]

northwards east of sites XX and XXI probably dates from this phase. Its continuation northwards out of the confines of Corstopitum is visible from the air in the playing-field of Corchester School and indicates that this road took over the functions of Dere Street and presumably superseded the earlier line as the main route to the north.

When search is made for other structures known to have been standing in the third century, remarkably little comes to light. Most of the strip-houses in the eastern and western sectors of the town cannot be precisely assigned as between the third and fourth centuries [or even the late second]. Many contain at least two phases, of which one may be third-century.[1] L subsided into the fort-ditch beneath it, like the first houses over the Vallum at Benwell, and was contemporary with the first period of the road which overlay those ditches; while XLIX had a coin of Commodus in fair condition on its earlier floor. The enigmatic site XLIV is presumably part of the same complex as the temples around it, and parts at least of site III must be contemporary with the cutting back of the hill north of site II, which was done before A.D. 296. Site II itself is the remaining building known from the third century, and both its importance as a civil building and the detail in which its history can be deduced justify a discussion in detail.

Site II: Mansio

This large house, situated north-east of the approach to the bridge, was excavated in 1906–7.[2] The reports cited contain sufficient material to permit re-interpretation in the light of more recent knowledge, though there are naturally deficiencies which make it impossible to be absolutely certain on every point. The notes which follow are my own interpretation and can be no substitute for re-excavation.

It seems clear that the excavators were correct in recognizing that this building was not the first on the site and that there were three main phases in the existing structure. These phases are represented in the accompanying plans in Fig. 6 (in which Phases I, II, III

[1] E.g. IX, XII, XLIX, L.　　[2] *AA* (3), III, 174 ff.; IV, 215 ff.

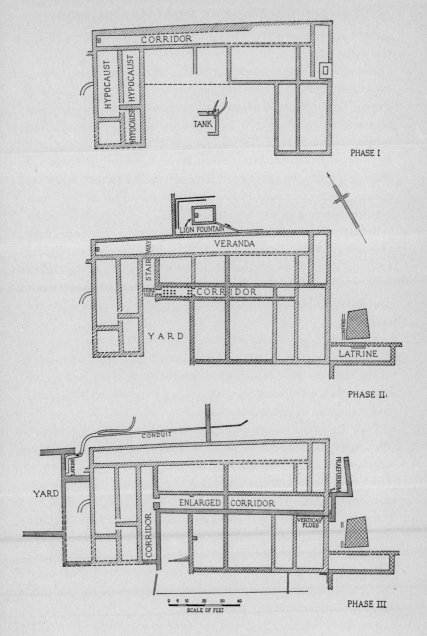

Fig. 6 *Development of the Corbridge* mansio

are broadly equivalent to Periods II, III, IV respectively of the reports).

Phase I. The house commenced as a corridor villa with wings projecting forward at each end. The main rooms lay in the central section, facing south on to the courtyard and the river beyond. The rooms in the west wing were heated by a series of linked hypocausts. The position of the stoke-hole is uncertain. A lightly built semi-circular wall projecting from the west side of the house and enclosing a flagged space may have screened a furnace from the wind. A similar screen protected a furnace added to the headquarters building of the Antonine fort.[1]

Storage of water in this period was by means of a tank in the courtyard, fed by a series of channels, which may have collected from the eaves-drips. In addition there was a sump in the eastern wing which perhaps served as a latrine. This structure is not bonded into the surrounding masonry and its period and function are uncertain.

The ground hereabouts slopes steeply towards the water and was partially terraced to take the Roman buildings. The northern wall of the main corridor of the house was (like that at the Red House baths further west) specially strengthened to retain the hillside and take the thrust of possible landslips.

Phase II. In the second phase the house was, in effect, reversed. The heavy outer northern wall was replaced by a much thinner structure, most probably converting the corridor into a veranda. The area to the north must now have been cut back into the hillside and levelled. This was preparatory to constructing the Lion Fountain, which stood in a small enclosure provided with a gutter to cope with the water splashed when the fountain was used by the household. The inhabitants seem to have been careless about their table scraps, for the outlet pipe was found almost choked with the oyster shells which they had tossed into the basin. However, they broke little pottery at any period.

The Lion Fountain replaced the tank to the south of Phase I. There is no doubt that running water was now available. The tank

[1] *AA* (4), xxx, 249.

was demolished and the eastern two-thirds of the courtyard occupied by two large new rooms. The former central chambers were slightly reduced in size by a new south wall. The corridor formed between these chambers and the new south rooms was warmed by a hypocaust. For this a stoke-hole was provided at the west end and a service yard occupied the western part of the old court. A wooden staircase on stone footings was constructed to lead south from the north corridor. As Professor Richmond has pointed out to me, it is likely that this led down to the stoke-hole (which had, with its hypocaust, been constructed in a specially dug pit). It is less probable that it served an upper storey, for which there is no other evidence.

Elaborate latrines were constructed at the east end of the building. The long, narrow room added at the south-eastern corner was provided with the necessary drain. Immediately to the north a massive concrete base was erected, either as another latrine (suggested by Professor Richmond) or as the stand for a water-tank.

Phase III. Violent destruction, marked by extensive burning, divided Phase II from Phase III. In the reconstruction the central corridor was widened and lengthened and the Phase II hypocaust abandoned. The stairs were not replaced. The stoke-hole seems to have been superseded by further rooms, including a southward extension of the former staircase compartment to make a corridor of access to the west wing and the new south chambers.

At the east end of the building a *praefurnium* was constructed to feed with hot air the new wall-flues of the eastern room of the east wing. The curious shape of the heating mechanism is explained by the pre-existence of the concrete base. In the same re-building the south-east latrine room changed its function. The drain went out of use and was superseded by a smooth plaster flooring continuous with the lining of the wall. This was probably intended to make the room water-tight. Within this same phase the decoration of the heated room seems to have deteriorated rapidly. Several new floors were laid and the walls were re-plastered and painted no fewer than four times. These facts strongly suggest that these rooms were used as baths in Phase III.

This arrangement would have left the house without a latrine, but the need was satisfied by the erection of a new set on the western end of the building. These were supplied with water by a conduit from the north-east, driven through the ruins of the Lion Fountain, and by subsidiary street drains. The outfall seems to have been south-westward across a new yard and thence towards the river.

It is uncertain at what period the terrace walk was constructed along the southern side of the building. It is, however, notable that a pipe stamped LEG VI V was employed in a surface drain for this walk fitted in Phase II or III.

Dating. Remains of a considerable stone structure underlie Phase I, associated with extensive burning. The *terminus post quem* given by the very small amount of pottery reported as sealed by Phase I features is at the earliest A.D. 140. No certain date can be given for Phase I, but it is tempting to see it as a Severan building replacing perhaps a destroyed second-century bath-house (with which the curious quay-like structure to the south—perhaps the underpinning for a latrine—is probably to be associated). The reports are unhappily not too precise on the destruction level. It may in fact represent a destruction of Phase I itself, putting it into the second century. Nevertheless, there were major alterations on other sites at Corbridge during the third century (e.g. site XX), and reconstruction of site II later in the century would be consistent.

The dating of Phase II and Phase III is more satisfactory. Not only did Phase II end in fire but a fresh coin of Carausius sealed between the two levels suggests that this event happened in 296. The house with the elaborate fountain then falls into the third century, while the last and largest state belongs to the fourth, almost certainly to the Constantian reconstruction, since there seems to be little gap in time. It is impossible to say when the building was finally abandoned, though the four re-decorations mentioned suggest that it survived well into the century. There is, however, no sign of a general reconstruction that might be interpreted as Theodosian.

The fourth century in the town

The chronology of the *mansio* has taken the history of civil Corstopitum into the fourth century. It was not, however, the only substantial civil building in use in that period. On site XX the open space of the later-third century received a large house, a fragment of which was re-examined in 1954.[1] The street front of this house was in the form of a narrow entrance passage flanked by two chambers (shops or porter's lodge), a design only paralleled in the frontier region by the *mansio* at Benwell in its second phase but common in Roman towns elsewhere.[2] The erection of this house was one part of a general re-modelling of the central area in the Constantian era. The front of site XI received a portico, the rooms of the south range being entered from the street and perhaps used as shops or offices.[3] On site IV a pottery store was established over the remains of the western temples, with an industrial site behind.[4] There are also signs of alterations to the eastern temples, and a furnace was established on temple III. The picture would therefore seem to be a spread of civil occupation into the central area, and the impression is strengthened by the sealing-off of the compounds into a single isolated area by the erection of a new wall closing the street between them.

Many of the strip-houses in the outer parts of the town (pl. V) must also have been in use in this period, as the dwellings, shops and factories of the civilians. Sites IX, XII and XLVIII were almost certainly in commission then and the same must be true of others.

The late fourth century

It has long been recognized that the destruction of A.D. 367 did not end the life of Roman Corbridge. The Theodosian reconstruc-

---

[1] *AA* (4), XXXIII, 226 ff.

[2] E.g. The Houses of the Faun and of the Tragic Poet at Pompeii.

[3] *AA* (3), VIII, 164; (4), XV, fig. 3, facing 254.

[4] *AA* (3), IV, 249. Professor Birley has pointed out to me that there is no need to postulate on the basis of the discovery of quantities of second-century samian an official store containing old but unissued stock. The samian all came from the area of the third-century temple VI, strongly suggesting that that structure had cut into a second-century deposit. The fourth-century pottery was quite separate, came from outside temple VI and can be reasonably associated with the later building.

tion appears to have extended to the civil as well as the military elements, though the civil details are obscure. Little has escaped the plough and other more drastic forms of interference, but late fourth-century occupation of indeterminate character was noted on top of the ruins of the Constantian house on site XX,[1] and a late structure of uncertain shape overlay the southern part of the east range of site XI.[2] From sites XII, XVII, XX and XXI the coins continued into the late fourth century, indicating activity after A.D. 367. There seems to have been a scare at some time under Magnus Maximus (perhaps not surprisingly), for a hoard whose issues end with Maximus was concealed in a furnace in site XII, but Hedley's analysis of the coins from Corbridge shows that money was coming into the town at least as late as A.D. 393.[3] Beyond that it is at present impossible to go, for neither arguments based on the presence of *minims*[4] and of wear on Valentinian issues nor the survival of the place-name element *Cor* convincingly prove the survival of anything resembling town life after the end of the fourth century. Indeed, the evacuation of the Wall must have removed both Corbridge's chief economic *raison d'être* and its main protection, and its demise as a town cannot long have been delayed.

Defences

The discussion above has left one major structural problem untouched. The question of town defences immediately poses itself when it is noted that many of the important official buildings are not included within the stout walls which surround the compounds. Only the granaries have their own enclosure wall, and even that is a slight thing, surviving from the late-Antonine period and never intended to be defensive. Even the compound walls themselves were probably not in the first instance constructed for defence against positive attack. Yet Gordon in the early eighteenth century was emphatic that a circuit of walls was visible on the site (a). MacLauchlan went further, confidently drawing a line along the

---

[1] *AA* (4), XXXIII, 249 f.   [2] *AA* (3), VII, 159 f.   [3] *AA* (4), XIV, 95 ff.
[4] These are not securely dated—Robertson, *Roman Coinage: Essays presented to Harold Mattingly*, 277 ff.

southern edge of the plateau to represent foundations of a wall remaining.[1] Unfortunately his line is not reliable. Doubts already
existed when sections were cut in 1906[2] and those trenches failed to
produce any trace of a wall. In addition it is now apparent that
MacLauchlan's line would cut through both site II and the various
buildings visible from the air in the south-eastern part of the town,
though this would not preclude a late wall.

Much more satisfactory results were obtained when excavation
spread to the north and north-eastern edges of the town. The line
there obtained is plotted on Fig. 5, and is visible from the air.[3] Details of the system were obtained in a section cut at the north-east
angle and carefully published.[4] It shows clearly two elements of
differing date. The earlier is a ditch of military type, 17 feet broad
and 7 deep, which had been deliberately filled with blue clay.[5] The
dates of construction and fill are unknown, but the ditch does not
seem to form part of any of the forts at present known. South of
the ditch lay a clay bank, varying in width from 13 to 17 feet (ex-
cluding the stone kerbs). This cannot have been a rampart associated with the ditch, for the berm between them could not have ex-
ceeded 3 feet. Its true purpose is explained by the discovery at one
point of a stone 'pavement' immediately to the north, laid partially
over the disused ditch. This 11 foot 'pavement', equipped with
'kerbs' front and back can hardly be anything else than the foundation of a defensive wall, the bank forming the normal rampart-
backing. Similar foundations were found west of the north–south
road and again further west immediately north of site XVII. At
the first point the published plan[6] seems to show that the wall has
narrowed to 8 feet, but at the second it is again 11 feet.[7] From the
air and from the excavated section it is clear that both ditch and
clay bank ran on the north and east sides of the town, and it seems
reasonable to suppose that the stone wall ran on the same line.

[1] *Watling Street*, sheet IV.   [2] *AA* (3), III, 161 f.   [3] Cambridge, DS, 15.
[4] *AA* (3), XII, 232, Fig. 2.
[5] A ditch of comparable dimensions was discovered in 1906 on the south edge of the
site, south of MacLauchlan's line, *AA* (3), III, 163 ff.
[6] *AA* (3), XI, pl. VIII.
[7] *AA* (3), VI, pl. XIII, facing 246. The occurrence of a 'peaty' deposit north of the wall
at a depth of 8 feet suggests the presence of the ditch here also.

Further evidence for the existence of defences on this side of the town was obtained by Mr Robin Birley in 1959. A trial hole dug on the east side of the Ministry of Works road immediately inside the northern field-boundary during work to widen the entrance revealed defences of more than one period. For details it will be necessary to await the publication of Mr Birley's excavation,[1] but it can be said that there were considerable traces of turf-work at the lowest level and stonework above. Whether the former represents a turf rampart or a backing and the latter the foundation or kerb of a turf rampart or a stone wall in the second period remains to be seen.

Such a town wall implies gates, and though none has yet been identified with absolute certainty there is substantial evidence for two and a possible trace of a third. For the first it is necessary to turn to the point at which the eastern road to the north crossed the line of the wall. Here two masonry piers were discovered, 8 feet thick from north to south and lying 27 feet apart. At the same point a drain running up from the south was found to make a significant bend into the road as if to pass through a passage.[2] Large stones found between the piers may well represent the remains of a *spina*, which would be required since the main piers are as far apart as the guard-chambers of a double fort-gate. The chief structural peculiarity is the apparent shallowness of the piers from back to front suggesting simple archways in a screen-wall rather than deep passages in a more military manner.

The other main exit from the town, the bridge over the Tyne, might be expected to have a similar structure at its northern end. Scrutiny of the excavation report for this area reveals a most interesting feature:[3] the road was narrowed for a distance of 23 feet from its accustomed 43 feet to the width of 27 feet, precisely the same as the distance between the piers at the northern exit. This narrowing was exactly delineated by insets in the stone kerbs of the third-period road, and equipped with a pair of covered drains run along its inner borders. The insets would accept a wall and bank only

---

[1] [Mr Gillam states that the *terminus post quem* for the defences is represented by a mortarium of *c.* A.D. 130.]

[2] *AA* (3), XI, 288, and pl. VIII. [3] *AA* (3), IV, 211.

slightly narrower than that found in the north-east part of the town and it may be noted that the road is reported to have been 'supported on each side by a bank of clay'.[1] The lack of any trace of a *spina* is a difficulty, but the proximity of Corbridge Mill may indicate the final resting-place of much stone from this part of the town. Moreover, if this was not a gate, it is difficult to offer an explanation for the insets, for a bridge abutment is ruled out by the fact that the road resumes its full width riverwards of the feature discussed.[2]

If these traces are rightly interpreted as gates, it is perhaps not unreasonable to draw attention to the crop-marks which occur at the point where the east–west road in the eastern part of the town would meet the line of the defences, and suggest that this point might repay excavation.[3]

Mausoleum (Shorden Brae, NY 975649)[4]

Aerial photography revealed the presence of a structure on the plateau west of the Cor Burn and a quarter of a mile from the Roman town, close to the presumed course of the Stanegate. The site was excavated in the summer of 1958.[5] For the present purpose it is sufficient to note that the site consisted of a massive hollow rectangular base for a substantial monument, standing in the centre of a square enclosure. The two southern corners of the precinct wall were ornamented with free-standing sculptures of a lion slaying a hart—and two more examples of the same motif, reported by Horsley, may[6] represent the missing northern pair. The presence of this motif confirms the identification of the structure as a funerary monument. Its size indicates a person of wealth or importance but his name is unknown. Datable material was scanty and the presence of a late burial outside the enclosure is probably fortuitous. The monument was apparently erected in the mid second century and it is probable that the deceased was a high official rather than a

---

[1] *Ibid.* 213.

[2] Towards the dating of these gates, it may be noted that the excavators associated the piers with the *first* phase of the (probably third century) north–south road, and the insets with the *latest observed* phase of the road which appears to be the original Dere Street and which lies here on a slope liable to erosion.

[3] Cambridge, BC, 77.　　[4] *JRS*, L, 215; Cambridge, DS, 17.

[5] [Now published: *AA* (4), XXXIX, 37 ff.]　　[6] *Britannia Romana*, 246.

rich private citizen. It seems to have been demolished in the fourth century for its building material.[1]

The people and status of the town

The civilians have left little epigraphic trace of themselves, though what remains reveals a highly cosmopolitan population. Persons with Greek connexions (39, 40) include a priestess of Hercules of Tyre, implying a regular cult and an acquaintance with the Greek language.[2] Christianity, too, was not unknown (b). Barates the Palmyrene (43), having buried his British wife at South Shields (107), probably came here as a contractor to the army during the third century. The little girl Ahtehe possessed a thoroughly Germanic name (44) and the boy and his female relative on (45) are perhaps Celtic. Only the two Julias seem to be properly Latin (41, 42).

These inscriptions reveal nothing of the status of this flourishing town. There is no trace either in the epigraphy or in the structures of the town's having had any autonomous administration or independent existence. The third-century date of its main development and the permanent presence of troops indeed make that inherently unlikely, and it is *prima facie* probable that the military occupation, however unusual its form, kept the civil settlement politically in the condition of an ordinary *vicus* like that outside any fort.[3] The only feature that singles out Corbridge from other *vici*, apart from its comparatively large area, is the possession of walls. Even though these may originally and primarily have been intended for the protection of the ordnance depot, it appears that the erection of private houses within them was permitted by the early fourth century at the latest.

2. A PORT OF SUPPLY
South Shields (ARBEIA)

South Shields is difficult to fit into any classification. Like Carlisle and Corbridge it is detached from the Wall while in some sense

---

[1] [The excavators suggest that this may have been to provide material for strengthening the town walls.]

[2] Cf. the companion altar to Astarte, CIG 6807, *AA* (4), XXI, 200 ff.

[3] [Perhaps one may conjecture from the presence of legionaries in special detachments that it was called *canabae* rather than *vicus*.]

belonging to the system. As well as being a fort, its function was as a port for supplying the eastern end of the Wall. At this point supplies were transhipped into lighters to be taken upstream at least as far as Benwell—where the master of the South Shields freedman Victor was probably stationed (pl. III, b). Also like Carlisle and Corbridge, it is related to south–north routes in this case by sea as well as by road, and it is clear that like Corbridge it owes the origin of its abnormal development to the Severan campaigns into Scotland. It is sad that so little is known of its civil side, for it is feasible that it became a town on the pattern of Corstopitum.

It is clear from Horsley[1] that little was visible of the Roman site in his day and there is no hint of extra-mural buildings in his account. Remains were certainly to be seen in Leland's time, but we have no specific details.

Structural evidence of a specifically civilian character is entirely lacking. We are obliged to rely on two, or possibly four, inscriptions, small finds and probability. Despite slight evidence of a pre-Hadrianic occupation of the fort on the Lawe and proof of Hadrianic and Antonine garrisoning, there is nothing to indicate the presence of civilians. Under the Severi the fort was re-modelled with a special compound and storehouses as a receiving depot for military supplies. The main activity seems to have been during the build-up for the campaigns of Septimius Severus and Caracalla. This seems the best explanation for the preponderance of lead seals bearing the portraits of Septimius, Caracalla, and Geta in the group found at South Shields.[2] One seal probably dates between 212 and 217, suggesting that traffic did not entirely cease with the abandonment of the conquest of Scotland.

This traffic implies a harbour, which one would expect to attract civilian traders and officials. It is notable that Hübner's dating of the tombstone of Regina, wife of Barates of Palmyra (107) (pl. III, a) is, on purely epigraphic grounds, attributable to the late second or third century. She may well have lived at South Shields at the time of this extraordinary shipping activity.[3] It seems reasonable to

---

[1] *Britannia Romana*, 449. [2] *AA* (4), XI, 101 f.
[3] [The widespread occurrence of second-century material well away from the fort may, as Professor Birley suggests, point to earlier beginnings for the settlement.]

suppose that her husband was the same Barates that died at Corbridge (43) and to follow Birley in believing him to have been a merchant rather than a soldier. If his profession, *vexil(l)a(rius)*, implies that he was a civilian contractor to the army, it would be wholly consistent with his appearing both at South Shields and at Corbridge in the Severan period. That Barates buried his wife at South Shields implies that his household was there rather than at Corbridge, at least at the time of her death.

Professor Richmond[1] has surmised that the freedman Victor (whose splendid tombstone (108) survives in good condition) had been set up by his master as a partner in a business. The master, Numerianus, was a trooper in Ala I Asturum which was in garrison in the third century at Benwell. This stone belongs to the same period as that of Regina and is probably a consequence of the same special activity. Victor's military connexion is at any rate certain. Perhaps he too was engaged in some form of contracting or ancillary service to the army. The costliness of his tombstone is interesting. As he was only twenty when he died it seems unlikely that he had himself built up a fortune. Clearly his master, though a private soldier, had prospered considerably.

Two other inscriptions now in the South Shields museum may mention civilians. A small altar to Dea Brigantia was dedicated by a man who gives his name as Congennicus which is Celtic and probably native. The second[2] is a stone set up in memory of a small boy by his father L. Arruntius Salvianus (109). The characteristically Italian name of the latter has suggested that he was the commanding officer of the fort. If this is true, the inscription cannot be used as evidence for a civil settlement.

Under the Constantian re-organization a change came over the fort. Not only were the new troops a specialist unit of lightermen (the Barcarii Tigrisienses), but also some of the Severan storage space was converted into accommodation for junior officers. This indicates that stores were no longer held here but were immediately transhipped.[3] The presence of the junior officers is due to the com-

[1] *The Roman Fort at South Shields*, 13.   [2] Figured by Bruce, *AA* (2), x, 244.
[3] *AA* (4), XI, 96 f.

plicated administrative machinery which this would require and perhaps also indicates a change from civilian contracting to direct military control of the whole of the supply organization. Certainly we have nothing clearly civilian from this period to set against the lavish tombstones contemporary with the earlier period of the fort as a service-corps establishment.

There is some evidence for occupation of the fort by another new type of unit following the restoration of the northern frontier by Theodosius. The main hall of the headquarters was now converted into storerooms and a persistent burnt layer at the topmost level on the site may represent light structures of this period.[1] However, here there was no destruction in A.D. 367, so the late-Roman soldiery was probably living in converted buildings of earlier periods rather than in huts constructed on top of ruins.

Topography[2]

The most useful evidence on extra-mural Roman finds is Hooppell's plan of the whole area (his plate V) and his notes which are reasonably specific in their details. In the making of Baring Street in 1874 a paved road was discovered approximately 275 feet south-east of the crossing of Baring Street and Fort Street. As far as can be seen from Hooppell's plan this seems to be heading for the south-east gate of the fort from a direction slightly west of south. This may be Horsley's Wreken Dike, visible in his day. It seems reasonable to accept it as Roman in view of the evidence below.

Cemetery

Close to the road were found 'a striking sculptured stone, which was conjectured with great probability to have been connected with some funeral monument' and a shallow stone trough.[3] Hooppell also reports the discovery of a considerable quantity of decorated and stamped Samian in the area. Some of this was found at a point about 500 feet south-west of the Roman road.

[1] *Nat. Hist. Trans.* VII, 126.
[2] [See now Birley, *Research on Hadrian's Wall*, 152 ff., including evidence for quays here and at Wallsend, and the possibility that South Shields was an island.]
[3] Hooppell, *Nat. Hist. Trans.* VII, 126 f.

The main evidence for the existence of a cemetery flanking this road was discovered later. Hooppell mentions 'many graves and skeletons' and a tombstone inscribed *D.M.*[1] Reporting on the bones found in the 1874–5 excavations he states that a cranium and other bones were found in inhumation graves near point *d* on his map (apparently on the line of the road and about 775 feet south-south-west of the place where it was cut by Baring Street). Also near this point were cremations in urns.[2] Cremation vessels from the cemetery now in the Museum in Roman Remains Park are of second- and third-century dates, with a preponderance of the latter.

In 1878 the *Regina* stone was discovered 'in effossionibus' (Hübner) at South Shields. Haverfield reports (EE, VII) that the tombstone of Victor was found in 1885 'eodem fere loco' as that of Regina. According to Bruce the *Regina* stone was unearthed 'a little to the south of Bath Street',[3] the main portion of the *Victor* stone 'at the intersection of James Mather Street and Cleveland Street' and the top of the same stone (found 'about three years' previously) 'at the east end of Cleveland Street, at a distance of perhaps 100 yards from the site of the present find'.[4] It is to be noted that the full details of the position of the upper portion of the latter stone were not published until three years after the discovery, while those of the lower were read to the Society of Antiquaries of Newcastle upon Tyne after a delay of only three weeks. If Bruce's estimate of the distance is accurate the upper part must have been found at a point about half-way between the intersection and the end of Cleveland Street.

If these locations are taken in conjunction with Hooppell's point *d* (which, by comparison with an Ordnance Survey six-inch map, lies on the south side of Bath Street, approximately 275 feet west of its intersection with James Mather Street), it will be seen that none of the points is more than 300 feet from the others. Bruce's statement[5] that the cemetery occupied 'more ground than the station itself' must either mean that he included the place of discovery of the Samian reported by Hooppell and mentioned

[1] Hooppell, 16. [2] *Ibid.* 23. [3] *AA* (2), x, 239. [4] *Ibid.* 311. [5] *Ibid.* 239.

above, or that some of the burials for which no location is given lay outside this area. Bruce is, however, clear that the cemetery did not approach closer to the fort than two or three hundred yards.

This fact certainly suggests that something lay between the cemetery and the fort. On so unusual a site as South Shields this something may have been an exceptionally large group of official extra-mural buildings, but the probability that it was the civil settlement is strong. This argument has been strengthened by the discovery in 1959 that the parade ground lay seawards north of the fort, making it unlikely that the *vicus* lay on that side. It is highly probable that the *vicus* whose existence has already been proved from the monuments should have grown up along the main road south of the fort.

The presence of both cremations and inhumations in quantity suggests that the burial ground remained in use for a considerable length of time. The presence of both second- and third-century cremations indicates that it was established before the Severan alterations in the function of the fort and continued to receive burials after the construction of the supply depot. I would therefore suggest that whatever caused the cemetery to be sited some distance from the fort was already operative in the second century.

The lack of specifically military tombstones is probably due to chance. Other evidence for civil occupation at South Shields is so scanty that it seems unreasonable to postulate a purely civil burial place. Nor are there any signs of a corresponding exclusively military cemetery.

Industries

There is a little evidence for civilian craftsmen working at South Shields. The *Regina* and *Victor* stones imply foreign sculptors capable of producing work of a comparatively high quality.[1] Jet wasters indicate local production in that trade. A small mould shows that metal-working existed, though not necessarily civil.

Most of these things, however, may have been—and probably were—made by travelling craftsmen. One class of objects,

[1] Probably Palmyrene, *AA* (4), XXXVII, 203 ff.

F

however, came from a genuinely local industry. This is the group of four fourth-century crossbow-brooches (two now at South Shields in the museum and two in the Joint Museum of Antiquities, Newcastle upon Tyne) which bear moulding on the bow, unparalleled elsewhere.

Summary

The conditions for civil settlement at South Shields ought to have been ideal. A flourishing port existed in the third and fourth centuries and, best of all, the site seems to have had the rare experience of remaining unscathed by hostile action throughout its life until finally ended around A.D. 400. Yet, except for one—perhaps quite brief—period, there are at present no certain material traces of such civilians.[1] The positioning of the cemetery is not *necessarily* due to the presence of a *vicus* in the second century, though a settlement at that date is perhaps more likely here than in many places. At the other end of the time-scale the presence of a Theodosian garrison does not prove the existence of a *vicus* in the late fourth century.

The importance and prosperity of South Shields in the Roman period is undoubted, and it is very much to be hoped that demolition of particularly hideous nineteenth-century property on the site will gradually provide opportunities to the active local archaeological society for investigation of its material remains.

3. HADRIAN'S WALL

The two Walls pose a number of special problems and provide sharp contrasts. The Antonine Wall is almost entirely without civil occupation, while Hadrian's bears the densest concentration in the entire region. The distribution of civil sites along the latter Wall is remarkably uniform. Kipling was not far wrong when he described it as a 'thin town eighty miles long ... a snake basking beside a warm wall' though it is a disjointed snake, interrupted by the empty spaces behind the turrets and milecastles where no *vici*

[1] [Except perhaps EE, VII, 998, 999.]

have ever been found. The Wall area is perhaps the clearest proof that where there was no official bar the presence of the army was an attraction so strong that physical difficulties in the way of settlement proved no deterrent. It is not easy to think of places less comfortable to live in than Housesteads or Carvoran, yet civilians flocked to both settlements. It can hardly be over-emphasized that the criteria useful in the study of the primitive societies of the prehistoric world have to be modified when an advanced culture is under examination. The further man advances materially and politically, the more he is able to control his en-vironment and the more human decision and political factors have to be taken into account. The Romans were quite capable of choos-ing how and where they would settle and altering the physical conditions on the grand scale to suit their convenience, whether by revolutionizing communications with roads, ports and canals or by drainage, irrigation and land-clearance. Professor Richmond has pointed out that the building of the Turf Wall implies that a vast strip of land was cleared for turf, apart from the felling of trees to provide timber for the immense number of wooden structures. Similarly, the construction of roads, forts and their ancillary works must have involved a great deal of clearing of forest, drainage and other improvements, all of them conducive to civil settlement. The activities of the Roman government in fact represent a revolution in the physical face of the region, just as the importation of a large number of troops, officials and followers must have made a tre-mendous change in the population density and social composition of a comparatively thinly peopled area. Apart from the basic military suitability of the terrain, the study of the occupation of the Wall area is essentially the study of a settlement in spite of, rather than because of, the nature of the land.

It has become conventional to describe the sites along the Wall in geographical order from east to west. This plan is followed here and the fortification of the Cumberland coast as far as Moresby has been included as part of the system, as in fact it was. The civil material from the outpost forts is examined in a subsection at the end.

THE WALL PROPER:
WALLSEND TO BOWNESS-ON-SOLWAY

The Vallum

An important point emerges if the evidence for date of *vici* is compared with their distribution. Only one *vicus* is certainly known to have existed along the line of Hadrian's Wall before the third century (Stanwix),[1] and in the strip between Wall and Vallum no civil buildings have yet been found that can be dated before the reign of Septimius Severus.[2] Moreover the only excavated native settlement in the strip seems to have been occupied only when the Vallum was slighted. Conversely, where private civil buildings have been excavated and found to lie over or north of the Vallum, they have been proved uniformly Severan or later (Benwell, Housesteads). It is therefore difficult to avoid the implication that the strip was, when the Vallum was in active use as a barrier, a zone prohibited to settlement and casual movement by civilians.[3] Thus not only would the Vallum act as a fence protecting structures and equipment lying outside the forts, but the strip could be used as a frontier control zone in which customs and security examination of large groups of people, caravans and herds of animals could be carried out without risk either of surprise attack or sudden attempts to escape on the part of the examined. The temporary cancelling of the Vallum during the period of Antonine disuse of the frontier is consistent with this explanation, and the strip did not fill then with civil settlements for the simple reason that the attraction—large garrisons—was for the present absent. The deliberate filling of the Vallum at forts in the early third century (after the late Antonine administration had put it back into use) is a clear act of governmental policy. The construction of private houses over the Vallum is in line with the Severan recognition of military marriages and converted the *vicus* from a nuisance, to be kept as far away from the military establishments as possible, into

---

[1] [Now with the addition of Housesteads *south* of the Vallum.]

[2] At Stanwix the bronze-smith's workshop seems to have lain on the slope well south of the Vallum.

[3] Cf. ch. III, 4, below.

quarters for troops which it was convenient to have close to the fort.[1]

Wallsend (SEGEDVNVM)

(*a*) Horsley, *Britannia Romana*, 135. (1732):

The ruins of a *Roman* station and town at this place are still very discernable; tho' it has all been plowed, and is now a very rich meadow.... The south rampart of the fort is about three quarters of a furlong from the river side, and runs along the brow of the hill, or at the head of a considerable descent from thence to the river. There have been buildings on this part, and to the south-west of the fort; but they are now so levelled and covered, that little evidence appears above the ground; yet the stones and remains of rubbish are easily discovered, when the surface is in any where removed: and some of these inequalities in the surface, which usually arise from ruins, yet remain, and may easily be perceived to be hillocks of stones or rubbish.

(*b*) Lingard, *Mural Tourification*, *AA* (4), VI, 140 f. (1807):

Mrs Buddle informed us that in trenching their garden to the east of the house many human bones were found: and in digging a cellar under the dining room a well [ ] feet deep, at the bottom of which were the bones and skulls of different animals, and the horn of a buffalo or reindeer.... A little to the west of the Station was opened 25 years ago an arched cavity, (arch of brick), in which were found many broken urns, (a dial and a cross—this is doubtful).[2]

(*c*) Hodgson, *Northumberland*, II, iii, 171. (1840):

In making railroads from the colliery, and digging for foundations of buildings about it, vast remains of Roman works have been found.... When the workmen, in 1814, were forming the gears of Fawden staith, they met much Roman masonry, and coins, a little above the high-water mark: and I was then present there when a very curious cauldron for heating water in was laid open, and removed....[3] It was, however, only

---

[1] *Vici* are known between the Wall and the Vallum at Benwell, Carrawburgh, Housesteads, Greatchesters, Burgh-by-Sands and probably Birdoswald. Chesters and Bowness-on-Solway, where the course of the Vallum is uncertain, should perhaps be added to this list.

[2] Both the well and the 'arched cavity' had already been found before September 1800 (Lingard, *First Notebook*, *AA* (4), VI, 133). Mrs Buddle's house stood 'parallel to the west rampart of the station and near the south-west angle' (Brand, *Newcastle*, I, 604, n. h), just inside the west rampart. Richmond points out that the arched structure may have been a potter's kiln (*RW* (11), 44).

[3] From the detailed description, here omitted, the 'cauldron' was a small oval hot

the last part of a considerable building that was remaining when I visited the spot, all the rest having been removed before I heard of the discovery. Many Roman coins were discovered in these excavations.

While there is nothing on this site specifically civil, the quantity of extra-mural buildings south and south-west of the fort implied by Horsley's report (a) is too great to be accounted for by military or official civil structures alone.[1] Details, however, of the development outside this fort are few. The bath-house lay 150 yards south of the south-west angle (c) and there is evidence for a well, perhaps a cemetery and possibly a pottery some distance west of the fort (b).[2]

Newcastle upon Tyne (PONS AELIVS)

[Two small stone coffins were found in Hanover Square, presumably south or south-west of the fort.[3] One was large enough for a child and contained bones and a Castor pot, the other would have taken a baby about three months old. The discovery of three altars further south-west in Hanover Street helps to suggest a cemetery and temple area stretching towards the river.]

Benwell (CONDERCVM)

It is fortunate that some excavation was possible at Benwell in the last decade before the war of 1939–45, for this site of exceptional interest was at that time largely swallowed up by the monstrously unattractive housing that now obliterates it. Unhappily the records available of the civil structures then uncovered are for the most part unsatisfactory. The descriptions which follow are partly the result of analysis of such reports and finds that survive.

Buildings between the fort and the Vallum

Temple of Antenociticus. This small, apsidal temple was patronized by officers, and there is no evidence for civilian worship.[4]

---

bath. The building was clearly a bath-house. MacLauchlan marks a bath (presumably the same structure) 150 yards south of the south-west angle of the fort (*Survey of the Roman Wall*, sheet I).

[1] [For streets outside the fort see MacLauchlan, *Memoir*, 7, footnote.]

[2] [A temple of Mercury south of Milecastle 1 has military dedications only].

[3] Black Gate Cat. nos. 352, 353.

[4] Especially G. W. Rendel, *AA* (2), VI, 169 ff.; also Bruce, *ibid.* 153 ff.; *NCH*, XIII, 549 ff.;

South, east and west of the temple other structures were reported, but in so fragmentary a state that it is impossible either to date
or to identify them. Close to the southern structure a cremation[1]
was found, presumably Roman, suggesting that the area was a
combined temple and cemetery region similar to that at Maryport.

Buildings overlying the Vallum

The excavations of 1933,[2] 1937 and 1938[3] (unpublished) revealed
that the Vallum had been deliberately filled during the Severan reconstruction of the Wall and that a series of buildings had been
erected over it in at least two areas.

(i) *West of the crossing*. The west arm of the Vallum diversion is in
two sections. Proceeding from the crossing the Vallum soon makes
a 15° turn northwards into the first section. In this, and immediately west of the Pendower fence, the excavators in 1937 found that
'buildings had been erected over its course, one being noted immediately north of the ditch, with its south wall collapsing over
the lip'.[4] The subsidence links this with the earliest third-century
structures at the crossing.

(ii) *The Vallum causeway and its gate*. Since 1938 six road periods
have been known. The third from the bottom, whose western
drain subsided with Building A, is Severan. The first must be
Hadrianic, together with the gate. Pivot-stones were discovered
in this Hadrianic level and in the fifth layer only. It is therefore
reasonable to suppose that the doors were removed under Lollius
Urbicus. The period of Marcus Aurelius remains uncertain. It
seems to me unnecessary to postulate a raising of the stone in a
period subsequent to the Severan to explain the non-appearance of
a pivot in the Severan level. The final obliteration of the Vallum
made such gates obsolete. Refurbishing in the fifth period (of

---

AA (4), XIX, 37 ff.; RW (11), 54 f.; there is some doubt whether or not the structure was
restored after 197, depending on whether the two altars found *in situ* are second century
or, as Professor Birley now thinks, are of the third century. Whether there was more than
one structural period is not absolutely certain, but it is clear that three inhumations inside
the apse are intrusive and may not be Roman.

[1] AA (2), VI, 171. [2] AA (4), XI, 176 ff. [3] AA (4), XIX, 1 ff.
[4] Ibid. 35.

uncertain date) probably represents an attempt to fortify what remained of the substantial stone-built *vicus* which had in the meantime grown up in place of the Vallum. The sixth, or top, layer is 'but a very light sprinkling of small stone' in W. L. George's words, and probably is the top dressing of the fifth period or a minor repair, rather than a reconstruction.

(iii) *Flanking the causeway* (references are to letters on plan, *AA* (4), XI, 180, Fig. 3, with additions made in 1938).

Phase I. Immediately after the filling of the Vallum early in the Severan period, a timber building was constructed east of the road, associated with a north–south drain (presumably the east side-drain of the roadway) and overlapping the north lip of the ditch (Building A—). A similar structure may have lain on the opposite side of the road, over the southern half of the Vallum. The structures of this period subsided into the ditch and were destroyed by fire.

Phase II. The subsided ruins of these buildings were levelled up with rubbish containing material of all the preceding periods, and a number of stone houses constructed within the first half of the third century, but late enough for no further subsidence to occur.

Building A, a strip-house more than 35 feet in length, overlay A—. There was a door in the north wall, at its eastern end (as surviving). A flagged floor, with hearths, was apparently associated with pottery as late as the middle or later part of the third century. This material was sealed by a heavy layer of burning (A.D. 296?).

Building B lay immediately south of A, was apparently contemporary with it and was also burnt.

Building C, another stone strip-house, was found complete in 1938 but the dimensions do not survive. It was situated opposite B and apparently overlay the south lip of the Vallum. It possessed double doors on to the road, perhaps as a shop-front, of which the northern half was later blocked. More than one period was discovered at the south-west corner of the building, but the significance is obscure. Fragments of querns were discovered in this building.

Building D lay north of C, also west of the road. Of the walls only traces of the south survived. The building possessed an oven and a clay floor, which overlay flagging perhaps to be associated with the Severan road.

Building F was discovered in 1938, but its position is now unknown. It was a slight structure, with a flagged floor and traces possibly of a kiln.

Phase III. This should perhaps include the modifications to C, but must certainly contain the reconstruction of A after destruction. A+ (as George entitled it) was given a new clay floor and five ovens perhaps of two periods, one of which overlay the north wall (of A, ?). There is insufficient dating evidence to place this phase, but pottery of the fourth century (none going beyond 367) is known from the site.

The full complexity of this site was not realized in 1933, and it was left to W. L. George in 1938 to discover in excavation traces of later periods and extra buildings. Unfortunately the war prevented publication, and the manuscript notes placed in my hands by the kindness of Professor Birley have lost their plan and photographs and are partly unintelligible. The figured samian was published in 1946 by Birley,[1] and the sequence of Vallum filling worked out by Dr Swinbank.[2] The summary presented above has been produced by studying with Mr Gillam such of the coarse pottery from the 1938 excavation as could be found, collating it with the reports mentioned and using the results to re-interpret George's notes. The results are hardly satisfying, but as the civil buildings on this site have now been destroyed it is impossible to hope for much advance in knowledge in the future.

Buildings south of the Vallum

Building 'E': *Mansio* (Fig. 7). This building was partially excavated in 1926–7 by J. A. Petch,[3] when flooding prevented complete recovery of the eastern part.

The notes which follow and the plan attached are based on the material contained in the published reports, though the interpretation will be seen to differ in some respect from that of the excavator.

Phase I. The building commenced as a simple 'barn-dwelling'

---

[1] *AA* (4), xxv, 52 ff.　　[2] *AA* (4), xxxiii, 142 ff.　　[3] *AA* (4), iv, 160 f.; v, 52 ff.

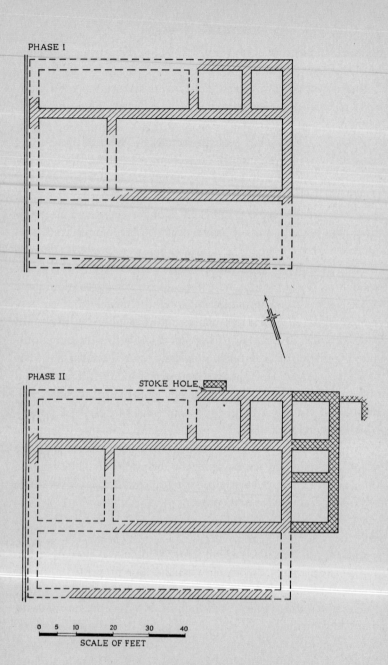

PHASE I

PHASE II

STOKE HOLE

0 5 10   20   30   40

SCALE OF FEET

Fig. 7 *The Benwell* mansio

74

or 'basilican villa', with nave and two aisles. This design is so common that I do not think it necessary to suspect with Petch that the central area might be an open court. As is frequent in these houses, a large square room was formed by walling off one end of the nave. The side walls of the nave were probably sleepers for stone or timber columns supporting an architrave. The north aisle was divided into rooms by cross-walls. The same may have existed in the wider south aisle, but no evidence survives.

Phase II. The eastern structures were an addition. Three new rooms were constructed in Phase II, as well as an additional structure on the new north-east corner, found in too fragmentary a condition to be interpreted. The arrangement of these rooms strongly suggests an entrance vestibule flanked by a pair of small chambers serving as a porter's lodge. Unfortunately there is no record of the state of the original east wall when excavated. It is therefore impossible to say whether or not there was a door into the nave at this point.

A further secondary feature is the stoke-hole built against the north side of the building. It is quite uncertain whether it acted as a furnace for some process or whether it fed hot air into the building by a flue now lost.

The date of Phase I is indicated by pottery from the foundation trench of the north outer wall of the building. On re-examining the excavator's report it became obvious to Mr J. P. Gillam and myself that this pottery formed a consistent group of *c.* A.D. 200. This places the construction firmly in the Severan period.

It is certain that the two phases are not merely stages in a single constructional process, for the original north-east corner was intended to be visible.[1] No post-Severan pottery is recorded. This is not surprising, since not only has the ground been subject to extensive modern disturbances but also the excavator was prevented from clearing the building. The beginning and duration of Phase II is therefore unknown.

South of 'E'. Traces of a further building were found by Petch in 1928 25 yards south of the old boundary of Benwell Park paddock[2]

---

[1] As is obvious from *AA* (4), v, pl. XVI, 2. [2] *AA* (4), v, 74, n. 8.

associated with samian which is unfortunately not illustrated and cannot now be dated.

Bath-house. This lay 300 yards south-west of the fort on the slope towards the river. Its plan[1] indicates that as at Chesters a large dressing room was added to the original scheme.

Summary

The structural evidence suggests a *vicus* gathered around the road south from the fort, concentrating on the site of the causeway across the Vallum and extending a short distance on each side over the course of the filled ditch and south along the road. The character and date of the structures close to the Temple of Antenociticus are wholly uncertain, but the discovery of a tombstone about 500 yards east of the fort[2] adds to the impression that this area contained temples and a cemetery.[3] Interest in the Vallum and its crossing has resulted in most attention, and therefore civil finds, in that region, but it is worth noting that Petch found nothing in trial trenching north-east of the *mansio*. However, the north door of Building A and the structures over the west arm of the Vallum imply an east–west road or alley, and confirm some depth of development behind the houses lining the main road.

This *vicus* probably originated in timber under Severus, suffered the vicissitudes of subsidence and fire and was re-built in stone within the first half of the century. The single Antonine sherd bearing as a *graffito* a woman's name (5) is insufficient evidence to postulate an earlier settlement.[4] The later history of the *vicus* is marked by another major fire (A.D. 296?), a second re-build in stone and the re-appearance of a gateway. The end is unknown.

Halton Chesters (ONNVM)

(*a*) Horsley, *Britannia Romana*, 142. (1732):

The remaining ruins of the out-buildings are to the south, and south-east of the fort.[5]

---

[1] Revealed in 1751, Brand, *History of Newcastle*, I, 607.
[2] *AA* (2), XII, 64, 136=*EE*, III, 184.   [3] [Cf. a lead coffin: *PSAN* (4), VII, 50 ff.]
[4] [Though an early settlement further down the hill remains a possibility.]
[5] This note is followed by Bruce (*Roman Wall* (3), 134).

(b) Hodgson, *Northumberland*, II, iii, 179. (1840):

The suburbs have covered a tract of fine pasture ground to the south.[1]

The presence of civilians at Halton is attested by two inscriptions, one recording a lady named Aurelia Victorina (58), the other a slave, Hardalio (59). The latter stone possesses the remarkable feature of having been erected by a *collegium conservorum*, the existence of which implies the presence of too many slaves to have been just employed in the commandant's household. This is most easily explained by assuming that they were employed in some industrial establishment in the *vicus* the existence of which received supporting evidence from the observations of Horsley and Hodgson (*a, b*). It is to be hoped that a dry summer may reveal in detail the buildings these antiquaries mention in the pasture south and south-east of the fort.

Chesters (CILVRNVM)

(a) Robert Smith, in Gibson, *Camden*, (2), 1054. (1708):

There was also a Statue of a woman, drawn down as low or lower than her breasts, and under it an Inscription, which I could not very well read; but however so much I read of it, as to find she was daughter of such a one, wife to another, lived so many years, &c.[2]

(b) Horsley, *Britannia Romana*, 143 f. (1732):

The ruins of the out-buildings shew themselves between the fort and the river. . . .

The sepulchral stones now at *Walwick grange*, which were found between that place and the *chesters*, seem to be a farther confirmation of this; for such monuments were often erected near their military ways.

(c) Hutchinson, *Northumberland*, I, 73. (1776):

On the south side, without the vallum and foss, many ruins of buildings appear, and some on the north.[3]

---

[1] This is repeated almost *verbatim* by Bruce (*RW* (3), 63).

[2] This is (37). [See *DN*, XI, 238.]

[3] It is not now clear to what the 'some on the north' refers. That they were Roman extra-mural buildings outside the Wall seems most unlikely. There was no sign of structures in this area in Bruce's day.

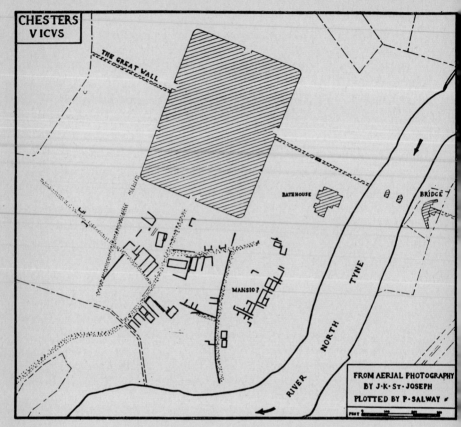

Fig. 8 *Shaded areas: military installations*

(d) Bruce, *Roman Wall* (3), 155 f. (1867):

Suburban buildings have left their traces between the station and the river, and ruins more extensive than usual are spread over the ground to the south. No habitations have been erected to the north of the encampment or the Wall.

Leaving for the present the immediate confines of the station, we may bend our steps a short way down the river on a visit to the cypress grove —the burial ground of CILURNUM.

This, which in Horsley's days formed a separate field called the Oxclose, is now included in the park of Chesters. Never was spot more appropriately chosen. The river here descends with more than usual rapidity over its stony bed, and bending at the same time to the left, exhibits to the eye the lengthened vistas of its well-wooded banks. No earthly music could better soothe the chafed affections of the hopeless heathen mourner than the murmur of the stream which is ceaselessly heard in this secluded nook.

From this spot have been procured several sepulchral slabs. . . .[1]

This is an idyllic spot, set on a gentle bank within a curve of the swift-running North Tyne. Even a Cistercian could hardly have chosen a more beautiful place, whether it be viewed in the deep haze of summer or the brilliantly crisp light of a snow-clad winter.

In the drought of 1949 the *vicus* at Chesters was revealed from the air in detail unequalled by any other in the region.[2] The plan (Fig. 8) shows features visible from the air, and to obtain a complete picture it is necessary to add the Military Way, and traces of buildings flanking it, between the bridge and the eastern postern gate, noted by Richmond.[3] The main road from the south gate, linking the fort with the Stanegate, was sectioned by Clayton (presumably at the point marked by the still-open trench which is a prominent feature in all the photographs) and found to be 27 feet wide and provided with stone kerbs.[4] The large patch of white visible from the air at the cross-roads in the *vicus* probably represents Clayton's spoil heap of road material. The pattern of roads in the *vicus* is odd,

---

[1] Bruce proceeds to describe in detail the cavalry tombstone CIL, VII, 590. The position of the cemetery as described is presumably the slope now known as Hodley Bank, the area between the road and river at the bottom left-hand corner of Fig. 2.

[2] *JRS*, XLII, 55; Cambridge, DI, 86; DO, 11, 12.

[3] *RW* (11), 96.   [4] Wallis Bridge, *Chesters* cat. 120.

and Richmond's suggestion that it might be caused by a Vallum diversion is important enough to demand testing with the spade at the earliest opportunity, for it would imply that as at Benwell the Vallum was still open or so recently filled as to threaten subsidence at the time when the roads were built and boundaries between properties in the *vicus* were being established. Few places potentially offer more to the excavator than the spot at which Vallum, Vallum crossing, roads and the stratification of civil buildings superimposed could be tested within a small area, and few places could be more pleasant to dig.

Most of the extra-mural structures are strip-houses of varying size. The most notable building visible from the air is that large range tentatively identified as a *mansio*. The same photograph reveals a complicated system of drains. The main outfall from the fort leaves the south-east angle and is joined by drains and street-gutters before it debouches into the river downstream of the *vicus*. The implication of official approval contained in the provision of a common drainage system for fort and *vicus* is important for what it reveals of the attitude of the military authorities towards the settlement.

One other important building lies without the fort, the bath-house excavated by Clayton, interpreted by Macdonald[1] and re-examined by Gillam in the snow of December 1956. The last operation I had the fortune to observe myself. For the present it is sufficient to note that as at Bewcastle it was found that a bath-house of standard Hadrianic type received drastic alterations in the third century, including the addition of the large *apodyterium* at the north end.

The cemetery has not been precisely located, but Horsley is most probably right in placing it along the road south (*b*, *d*), south of the stream which divides the park of Chesters. The absence of buildings south of the 'ha ha' is some slight confirmation of this, though the evident remains of ridge and furrow here raise the possibility that such structures have been destroyed by the plough.

The civil tombstones add some interesting information. Fabia

[1] *AA* (4), VIII, 219 ff.

Honorata, if her memorial is rightly assigned to Chesters, is certainly to be associated with official circles and not the *vicus* (36). She was perhaps a visitor in the *praetorium*—or the *mansio*—and what more delightful spot for the daughter of a colleague of the fort commandant to spend a holiday? Two more women, of German affinity and lower social status, are recorded on (37), and it is possible that the same stone formerly remembered yet another woman. One other stone should perhaps be included—the bust of a person of uncertain sex in the Chesters Museum (*Chesters cat.* no. 11). But the most important stone is not a memorial but a dedication to an unknown deity (38). This altar records a veteran and suggests the presence of his family, though it unfortunately gives no indication of his date or unit. In contrast another veteran is known from a diploma found at the south gate to have been discharged in A.D. 146, though again his unit is uncertain.[1] The suggestion of an Antonine *vicus* is important.

Carrawburgh (BROCOLITIA)

(*a*) Horsley, *Britannia Romana*, 145 f. (1732):

The buildings without this fort have been chiefly on the west side, where about a year ago they discovered a well. It is a good spring, and the receptacle for the water is about seven foot square within, and built on all sides with hewn stone; the depth could not be known when I saw it, because it was almost filled up with rubbish. There had also been a wall about it, or an house built over it, and some of the great stones belonging to it were yet lying there. The people called it a cold bath, and rightly judged it to be *Roman*.[2]

(*b*) Lingard, *Mural Tourification*, AA (4), VI, 150. (1807):

100 yds. east of the station is a castle stead. The burying place is between it and the station. Bones etc. found in it.[3]

---

[1] *AA* (2), VIII, 217. A fragment of another diploma was also found here.

[2] This well was the shrine of Coventina. When it was re-discovered and cleaned out by Clayton in 1876 the 'rubbish' proved to be a mass of sculptures and other votive objects of every kind. Full descriptions were published by Clayton and others (*AA* (2), VIII, 1 ff.) and Bruce (*Commentationes in honorem Theodori Mommseni*, 739 ff.), and a summary and plan are published in *RW* (11), 108 f.

[3] The 'castle stead' is milecastle 31. This seems to be the only evidence for the whereabouts of the cemetery.

(c) Hodgson, *Northumberland*, ii, iii, 183. (1840):

The suburbs have been partly to the south, but principally on a slope under the west wall, having in front of them a small stream, and by the edge of it a very copious spring of pure water.... In 1817 the shaft of a column was lying near this spring; but some years before, much of the works about it were removed for building purposes by the tenant of the contiguous lands. On the left of the strand of this, and about 100 yards from the south-east corner of the station, we also observed another spring regularly cased and covered with masonry.

The existence of a *vicus* is proved epigraphically by three inscriptions (23, 24, 25). The concentration of extra-mural buildings west of the fort was noted by Horsley (a), and by Hodgson who also observed a slighter development to the south (c). These observations have been confirmed by aerial photography (pl. IV, b), which reveals considerable traces of structures on both sides of the Military Way immediately outside the fort. These extend to the south-west angle of the fort, but it is clear that the narrowing of the dry ground southward prevented as large a growth there. Detailed interpretation of this western area is confused by the uncertainty whether some of the marks which seem to overlie the banks and ditches are in fact buildings or whether they represent trenches cut by Clayton when excavating the baths in 1873.[1] The banks and ditches themselves are uncertain in purpose, for it is not clear whether they are part of early and elaborate defences or are terraces intended for housing or cultivation.

The precise date of the civil development at this site cannot without excavation be ascertained, but the third- or fourth-century indication of (24) is borne out by the layout of the *vicus*. The fact that the buildings west of the fort clearly overlie the Vallum is not conclusive, since the Vallum had already been obliterated here at Carrawburgh in the second century for the insertion of the fort and it is uncertain how far on either side this filling may have extended. The key to the dating should be the disposition of buildings along the sides of the Military Way—if it were properly dated!

Hodgson's note of buildings south of the fort probably refers

[1] Bruce, *Lectures*, 1873, 17 ff.

mainly to surface indications on the site of the Mithraeum similar
to those which appeared in the summer of 1949. Excavation here
in 1950 revealed a temple of exceptional interest, but one that in all
the periods of its use had been sponsored by fort commandants
and was without trace of civilian worship.[1] It was originally con-
tructed under Severus, enlarged late in the reign of Caracalla and
subsequently twice refurbished in the same century. Destroyed in
A.D. 296, it was soon rebuilt but succumbed to deliberate desecration and ruin some time before A.D. 350.

Immediately south of this temple an altar to the Nymphs and
the Genius Loci was discovered in 1957. This also was dedicated by
a Severan fort commandant, and being unweathered (except on the
top) represents another shrine. Richmond notes surface indications
of a substantial building south-east of the Mithraeum.[2]

On the western slope of the damp valley in which the Mithraeum
stood, and a little south of the Military Way, it is still possible to see
the overgrown remains of the Shrine of Coventina.[3] The name and
appearance of this water-goddess are known from the considerable
quantity of altars and other religious material thrown into the
sacred well. Information on the duration and popularity of the cult
is provided by the coins cast in by visitors to the shrine. The structure itself was presumably not constructed before the reign of
Hadrian. Coins[4] in very large quantities start with the Flavians and
continue to Commodus, with the peak in the first half of the second
century. The quantities are drastically reduced in the third century,
though the series continues (with a minor revival in the third
quarter of the century) into the fourth. Renewed generosity from
visitors is apparent in the age of Constantine (when paganism *ought*
to have been declining!), and the coin series continues late. But despite this apparent long life of the cult, the coins of the third and
fourth centuries are numbered in hundreds rather than the thou-
sands of the earlier reigns, and its heyday was clearly in the second

[1] *AA* (4), XXIX, 1 ff; cf. *AA* (4), XL, 105 ff.
[2] *RW* (11), 111. [Shrine excavated 1960: *AA* (4), XL, 59 ff.]
[3] See (*a*) and references thereon.
[4] [Professor Birley points out that many of the coins are worn and that allowance must
be made for dedication of non-contemporary coins.]

century when the worship must have come largely from the army. Even in its later days some of the most notable dedications are military. Its survival late in the fourth century seems to be a sign of the tolerance of the earlier Christian iconoclasts towards local cults (as opposed to the greater rivals) which was noted in the Mithraeum.[1] Perhaps the most interesting find was a pair of pots specially made for dedication at this shrine. One bore the inscription added before firing: *Coventina(e) A(u)gusta(e) votu(m) manibus suis Saturninus fecit Gabinius.* The title given to Coventina bears out the impression made by the dedication by a prefect and by offerings of gold coins that the cult received considerable support from persons in authority.

At some time in the first half of the fourth century the water-level was raised in the valley, subsequent to the disuse of the Mithraeum.[2] This apparently artificial and deliberate change must reflect some activity whose results must have been of some importance to the *vicani* but whose nature remains as yet unknown.

Housesteads (VERCOVICIVM)

(*a*) Hunter, *Philos. Trans.* XXIII, 1131. (1702):

The Stone Tab. 1, No. 2, lies against a Hedge a quarter of a mile from this place. . . . The two Altars, Tab. 1, Nos. 4 and 5, are very legible; I found them on a rising ground South of the *Housesteads*; they call it *Chapel Hill*, and suppose a Foundation, which is visible there, to have been a Chapel; and say that within the memory of their Fathers they used to bury their dead here: I dare not determine in this point.[3]

(*b*) Robert Smith, in Gibson, *Camden* (2), 1053. (1708):

The extent of this City, is, as they told me, and as I guessed also by my eye, almost seven hundred yards one way, and about four hundred from south to north the other. It lies all along the side of a pretty steep Hill; but

---

[1] *AA* (4), XXIX, 42 ff.   [2] *Ibid.* 43 f.

[3] The first inscription is (67). Birley and Keeney point out that it may have been discovered near the structures west of the Knag Burn and south-west of the fort (*AA* (4), XII, 235; compare (*b*), (*f*), below). But the location is too vague to be sure. The two altars are CIL, VII, 640 and 638 (see (*c*), below). It seems clear that Hunter, Robert Smith and Gordon saw a distinct structure on Chapel Hill. It is less certain that Stukeley did the same ((*d*), below), and nothing remained by 1884 when the ground was trenched (and again in 1932) (*AA* (2), X, 171; *AA* (4), X, 91 f.).

that part of the City, where the Vallum or square Trench seems to have been, is not by far so large. . . .

Nigh the place where all these and other rarities were found, there was also a Column above two yards in length, and two foot diameter, lying sunk in the ground at one end. The people of the place have a tradition of some great house or palace that was at this place. This is at the Southermost part of the East side of the City, in a bottom; three hundred yards West of which, upon a little eminence, are to be seen the foundations of a Chapel; and the Inhabitants do still call it the *Chapel-steed*. . . . It is very surprising to see the vast rubbish of old buildings that yet remains here, with the track of the Streets, &c.[1]

(*c*) Gordon, *Itinerarium Septentrionale*, 75 f. (1724):

At the Foot of the Hill is a rising ground, whereon seem to be the Vestiges of a round Temple, within which are five or six Altars with *Roman* Inscriptions.[2]

(*d*) Stukeley, *Iter Boreale*, 61. (1725):

But when we were led lower down into the meadow, we were surprised with the august scene of Romano–British antiquities, in the most neglected condition: a dozen most beautiful and large altars; as many fine *basso relievo's*, nearly as big as the life, all tumbled in a wet meadow by a wall side, or one on top of the other to make up the wall of the close. . . .[3]

Mr Gale and I laboured hard at the inscriptions, and made out what we could of them under all disadvantages. Along the same wall, as we walked on further, we found more altars and carved stones of various sorts: but at length the farmer carried us up to a knoll in the middle of the meadow called Chapel-steed, where undoubtedly was the Roman temple: there we saw three or four most beautiful altars; and a little further, under another wall, a pretty sepulchral carving of an old soldier's upper part in a niche.

(*e*) Horsley, *Britannia Romana*, 148. (1732):

The vast ruins of the *Roman* station are truly wonderful, and a great

---

[1] The approximate dimensions given are reasonable. The distances as at present known correspond almost exactly. The last sentence seems to refer to the site in general and not to Chapel Hill.

[2] Gordon describes CIL, VII, 635, 638, 640, 651, 653 and 658. All are military dedications and each except the last was erected by a different prefect of *cohors I Tungrorum*.

[3] The first group of stones included a relief of Victory and one of three Matres and a number of 'soldiers'—military tombstones (or possibly reliefs of armed gods, e.g. Mars).

number of inscriptions and sculptures have been found, and many yet remain, at this place. The town or out-buildings have stood upon a gentle declivity to the south and south-east of the station, where there are streets or somewhat that look like terraces.[1]

(*f*) John Hodgson *AA* (1), 1, 272. (1822):

... on the west side of Knag Burn, where it enters the inges, the ground is irregular, with the remains of considerable buildings.[2]

(*g*) Bruce, *Roman Wall* (3), 189. (1867):

The suburbs of the station may now engage our attention. Turning to the east it will be noticed how much the Knag Burn contributes to the strength of the camp. On both sides of the burn the foundations of houses have been found. A villa of considerable pretensions stood upon a shelf of the rock, on its eastern side. ...[3]

(*h*) *Ibid.* 191. (1867):

Immediately in front of the station, towards the south, are extensive traces of suburban buildings. They extend in streets on the slope of the hill, having a full exposure to the mid-day sun. To the west of these the ground has been turned up in terraces for the purposes of cultivation. When the sun is low these lines of streets and gardens show strongly. ...

In draining the marsh, a few years ago, considerable quantities of human bones were found. ...

In the centre of the meadow, and directly fronting the station, a small knoll rises above the general level. From the number of altars and other remains found on it it has been named Chapel Hill. A little to the west of this, and in the fork formed by two streamlets, which unite and flow into the Knag Burn, is the site of the Mithraic cave which was discovered in 1822. ...[4]

---

[1] Horsley clearly perceived the distinction between the fort and *vicus*. Unlike Bruce he wisely did not try to distinguish between streets and terraces from surface indications.

[2] No structural remains were found here in 1932, but traces of occupation were clear (*AA* (4), x, 92). Compare Bruce ((*g*), below) and note thereon, and Birley and Keeney (*AA* (4), XII, 234 f.).

[3] The 'villa' is clearly the bath-house, fragments of which are still visible. The structures mentioned on the west side of the burn are presumably represented by the column drum, perhaps the site of a temple of the Matres (Bosanquet, *AA* (2), xxv, 196 f.). These western structures were also noted by J. Hodgson.

[4] The Mithraeum was excavated in 1822 (*AA* (1), 1, 273 f.) and re-excavated in 1898 (*AA* (2), xxv, 255 ff.). Conflation of the two accounts leaves many details obscure. Its

(i) Bruce, *RW* (3), 152 ff. (1885):

... there is a very abundant runner of excellent water at the bottom of the slope in front of the station. The spring yielding this runner was not discovered until the summer of 1844 [*sic*], up to which time it had been concealed by loose stones and herbiage. The spring may now be seen enclosed by four upright flag-stones, and these are surrounded by walls of masonry forming an oblong building, circular at its northern end but rectangular at the other. These arrangements date, doubtless, from the Roman area. . . .

Towards the close of the year 1883, two large altars, dedicated to Mars Thingsus, and two female deities named *Beda* and *Fimmilena*, together with an arch-shaped sculptured stone, were found at the bottom of Chapel Hill, on its northern side. . . .

The spring, noted on the previous page, is just to the north of the spot where these altars were found.[1]

Since the eighteenth century the *vicus* at Housesteads has been perhaps the best-known and certainly the most fully published in the region. In 1904 Bosanquet admirably collected the evidence then available,[2] and the process was repeated by Birley and Keeney at the close of the excavations of 1931–4.[3] Here I propose merely to summarize the evidence now available on this site and comment on such features as are of particular importance for this study.

Excavation and aerial photography[4] show the main concentration of civil structures to lie on the slope south of the fort, with a

---

external dimensions seem to have been 59 feet by 21. One of the altars was dated to A.D. 251 (CIL, VII, 646). Two altars to Cocidius (*AA* (2), XXV, 262 f.) from the same site need not indicate another temple: the collection of cults represented in the London Mithraeum bears out Bosanquet's observation on the catholicity of dedications permitted in Mithraea. Compare, too, the relief of a mother goddess found in the Carrawburgh temple (*AA* (4), XXIX, 30 f.).

[1] This passage was brought to my notice by Professor Birley, who pointed out that the spring is still visible. The passage is doubly important, for it establishes another shrine (an apsidal structure, perhaps dedicated to a water deity) and firmly locates the provenance of the altars and sculpture mentioned. It is certain from *AA*(2), X, 170, that the date of discovery of the spring should read 1884. [See *AA* (4), XXXIX, 301 ff. for excavation in 1960 by R. E. Birley.]

[2] *AA* (2), XXV, 193 ff.

[3] *AA* (4), IX, 226 ff.; X, 85 ff.; XII, 247 ff.: summary XII, 226 ff.

[4] Cambridge, DI, 78; DS, 31.

few extra houses flanking the road eastward from the south gate and between it and the Military Way (Fig. 10). Buildings II, IV, and IX (these figures are the reference numbers used in the reports on the 1931–4 excavations) were first erected in the early third century, IV being originally in timber. IX contained a small shrine which was a secondary structure, erected *c.* A.D. 229 as shown by a deposit of coins. These third-century buildings seem to have had a fairly long life, for IV contained five phases in timber. The structures are curiously scattered, strongly suggesting the presence of other third-century houses as yet undetected.

Buildings I, III and VIII were found to be fourth century in date, while the rear portions of XIII and XIV, being later than IX, are probably to be assigned to the same period. The remaining eighteen buildings examined in 1931–4 are undated.

From the early third century the road south from the fort was partially obstructed by the erection of building II and in the following century also by IV. There is no evidence that the roadway was restored till the later third century or the fourth, the *terminus post quem* being a coin of Claudius Gothicus under the existing metalling.[1] During the third century, therefore, the direct line south does not seem to have been in use as a through route. The restoration of the road in the fourth century does not necessarily mean that it was more than a street or service road giving access to the houses. Indeed, the fact that its surface was continuous with the paving inside the front of VIII supports the possibility that it was a private construction by the *vicani* rather than an official highway.

The back lane which served the houses on the east side of the street south was probably already in use in the third century, for its course is determined by the rear portions of II and IX, while it in turn seems to dictate the shapes of XII, XIII and III. Another road, which runs south-westward from the south gate is not securely dated, but it is difficult to avoid the suggestion that it replaced the south line as the route towards the Stanegate in the third century. There is, then, at present insufficient evidence to prove whether

---

[1] Building XXI, which overlies the Vallum and the original causeway, is presumably to be associated with the new road.

there was any considerable change in size or plan in the *vicus* after the end of the third century.[1]

The end of the excavated part of the external settlement seems to have come in A.D. 367, for no material was produced later than the *barbarica conspiratio*.[2] Within the fort there are signs of changes at a late date, perhaps indicating a need for increased accommodation, possibly for the families of troops. A late structure containing an apse was erected later than barracks I and VII[3] and a number of buildings of uncertain date were inserted immediately behind the wall on each side of the fort.[4]

A predecessor to the visible *vicus* was suggested in 1935 by discussion between Bosanquet and Birley of the results of trenching in 1898 south of the Vallum,[5] between it and the field-wall which runs north of Chapel Hill. The ground was revealed 'to be full of Roman remains, walls, pottery and even leather and woodwork well preserved in the deep wet peat'.[6] This area produced an unusually high proportion of samian, suggesting a second-century date. Yet the ground must have been unpleasantly damp to live upon and is reminiscent of the marshy area south-west of Chesterholm *vicus* used as a cemetery. Moreover, it is precisely the area where came the heaviest concentration of inscriptions from House-

---

[1] The dating of the Knag Burn Gate, sometimes associated with increased trade in the fourth century, is insecure. When re-excavated (*AA* (4), XIV, 172 ff.) only one period remained, apart from the original Hadrianic Wall into which the structure was inserted, but the presence of a quantity of samian in the earlier excavations (*AA* (4), XII, 246, etc.) arouses suspicions of occupation before the fourth century. Nor is there any satisfactory parallel known to me by which to *date* the structure on plan, for as a freestanding gate in a linear frontier-work its design will not necessarily bear a close relation to contemporary fort gatehouses. Dr John Mann suggests to me that the gate may not have been intended primarily for civilian use, but that it replaced the north gate of the fort for horses and vehicles when the ramp outwards from that became inconveniently steep in consequence of raising the threshold.

[2] *AA* (4), XII, 247.

[3] *AA* (2), XXV, 242. [Pottery from the 'intrusive' structures and also from the granaries was almost entirely later than 367, according to *AA* (4), IX, 224.]

[4] Bosanquet also noted 'the comparatively frequent occurrence within the barrack rooms of fragments of bracelets made of glass, paste, and jet, and of beads and similar trinkets . . .' (*ibid.* 235), but the purchase of souvenirs, the unauthorized but temporary presence of women in barrack rooms and the personal taste in adornment of auxiliaries are all contingencies which must not be overlooked before accepting the residence of women and children within the barrack blocks.

[5] *AA* (4), XII, 239 f.   [6] *AA* (2), XXV, 205.

steads (including those from the Temple of Mars Thincsus and the Alaisiagae)[1] and lies immediately below the site of the temple recorded by the early antiquaries (*a*, *b*, *c*). A local tradition of burial in this area survived into the eighteenth century (*a*), and bones were found at an unspecified point in draining the marsh in the nineteenth (*h*). A sacred spring was also found here (*i*). There is therefore good reason to suspect a cemetery in a similar relation to the Vallum as that at Greatchesters, and close to the temples.

[R. E. Birley's excavations in 1960 and 1961[2] immediately north of Chapel Hill have gone far to resolve this apparent conflict of evidence. Civil occupation has been shown to have started here in the Hadrianic period and included substantial stone buildings in the second half of the second century. This occupation may have spread extensively here south of the Vallum. At the point excavated it ended close to the end of the second century and the area was used in the succeeding periods for religious and funerary purposes (including almost certainly the temple of Mars Thincsus). It seems to me unnecessary to postulate destruction in 197 to explain the change in use. The Severan abolition of the prohibited zone north of the Vallum was probably enough to attract the civil population up the hill towards the fort.]

Evidence for cemeteries elsewhere is unsatisfactory. For one lying near the Knag Burn there is only the probable existence of a temple (*b*, *f*, *g*) and the uncertain provenance of CIL, VII, 693 (*a*). For a cemetery west of the Mithraeum[3] there is slightly more evidence—a relief probably a tombstone and a block which Hodgson thought probably a pedestal for a statue.[4]

The epigraphic evidence is small but important, for it includes one of the rare communal dedications (65). It is unfortunate that this fragment was unstratified and undatable. (67) seems to include a single woman among a long list of men including some German names, perhaps members of either the *cuneus Frisiorum* or the *numerus Hnaudifridi*. (66) the relief of *genii cucullati* from house IX is representative of the religious life of the settlement (in

---

[1] *AA* (3), XIX, 185 ff. [2] *AA* (4), XXXIX, 301 ff.; XL, 117 ff.
[3] See (*h*). [4] *Northumberland*, II, iii, 194 f.

contrast to the dedications from the temples of Chapel Hill which are firmly military in character), to which perhaps should be added a small altar[1] to Nemesis erected by Apollonius *sacerdos*, a title which suggests a shrine. Nothing else is known of the epigraphic output of this flourishing *vicus*, a situation so strange as to suggest that its main cemetery and temple area remains undetected.

Chesterholm (VINDOLANDA)

(*a*) Horsley, *Britannia Romana*, 149 f. (1732):

The town or outbuildings here have been chiefly to the west, and south-west of the fort; there being a small brook to the south-east, and a descent from the station to it.

(*b*) Hodgson, *Northumberland*, II, iii, 197. (1840):

In a swampy part of a close to the south-west of the field in which the station stands, an old inhabitant of the place, in 1810, told me that urns had been often found—sometimes four or more together, covered with a square flat tile, and having a stong oak stake driven into the earth close by them. A little to the south of this sepulchral ground, a dry green hill was pointed out to me as the Chapelsteads.[2] Sepulchral stones have also been found in the fields on the north side of the Causeway. . . .

(*c*) MacLauchlan, *Memoir . . . Roman Wall*, 43 (1858):

Coadley-gate, is the name of the farm-house close to Chesterholm; near to it is a Roman mile-stone, still standing, and close by it a tumulus; between this and High-shields there is another very flat mound, which possibly is an ancient tumulus also; it is a little west of the bridle road.[3]

Chesterholm *vicus* became of particular importance on the discovery there of one of the four communal inscriptions (32), almost certainly third-century in date. The remaining inscriptions add little to this, though (34) is interesting as the sole example in the region of the wife of a *singularis consularis*.

The structural remains are most impressive from the air and

---

[1] CIL, VII, 654.

[2] [Kingcairn Hill—this puts the cemetery at least 500 yards from the fort. Another cemetery lay about 600 yards west of the fort at Archy's Flat (Wallis).]

[3] The second tumulus (?) seems now to have disappeared.

exactly conform to Horsley's observations (a).[1] Some of the houses are clearly aligned on a road issuing from the west gate and curving northwards in the direction of the Stanegate; others are differently placed and the streets or alleys on to which they face are not visible. Excavation in 1930 near the point at which the communal inscription was found in 1914 revealed part of a stone building dated by pottery soon after A.D. 200.[2] A timber structure 20 feet further north lay outside the ditch of an early fort but no dating evidence is available. [Excavation in 1959 by R. E. Birley near the south-west angle of the fort revealed two stone buildings, one being a workshop apparently occupied from the middle of the third century to the middle of the fourth.[3]]

The bath-house, visible in the aerial photographs, has been known since the early eighteenth century. Re-excavation might yield useful evidence in the light of recent work on similar buildings in the region.

Horsley realized that the position of the *vicus* was dictated by the terrain. Further indications of its limits are provided by the location of cemeteries to the south-west of the settlement and north of the Stanegate (b, c).

A rare feature of the site is the tombstone of Brigomaglos indicating some degree of Romanization in the area in the post-Roman period. It is, however, insufficient to prove the survival of the *vicus* or its people as a community into the Dark-Ages.

Greatchesters (AESICA)

(a) Horsley, *Britannia Romana*, 150. (1732):

On the south side of the fort has been a regular entry.... From this gate there goes a paved military way to *Hadrian's vallum*, which is distant about fifteen chains from this entry; which way is also continued till it joins the other military way, which I have often spoken of.[4] The outbuildings are most considerable on the south side, tho' there are also some on the east.

---

[1] Cambridge, DO, 23.

[2] *AA* (4), VIII, 211. [Professor Birley tells me that he found second-century material in a building towards the west end of the main field in 1930.]

[3] *AA* (4), XL, 97 ff.

[4] The 'other military way' is the Stanegate, here a third of a mile south of the Vallum.

(b) Hodgson, *Northumberland*, II, iii, 203. (1840):

The burial-ground of the fort is supposed to have been near the spot called Mill Hill, a little to the west of Walltown Mill, where, in 1817, a great number of stones, well squared on five sides, but rough on the sixth, were dug up to repair the mill. They were laid on fine sand, and had the rough side upwards. Many foundations have been dug up on the same hill; and a stone, which had the figure of a woman upon it, and had lain at the gate from the mill to the station for many years, was broken and put into the end of the mill in rebuilding it in 1817.[1]

This *vicus* is attested by excavation, epigraphy, aerial photography and antiquarian observation alike. Aerial photographs show buildings south of the fort, east of the road from the south gate.[2] One strip-house stands about 50 feet from the fort ditch, with its end to the road. Two more are at right angles to this structure, and are sited just south of the south-east angle of the defences. All these were excavated in 1897, but details were published only of the western of the last two.[3] This measured 44 feet by 27 feet, and no interior features were recovered. In the same season the baths, which are visible on both photographs, were excavated and planned.[4] By analogy with Chesters and Bewcastle it seems probable that this was a Hadrianic structure, with third-century modifications including a large *apodyterium*. It was apparently destroyed late in the third century. Other extra-mural structures, though less in extent, were recorded east of the fort by Horsley (a). The photographs show roads but no buildings in this area. All the civil buildings lie between fort and Vallum are therefore probably third-century or later.

The cemetery seems to have lain south of the Vallum and east of the road from fort to Stanegate. Four structures, probably tombs, are visible and two or possibly three more lie in a corresponding position in the next field east. In the south-west corner of this latter field are the remains of the mill west of which Hodgson reported a mass of fallen masonry (b). The Roman date of two groups of tumuli, north of the Vallum, west of the road, and north of the Stanegate is less certain.

[1] The stone is (51).   [2] E.g. Cambridge, DO, 29.   [3] *AA* (2), XXIV, 44 f.   [4] *Ibid.* 45 ff.

The *vicus* is well represented epigraphically. (48) and (53) record womenfolk of auxiliary soldiers, and the former strongly suggests local recruiting of troops. Nine women are recorded altogether, including the relative of a legionary centurion (50). Two dedications are erected by women, one (46) to Jupiter Dolichenus— a deity popular with the army—and one (47) to Veteres (Vitiris or Huitris).[1] The almost completely spelled-out formula DIS MANIB(us) on (49) and the only partially abbreviated DIS M(anibus) on (51) argue for a comparatively early date for the arrival of the first civilians and therefore probably, but not certainly, for the beginnings of the *vicus*.

Carvoran (MAGNIS ?)

Stukeley, *Iter Boreale*, 59. (1725):

A little upon the south side of the *wall* was a great Roman city and castle. We traversed the stately ruins: it stood on a piece of high ground, about 400 foot square; had a wall and ditch; vestiges of houses and buildings all over, within and without.

Since Stukeley visited Carvoran destruction has been rife within the fort and without. But the one civil inscription definitely associated with the site (27) confirms the existence of a *vicus*. The other stones (28–31), which probably came from this site, record six other women, and (28) suggests a Celtic, if not local, peregrine family. (29) attests a devotion to the nymphs by two ladies, which may be paralleled by (54) (Greta Bridge) and, not so closely, by (96) (Risingham). The religious life of the settlement is also probably reflected in the numerous dedications to Vitiris, which Professor Richmond associates with the *vicus*.[2]

No certain indications now remain of the location of the *vicus* [but Robert Smith was able to distinguish 'several long streets, and foundations of houses' south of the fort in 1708, and it seems that something of this was still visible when Hodgson wrote his notes in 1810. Horsley seems to have seen traces of buildings on the west

---

[1] The latter is particularly interesting in view of the association of such dedications with the *vicus* suggested by Professor Richmond at the next fort to the west (*RW* (11), 163).

[2] *RW* (11), 163.

side as well.][1] It is unlikely to have lain east of the fort, for burials have been found there from time to time,[2] nor in the marshy area to the north. It is probable that the main civil development concentrated around the junction of Stanegate and Maiden Way immediately south of the fort.

Whitley Castle

South from Carvoran—to diverge for a moment from the line of the Wall—runs the Maiden Way to Whitley Castle and on to Kirkby Thore. Although it runs through some of the wildest country in the region, the land against which the Vallum was constructed, it has but the single fort of Whitley Castle between its termini, and is without signal stations or fortlets. It is therefore probable that it was not a regular patrol route and that its function was not primarily the control of these hills. The function of Whitley Castle was almost certainly the protection of the Alston lead mines against attack and theft from without and, if convict rather than military labour was employed, against risings among the miners. No more appropriate spot can be imagined for a Roman Dartmoor.

This is not a site where one would expect civilians to settle from choice. The evidence is a letter by Hedley,[3] reporting shoes 'dug out of an old dunghill, undoubtedly Roman, as well as the shoes. . . . Those of the Ladies had been much ornamented and escaloped, &c. in the upper leathers, with ears for lace-holes.' A child's shoe is illustrated.[4] The description both of the finds themselves and of the place of discovery is immediately reminiscent of Bar Hill, and it seems reasonable to adopt the same explanation in view of the lack of other signs of civil occupation—that the shoes most probably belonged to the household of the commandant. Where the labour-force for the lead mines[5] lived is unknown, but in any case it is improbable that any woman among it would have worn such elaborate footwear.

[1] See Birley, *Research on Hadrian's Wall*, 192 f.
[2] Bruce, *Roman Wall* (3), 240; Richmond, *RW* (11), 164.
[3] *AA* (1), II, 205 f.   [4] *Ibid.* pl. XII.   [5] *CW* (2), XXXVI, 109.

Birdoswald (CAMBOGLANNA)

(a) Horsley, *Britannia Romana*, 152. (1732):

The fort of *Burdoswald* stands upon a large plain, at the head of a steep descent towards the river, having the outbuildings chiefly on the south-east.

(b) Bruce, *Roman Wall* (3), 261. (1867):

The field on the east side of the station contains the foundations of several suburban buildings.

The epigraphy of Birdoswald supplies evidence for four civilians, all children. The boy of (6) was the son of a tribune, presumably the fort commandant, and the two of (7) were probably children of a third-century Dacian soldier. The fourth child is more interesting, for his tombstone is proved stratigraphically to be pre-Severan (8). The occurrence of the name Aurelius therefore suggests a date in the second half of the second century. Unfortunately his status is unknown.

The marshy nature of the ground west of the fort may have discouraged extra-mural development there.[1] To the south, in the triangle formed by the fort wall and two precipitous cliff-edges, a highly complicated series of timber structures has been interpreted by Richmond as military. The evidence for a *vicus* concentrates on the area east of the fort. Horsley's statement (a) is somewhat ambiguous, for he may either refer to signs of the military activity around the south-east angle or to something different further east. Bruce is clearer (b). His statement is supported by discovery of tiles, window-glass and pottery east of the fort in 1897[2] and confirmed by the proof in 1933 that the well-known bumps outside the east gate in fact cover stone buildings, with the sole exception of the ridge running north–south which was an excavator's spoil-heap.[3] These buildings contained at least three phases. Stone walls were also found in alignment with the east wall of the fort and between 40 and 50 feet from it,[4] perhaps parts of the same group of buildings.

---

[1] [But see Birley, *Research on Hadrian's Wall*, 203, for a fourth-century cremation cemetery, found in 1959 200 yards west of the fort.]

[2] *CW* (1), xv, 184.   [3] *CW* (2), xxxiv, 130.   [4] *Ibid.* 128 f.

These walls were later than the lock-spit for the unfinished outermost ditch of the fort. No details of these structures are available. The evidence seems sufficient to suppose the existence of a *vicus*, but confirmation would be welcome.

An unusual development was the structures discovered south of the fort in 1928 and subsequent years.[1] These were wooden huts of varying size and plan, interpreted as builders' huts in use during the construction of the stone fort. Stratigraphically they were later than the filling of the Vallum (here obliterated almost immediately after original construction) and earlier than the outermost ditch of the fort. In passing, it is perhaps worth making two points. On the published evidence it seems that the position of the fort-ditch chronologically—and therefore the date of the wooden buildings —depends not on an assumption that it was contemporary with the stone fort in construction but on its relation to the Turf-Wall ditch at the east gate, on the fact that 'the outer multiple ditch, fully dug, ran straight into the Turf-Wall ditch on the north, as if contemporary with it: that is, it was not dug in a mass of solid filling as if it were crossing that ditch when obliterated'. The Turf-Wall ditch cannot have been intended to be left open when the fort was complete, for that would render the east gate useless. Therefore the digging of the outer ditch and demolition of the huts must come before the fort was in full working order. This confirms the temporary nature of the huts cut by the ditch. It does not, however, necessarily indicate that such huts as were not obliterated by the ditch were pulled down at the same time as these. Indeed, the southernmost group was twice rebuilt. Nevertheless, the identification should give a wise excavator finding wooden structures outside any fort cause to hesitate before proclaiming the discovery of a timber *vicus*.

Castlesteads (VXELLODVNVM)

[(a) Richard Goodman, letter to Gale (Hutchinson, *Cumberland*, I, 115). (1727):

The fort is an oblong square, from the southeast front, the ground is

---

[1] *CW* (2), XXIX, 311 f.; XXXII, 143 f.; XXXIII, 254 ff.; XXXIV, 124 ff.

declining towards the river Irthing, on which ground, there are still visible, the foundations of walls and streets, but removed for the sake of buildings and tillage; . . .

(b) Gale to Goodman (Hutchinson, *op. cit.* 119). (1728):

On the ground where the bath was formerly discovered,[1] nothing was found but the pedestal of a column. At some little distance from the fort, the foundations of a building were found, and about it a quantity of ashes and some wheat, the grain entire but turned black.[2] here the largest altar was recovered; it is cracked, perhaps by the effect of fire.

Goodman's comments, to which my attention was drawn by Mr A. L. F. Rivet, carry conviction and it seems necessary to record a likely *vicus* pending more accurate knowledge of the nature of the structures without the fort. It is not clear which altar was found in Gale's building, though it seems possible that it was the altar to Discipulina Augusta figured by Hutchinson. This may indicate an official structure, but the stone may on the other hand have been re-used. Confirmatory exploration is much needed on this site.]

Stanwix (PETRIANA)

(a) Horsley, *Britannia Romana*, 155. (1732):

For here is a plain *area* for the station, and a gentle descent to the south, and towards the river, for the out-buildings. And by all accounts, and the actual evidences, it is upon this descent, and chiefly to the south-east, that the *Roman* buildings have stood. Abundance of stones have been lately dug up in this part. I was told of some, which by the description of them resembled the stones of an *aquaeduct*.[3]

(b) The Bishop of Cloyne *in* Lysons, *Magna Britannia*, IV, cxxxix. (1816):

The site is a good one on a south bank sloping to the Eden. The church stands within the area of the station, and the descent to the river is covered with ancient ruins of houses that extend into the streets of Carlisle itself, which I have before contended was a British town occupied by the Romans and used as a *vicus* or suburb to the garrison.[4]

---

[1] It was found by the admirable Mrs Appleby. [2] Cf. Papcastle.

[3] While Horsley clearly knew plenty of evidence for buildings on the slope, he does not seem to have any very precise idea of the limits of the fort here. In fact he has to fall back on general principles on the siting of forts and *vici*.

[4] What the bishop meant by 'houses extending into the streets of Carlisle' is obscure.

For so large a fort, with the most important garrison on the frontier situated at a key position in the system of communications and defence, the traces of civil occupation are remarkably slight. A tombstone (110) indicates a *vicus* with at least one inhabitant who was a citizen, since it is unlikely that the lady who set it up would have omitted to mention that her husband was an officer had he been so. On the position of the *vicus* both Horsley (*a*) and the Bishop of Cloyne (*b*) are vague but suggest that considerable signs of buildings were visible on the slope towards the river south-east of the fort.[1] Bruce's statement[2] that 'The suburban buildings of the station stood upon the sunny slopes to the south and south-east' is, in so far as it is not derived direct from Horsley and the bishop, rendered useless by being based upon MacLauchlan's estimate of the size of the fort. MacLauchlan thought of a square fort of $2\frac{1}{2}$ acres, with sides of about 330 feet and an east wall lying approximately 60 feet east of the church.[3] This area is but the north-west quarter of the $9\frac{1}{3}$ acres now known to have been included in the defences of the fort.

Slight traces of occupation of an indeterminate character were found in 1931 by F. G. Simpson about 200 feet west of the west rampart,[4] close to but not definitely associated with an altar fragment dated to A.D. 167. More illuminating was the discovery in 1930 in King's Meadow below the fort of the contents of a bronze-smith's workshop.[5] The presence of tiles with this material does not prove that the workshop stood upon this spot, and indeed the regular flooding attested by the 15 feet of silt above the finds renders it extremely improbable that it did. The bronze material has almost certainly slipped or been dumped from the slopes above. The objects in the collection include both brooches and minor items of military equipment, such as cavalry identity plates. The mixed production of the workshop suggests that its proprietor was civilian, though it is not unknown even now for official establishments to do work outside the regulation programme. But the

---

[1] [See also Hodgson's report of masonry on Stanwix Bank, Birley, *Research on Hadrian's Wall*, 206.]

[2] *Roman Wall* (3), 292.   [3] *Memoir . . . Roman Wall*, 75.

[4] *CW* (2), XXXII, 147 f.; *RW* (11), 208.   [5] *CW* (2), XXXI, 69 ff.

existence of such a civilian workshop does not necessarily imply any considerable *vicus* market for the products. The commandant's household was one source of patronage, sales to troops for female relatives and friends elsewhere another.

To the south-west there is perhaps a hint of a cemetery in reports of a Tuscan capital and Roman pottery at a point 300 yards from the fort. In addition, a large number of horse bones reported by Pennant[1] in the cliff near Hyssop Bank may possibly provide a parallel to the curious 'horse-burial' rite of the Trajanic military cemetery of Heidelberg-Neuenheim. Alternatively, and more probably, it may have been the knacker's yard of the *ala Petriana*. On the east side an inhumation is reported in Rickerby Park near Brunstock Beck,[2] a half-mile from the fort.

The dating of the civil occupation is an interesting problem. The style of the tombstone mentioned strongly suggests a date as early as possible after the Hadrianic foundation of the fort. The bronze material was dated by R. G. Collingwood to the mid-second century, on a typographical study of the brooches, though unfortunately his catalogue by omitting the pottery 'as not deserving detailed description' removed a possible check on the dating. This evidence is little enough, but the apparent lack of third- or fourth-century finds is interesting. It is possible that the Bishop of Cloyne's guess was right and that the town of Carlisle came to serve in place of a *vicus*, attracting the civilians and inhibiting the growth of any considerable civil settlement across the river in the later period.

Burgh-by-Sands (ABALLAVA)

The chief evidence for a *vicus* is an observation from the air by Dr St Joseph, who reported buildings of a civil settlement east of the fort.[3] The site was not photographed, and it is now impossible to recover details. The possibility that the structures might have been the military bath-house is ruled out by the fact that the baths were found and destroyed in making the former canal cutting near the vicarage, south-east of the fort.[4] The position of these structures

---

[1] Cited: Hutchinson, *Cumberland*, II, 579.   [2] *CW* (I), XII, 374.
[3] *JRS*, XLI, 55.   [4] Hodgson, *Northumberland*, II, iii, 223.

north of the Vallum gives a strong presumption of third-century or later date.

Bowness-on-Solway (MAIA)

MacLauchlan, *Memoir . . . Roman Wall*, 87. (1858):

The whole of the ground on the south-east of the station appears to have been built upon, and even now parts of walls are in existence, and stones have been recently dug up.

Knowledge of the civil occupation at this site is slight. The only civil tombstone is the fragment from the cemetery of the church (12). A *vicus* is suggested by the trader's vow (11)—even though he may have been no more than a bird of passage. Its existence is more certainly indicated by MacLauchlan's report of buildings south-east of the fort and its position given more precision by Professor Birley's observation of surface indications in the field west of the churchyard.[1] The general position of the *vicus* as known is therefore on both sides of the road from the south gate, but its extent is quite uncertain.

THE CUMBERLAND COAST

The Hadrianic system was continued along the coast beyond Bowness at least as far as Moresby. Forts, fortlets and towers correspond to the structures on the Wall and a road continues the Military Way (though not necessarily contemporary). The sea fulfils the function of the Wall itself. One feature only is missing, for civil purposes perhaps the most significant, the Vallum. It was presumably felt that the comparatively gentle land of northern Cumberland, easily controlled by the inland forts, presented no serious risk to the rearward side of the frontier fortifications. There is therefore no reason why, unlike the Wall proper, these forts should not have had pre-Severan settlements close to their walls, and it is perhaps an indication of the generally slow growth of civil settlements throughout the region in the second century that there is as yet little evidence of such development. On the other hand, not much work has yet been done on these sites, and new evidence may appear at any time.

[1] *CW* (2), XXXI, 144.

Beckfoot (BIBRA)

Knowledge of the civil occupation at Beckfoot is scanty. The aerial photograph shows a few buildings of the strip-type flanking the road from the south gate, establishing the existence of a *vicus*.[1] A large stone structure lies immediately outside the gate, on the east side of the road, and another, smaller building can be seen nearly opposite. In the next field south traces are visible of similar buildings on each side of the road.

In 1880 Robinson reported extra-mural structures 130 feet north of the north-east angle of the fort, but wisely forbore to elaborate until further details should be known.[2] His sketch suggests something more elaborate than strip-houses.

A cemetery lay on the seaward side of the road leading north from the fort.[3] To the south a particularly interesting cremation cemetery is indicated by finds of pyres with biers *in situ* on the cliff-edge 400 yards from the south-west angle. Further finds in 1957 included a cremation of the second half of the second century and an inhumation in a slab tomb, presumably of later date. An early fourth-century pot, containing cremated bones and bearing the graffito of a woman (3) was found 200 yards south of the south-west angle and presumably belongs to the same cemetery.

Maryport (ALAVNA)

Stukeley, *Iter Boreale*, 50. (1725):

On the north side of this *castrum* lay the city OLENACVM, of a great extent, as is plain from the ruins of it, but dug up all about. The family of the Senhouses, and the Eaglesfields whose heiress they married, have been continually digging here; and the ruins are still inexhaustible: the dwelling-house and all the outhouses are built from it, as from a quarry: hundreds of cartloads of hewn stone now lie there.

One may trace many square plots of the houses, and of the streets, paved with broad flag-stones, that are visibly worn with use.[4]

---

[1] Cambridge, DU, 28.   [2] *CW* (1), v, 142.

[3] *CW* (2), XXI, 270 f.; LVIII, 57 ff.; cf. LXII, 71 f.

[4] This account is not matched by any other, but it is first-hand, and its location of the *vicus* is confirmed by excavation and aerial photography. Olenacum is now believed to be Old Carlisle, not Maryport.

Stukeley enthused over Maryport and its civil settlement as on few other sites in the region. He placed the civil town to the north-east of the fort and all the direct evidence confirms his observation. Camden's remarks on coastal works further south[1] are too vague to prove the existence of a Roman port, and the Roman date of Bailey's finds near the mouth of the river[2] was rightly held un-proven by R. G. Collingwood.[3]

Detailed information about Stukeley's 'city' has to be gleaned from comparison of Joseph Robinson's account of his intelligent excavations in 1880[4] with recent observation from the air.[5] This may most conveniently be tabulated by numbering the fields northwards from the fort and taking the plot next north as the first.

Field I. Robinson recorded that there were finds at every point he dug, including structures on each side of the road which leaves the north-east gate of the fort and travels diagonally across these fields. He excavated a single strip-house as a specimen, implying that the others were similar. This building lay on the west side of the road, its short side as usual butting onto the street, at a point 99 yards from the gate. Its width was 17 feet, certain length 40 feet 6 inches. The door lay in the centre of the south-west wall, and therefore presumably opening on to an alley. There appears to have been an internal division. Finds included a quern, slates, coal and a crude carving of a *SIG(nifer)*. Interesting also was the dis-covery in the centre of the structure of a cremation associated with a coin of Faustina presumably before the house was built.

Field II. The road was here found to be 21 feet in width. Founda-tions mentioned by Robinson are doubtless those of the strip-houses visible flanking the road. Iron slag and coal were found at a spot 'almost like the hearth of a smithy', suggesting industrial activity. A pair of walls, 20 feet apart and traced for 53 feet prob-ably represent one of the houses. A conduit ran under the road and burials were found on its east side.

[1] *Britannia* (6), pt. i, 769.   [2] *CW* (2), XXIII, 146 ff.; XXVI, 417 ff.
[3] *CW* (2), XXXVI, 94.
[4] *CW* (1), v, 237 ff. [For development eastwards see also Birley, *Research on Hadrian's Wall*, 223.]
[5] Cambridge, DL, 24; and my own air photograph.

To the west the aerial photographs seem to show a number of irregular enclosures and rectangular structures not apparently aligned with the road. However, it is a question whether these crop-marks are not largely the product of Robinson's extensive trenching.

More remarkable is the group of structures found in the south-east corner of this field, at a point approximately 100 yards south-west of the seventeen altars. Robinson's plan of the main structures was conveniently reproduced by Collingwood.[1] The buttressed circular building, 34 feet in diameter, was perhaps a tomb, if the 'pyre' and 'cist' were correctly identified. It may be compared to that at High Rochester,[2] though twice as large. As at High Rochester the structure contained a coin, in this case of Antoninus Pius.

The rectangular building, 46 feet by 25 feet, with a projection of 6 feet at the west end, is unusual but not now unparalleled. The Mithraeum at Carrawburgh is comparable in size and similarly possessed a rectangular projection (albeit shallower) at one end and an internal subdivision or ante-chapel at the other. Robinson's interpretation of the building as a temple is thus not to be scorned. Structurally most interesting is the section of stonework which Robinson successfully identified as the fallen outer wall of the western projection, giving a height of not less than 16 feet to the eaves (or 18, if his plan is preferred to the text). Collingwood[3] suggested that this was due to violence in A.D. 197 since 'it does not appear that the foundations were in any way disturbed'; but a re-examination of those foundations, preferably producing some dating evidence from this building, would be of assistance in judging the problems posed.

Several altars were discovered in the immediate vicinity of these buildings, as well as a platform which appeared to be the emplace-ment for an outdoor altar. In addition a large number of burials were unearthed. The area in fact presents the typical appearance of a sacred place, with temple, isolated altars and burials ranging from the humble grave to the monumental tomb.

Field III. The aerial photographs (cf. pl. VIII) reveal at least three

---

[1] *CW* (2), xxxvi, 91.   [2] *NCH*, xv, 104 f.   [3] *Op. cit.* 92.

stone houses bordering the road on its west side and another on the east. No details are known.

Field IV. Robinson recorded a most remarkable cremation-cemetery north-west of the road. Some of the burials were covered by slabs, others were without protection. Two monuments bearing snakes in relief were found, one the famous 'Serpent Stone'.[1] This pillar bore on its reverse a human head, also in relief, flanked by curious zoomorphic, snake-like objects, reminiscent of the flaps or lobes attached to heads which appear on certain Celtic stone monuments.[2] The Celto-Ligurians were fond of columnar stones bearing human heads (sometimes an actual skull contained in a niche) and the origin of the motif is perhaps to be sought in continental Europe.

The pavement in front of the 'Serpent Stone' covered four cremations. It was very sensibly replaced in position by Robinson, at a depth sufficient to clear the plough. Other graves, covered by slabs, were reported by Bruce alongside the Roman road to Old Carlisle and presumably represent part of the same cemetery.[3]

Despite all these details little is definitely known of the history of the *vicus*. It is reasonable to follow Dr Jarrett[4] in thinking that the civil settlement superseded a cemetery near the fort. It seems likely that the house excavated in Field I was later than the burial, itself not earlier than the reign of Marcus Aurelius. The coin in the circular structure is unfortunately not conclusive evidence of its date, but taken with the altar of C. Caballius Priscus, apparently of the second century, it suggests that the temple area was also active in the second century. The date of the cemetery marked by the serpent stones is unknown, but its distance from the fort and the fact that no civil buildings are known in its immediate area or beyond would be consistent with its being contemporary with the *vicus* and marking its outer limit.

The epigraphy is not very illuminating. The eight civil inscriptions record five women (70–1, 72, 73, 76, 77),[5] one old man (74)

---

[1] *Netherhall cat.* no. 55.   [2] Cf. Powell, *The Celts*, 133 ff.   [3] *Roman Wall* (1), 362.
[4] Unpublished B.A. dissertation, University of Durham.
[5] A further woman's tombstone may be represented by Hutchinson, II, pl. ii, no. 14.

and a boy (75). Two of the women were probably members of a commandant's family (70–1, 72). The quantity of civil inscriptions is only surpassed by Risingham, but the information supplied is small.

The later history of the *vicus* is extremely obscure. Jarrett reports pottery from Maryport dating after A.D. 369, but the character of the occupation it implies is unknown. Bailey thought he had detected a rampart enclosing the *vicus*[1] but altered his opinion when R. G. Collingwood found beneath it (at a point unspecified) a *vicus* building and pottery probably third century. This does not rule out a late-Roman date, but much more evidence is required. The Ordnance Survey investigator believed it to be part of a mediaeval field-system.

Moresby (TVNNOCELVM ?)

George Wilkinson, identified by Birley as the author of the note in Jefferson, *Cumberland*, II, 448. (1842):

The *vicus*, or town for the camp followers, lay, as usual, to the south of the station; the foundations of its walls were very conspicuous a few years ago, when the neighbouring field was drained.

A *vicus* existed in the field south of the fort at Moresby and possibly extended into the next. This is indicated by George Wilkinson's passing remark and confirmed by Professor Birley's report[2] of several buildings, though one in which (lying about 12 yards from the rampart) Mr J. B. Jackson observed cement floors and roofing-tiles when a telephone pole was being erected may have been the bath-house. Birley also records that the next field to the south-east is known locally as 'Sooty Field', perhaps indicating the discovery at some period of a hypocaust. Such is the sum of knowledge about this *vicus*.

THE OUTPOST FORTS TO THE NORTH

These outposts fall into two groups, both geographically and historically. The western, Birrens, Netherby and Bewcastle, are Hadrianic in origin, the eastern, Risingham and High Rochester,

---

[1] *CW* (2), XXIII, 151 ff. [2] *CW* (2), XLVIII, 71.

though probably representing Agricolan temporary camps and Antonine stations, are as they stand strong points in the new Severan frontier system. Of these all but Bewcastle have produced civil material.

Birrens (BLATOBVLGIVM)

Epigraphy gives one indication of a *vicus* at Birrens.

The freedman Celer (9) is to be assigned to the *praetorium*, [but the wife Flavia Baetica (10) I had thought was one of the rare early lawfully wedded military wives resident in a *vicus*, but Professor Birley suggests that centurions' wives were accommodated in the fort. There is good reason to put both into the Antonine period.]

There is some evidence for extra-mural buildings, but none of it suggests *vicus* structures. The earlier evidence is given in full by Christison in his general discussion of the site[1] and I shall do no more here than outline and comment upon it. The exact provenance of most of the inscriptions from Birrens is unknown. Christison pointed out that the most precise statement was Nivison's that before 1831 'many splendid specimens of Roman antiquity, particularly large stones neatly cut and ornamented, with inscriptions perfectly legible. . .' were found in the annexe on the west side of the fort. This is vague enough.[2]

Also outside the fort was the structure from which came three dedications including the relief of Brigantia, erected by Amandus the architect.[3] If it was a temple, it was a temple patronized by the military authorities.

Roy's plan[4] shows three rectangular structures, one with a projection to the west, lying at the south end of the annexe and overlooking the Mein Water. In view of their position it is legitimate to wonder whether they represent the bath-house which was not found inside the fort.

---

[1] *PSAS*, xxx, 81 ff.

[2] It may or may not include the altar to Minerva (CIL, VII, 1071)—but even so, as emphasized by Christison, the activities of the finder of the altar are anything but precisely located. In any case, the altar is not civil, but a dedication by a prefect of *cohors II Tungrorum*. And perhaps the head in the Dumfries Burgh Museum (*JRS*, XLII, 63 ff.) is included.

[3] CIL, VII, 1062; see *PSAS*, xxx, 84. [*Dumfr. & Gall.* (3), xxxviii, 131 f.]

[4] *Military Antiquities*, pl. XXIV.

The last piece of evidence relating to extra-mural buildings is a series of rectangular dark crop-marks seen from the air north of the annexe.[1] In 1951 Dr St Joseph was inclined to identify them as a *mansio*: he now feels that the unsuitability of the ground makes that improbable. It may perhaps be remarked that if these marks represent structures, they are very large structures and bear no resemblance to the normal houses of a *vicus*.

Netherby (CASTRA EXPLORATORVM)

(a) Leland, *Itinerary*, ed. Hearne (3), VII, 56. (1539):

Ther hath bene mervelus Buyldinges, as appere by ruinus Walles, and Men alyve have sene Rynges and Staples yn the Walles, as yt had bene Stayes or Holdes for Shyppes.

(b) Bainbrigg, (British Museum), *Cotton, Iulius F. VI*, 319=*CW* (2), XI, 354. (1601):

De portu ad Netherbie.

Certo certius portum his Aesicae extitisse, quia latera navium, anchora et annuli ferrei quibus naves alligari soleant inveniuntur, sed propter aggestas arenarum moles, quae e mari diiciuntur, per aliquot milliaria mare longius excluditur, et portus, qui naves admittere soleat, iam obstructus est. antiqua urbecula cadaver iacet.

(c) Stukeley, *Iter Boreale*, 57 f. (1725):

The foundations of the Roman *castrum* at Netherby appear round the house, or present castle: it stood on an eminence near the river. . . . A little lower down has been some monumental edifice, or burial-place, where they find many urns and sepulchral antiquities.

(d) Richard Goodman, *Surtees Society*, LXXVI, 77. (1732):

You may please to remember that there was a gradual descent, from the principall and oblong fort on the north-west angle, towards the river Esk, in which there are severall streets very visible. In one of them, which runs north and south on the west side towards the river, by digging among the ruins for stone, were two rooms discovered parallel to the street. . . .[2]

[1] Cambridge, E 57, see *JRS*, XLI, 57.
[2] The building mentioned in the last sentence is the bath-house, discovered in October 1732, the plan first published in *Gent. Mag.*, 1750, XX, 27 (reproduced *CW* (2), LIII, 16) and discussed in detail in *PSAS*, LXIII, 483 f.

(e) Hayman Rooke, *Archaeologia*, IX, 222. (1789):

I shall only mention one [antiquity] that was found last spring [1788] in making a plantation near the house. . . . When it was taken up, ashes and bits of burnt bones lay scattered about, but no urn.[1]

The landscaping activities of past Grahams from the middle of the eighteenth century have disposed most effectively of the visible signs of Roman occupation, and a miscellaneous collection of Roman antiquities is small recompense for a fort and *vicus* beautified away.

Stukeley gives the position of the fort as at the top of the eminence now covered by the house and gardens of Netherby, the seat of Sir Fergus Graham, Bart. The *vicus* is best attested by Goodman's letter to Gale (d), which locates on the slopes from the north-west angle to the River Esk a number of extra-mural streets. One of these, west of the fort, ran north to south and the site of the bath-house lay alongside it. Despite the dedication to Fortuna by a tribune of the period of Severus Alexander,[2] the basic plan follows the Hadrianic pattern and it does not seem that this was a new structure in the third century. Nor is any sign reported of the typically Severan large *apodyterium*.

The position of the cemetery recorded by Stukeley is unfortunately not precisely stated. It is presumably the same as that pointed out to Pennant in 1772 in 'a shrubbery'.[3] The plantation of 1788 in which the cremation grave and tombstone of Titullinia Pussitta (78) were discovered is also now unknown (e), but search in estate records might one day throw light on these points.

Neither the status of this lady (whom Birley is inclined to put in the third century) nor of Iavolena Monime (79) is known. Reports of a quay contained in the notices of Leland and Bainbrigg suggest an interesting comparison with South Shields and perhaps Carriden where considerable civilian development accompanied the activity of a primarily military port.

Occupation of the fort is not certainly proven after the second

---

[1] This is the grave of Titullinia Pussitta (78).   [2] CIL, VII, 954; cf. CIL, VII, 965.
[3] *A tour in Scotland* (3), II, 70.

quarter of the third century[1] and it is omitted from the *Notitia*. The fort may have provided a centre for a Dark Age ruler in the later sixth century; but H. M. Chadwick's suggestion that it was the capital of Gwenddoleu, killed in the battle of Arthuret in A.D. 573,[2] need imply no more than that it provided a ready-made strongpoint. Continuity of occupation from the Roman period is hardly even a matter for speculation.

Risingham (HABITANCVM)

John Bell, *AA* (1), III, 157 and map pl. II[3]—reporting on his visit of October 1842 or 1843:

The principal entrance of the station has been on its western side, between which and Watling Street, here raised on a considerable embankment constructed for a level access on to the bridge, there must have been another bridge crossing Chesterhope Burn, of which there is not the least vestige. The road from this entrance to Watling Street has been paved with large stones, which are still to be seen amongst the grass; and on the southern side of this road is the dunghill of the station, which I have no doubt would also be productive of numerous Roman remains. From the land being designed for a crop of hay next summer, we could not examine it further. On the embanked part of Watling Street, near where the road to the station turns off, are the grass-grown remains of a square building. . . .[4]

Habitancum is a tantalizing site. It has more civil inscriptions than any other in the region; it was the official station of a *beneficiarius consularis* in the third century;[5] it has produced less structural evidence than any comparable site. Yet after deducting those inscriptions which may reasonably be associated with the commandant's *familia* (95, 97, 105 ?), sufficient are left to indicate a *vicus*. The daughter of Blescius Diovicus (99) is surely a native inhabitant of

---

[1] *CW* (2), LIII, 34.   [2] *Early Scotland*, 143.

[3] Which should be read in place of the reference given in Birley, *Roman Britain and the Roman Army*, 85, n. 74.

[4] The map shows a structure approximately 50 feet square lying between the Chesterhope Burn and Dere Street, immediately to the north of the point at which a still-extant field-boundary turns southwards to run along the embankment. This is presumably the building mentioned in the text. It seems to be about 100 feet south of the junction of the roads.

[5] CIL, VII, 996.

the *vicus*. Similarly, it is far more probable that the wife of Fabius (96) dwelt in the civil settlement than in the *praetorium*.

There is so far little sign on the ground or from the air of the *vicus*. Destruction has been rampant. To the north the River Rede has eroded up to the fort itself and on the other sides prominent riggs attest ploughing from an early date. It is not even certain whether the building on Dere Street recorded by John Bell was Roman or not. It is, furthermore, quite uncertain what he saw and described as the 'dunghill' of the fort. It is tempting to think of a *Schutthügel*. If this were correct, a civil settlement would be less likely on this side. Further away from the fort shrines may some day come to light like those which probably once accompanied dedications such as (96) and 'Rob of Risingham'.

Equally unfortunate is the fact that the civil inscriptions cannot be dated with any precision. We do not even know whether the re-building of the fort-wall which employed (102), (103) and (105) fol-lowed destruction in A.D. 296 or 343.[1] Perhaps the only fact that can be confidently asserted about the civilian population is its cos-mopolitan character. Theodotus the freedman (97) and the family into which Aurelia Lupule (102) had married were of Greek origin, in the latter case possibly from Africa. Aurelia Quartilla also dis-plays the African formula *D M S* on her epitaph (103). Inscription (100) may belong to this group as well, for it shares with (102) the formula *S T T L*, rare in this region. It is clear that Blescius Diovicus' daughter and Iuliona (106) were both Celtic and equally certainly the ancestors of Satrius Honoratus (105) came from Etruria. The problem remains to find where and when the *vicani* lived.

High Rochester (BREMENIVM)

High Rochester is a site at which a trading community might be expected. It was both a road junction of some importance and, in the third century, became the station furthest forward on the great road by which such centres of friendly tribes as Traprain Law were supplied with Roman wares. It was, moreover, held most powerfully in this and the succeeding century. But the pre-

[1] *NCH*, xv, 114.

sence of a *beneficiarius consularis* at Risingham might suggest that the centre for customs control and trade was further south than Bremenium.[1]

Positive evidence for a *vicus* is lacking. No structural traces are known, either on the ground or from aerial photographs. Of the inscriptions, (60) and (61) record in the third century the wife and a freedman of the commandant. Felicio (63), another *libertus*, may have been here in the same capacity as his colleague at Risingham. (62) is obscure, but certainly records a woman who died in the early third century. The provenance of a further feminine tombstone is uncertain (64). Hermagoras, *alumnus* of another third-century commandant, should perhaps be added to the list. Unfortunately his age is not recorded.[2]

High Rochester certainly had its civilians in the third century if not at other times. But two at the very least were residents in the *praetorium*, and it is quite uncertain whether there were any *vicani* at all. The very strength of the fort is itself ominous: life may have been too dangerous in this wild country even for soldiers' families. If a *vicus* is ever found, it will most probably be to the south-east along Dere Street and the Coquetdale road. Altars and graves might be permissible on the ground to the north of the fort, but buildings would have blocked the elaborately planned artillery fire-pattern.[3] It is perhaps significant that the well-known tombs by the side of Dere Street lie over a third of a mile south-east of the fort.[4] This *may* indicate intervening buildings. More cannot yet be said.

4. WEST OF THE PENNINES

The Roman traveller emerging from the south or west gates of Carlisle had before him one of the most variegated and heavily occupied areas in the north. South the great highway ran up through the valley of the Eden until it forked at Brougham, one branch leading on south through the valley of the Lune towards the headquarters of the Welsh Command at Chester, the other turning

[1] CIL, VII, 996.   [2] NCH, XV, 151, no. 30.   [3] Cf. NCH, XV, 99, fig. 21.
[4] PSAN (4), VI, 246 ff.; NCH, XV, 104 f.

left and climbing up into the Stainmore Pass towards its destination, the legionary fortress and later colony and provincial capital, York. South-west from Brougham another military road linked the forts that controlled the deep valleys of the Lake District from the south. West and south-west of Carlisle itself lay the marshes and low, fertile hills of the Cumberland plain, protected on the seaward side by the coastal defences, from the Pennines by the forts on the highway to the South and to the south-east from the fells and the Lakeland mountains by a line of forts on the Carlisle–Moresby road.

THE CUMBERLAND PLAIN

Much of this district is marked by glacial eskers and low, well-drained ridges of sand. Very many of these have now been revealed from the air as the sites of native farms (pl. VII). Perhaps the most notable is the group around the fort of Old Carlisle (Fig. 9), but there are many others. They are mostly simple, fairly rectangular ditched enclosures, sometimes with subdivisions and occupation floors. At Wolsty Hall the second-century farm was oval and contained a large stone and timber hut, the third- and fourth-century farm rectangular. The form of agriculture cannot yet be proved though there are some indications. So far no corn-drying kilns or storage pits have been found, but the large number of Romano-British querns from the Carlisle area, together with pollen evidence from further east (at Birdoswald), suggests that cereals played a significant part. Few of the sites have any sign of small enclosures suitable for penning sheep or cattle, but many seem to be the centres of large irregular fields.[1] The lack of any sign of granaries, storage pits or drying-kilns is probably due to the slightness of excavation on these sites so far, but may possibly be explicable in terms of sale to the army immediately on harvesting. The sites certainly seem to concentrate on military centres and there can be little doubt that their market was largely the army. Parched grain

[1] There are ditches, apparently parts of field boundaries, radiating out from a number of sites: e.g. Jenkins Cross (NY 286482), Wreay (246455), Wiza House (258454), Greenhill East (255456), Greenhill West (248452) and Wolsty Hall (106511). However, they may in fact represent drainage works relating to the farmsteads themselves rather than field boundaries.

I

has frequently been found outside the fort at Papcastle, and it is possible that processing was by corn-merchants who acted as middlemen. Certainly the idea of military granaries outside forts seems implausible.

It is inherently probable that the new taste for Roman manufactured articles should encourage native farmers to sell their produce in the urban centres where those articles and the money with which to buy them might be obtained. The few sites of this type that have been excavated have all produced Roman material,[1] and the onus of proof is now with those who would disbelieve their Roman date. The presence of Roman factory-made goods proves that these farmers had a surplus to sell and demolishes the idea that official requisitions reduced the native country population to a lower standard of life than they had enjoyed before the conquest. In fact the indications in this region are of a larger population living in growing prosperity in the security of the new age. The essential point is the likelihood that these farms existed on a system of sale of produce and purchase of goods. This is a revolution in agricultural economics, that divides the Roman from the prehistoric world. It also helps to explain the prosperity of Carlisle as a Roman town and to demonstrate that the Cumberland plain could have been viable as a local government unit, economically as well as politically.

Certain of the *vici* of this area have already been examined as part of Hadrian's Wall and its coastal prolongation: Burgh-by-Sands, Bowness, Beckfoot, Maryport and Moresby; and the centre of the region, Carlisle, has been seen in its role as a town at the junction of main routes. The three remaining *vici* all lie on the south-eastern rim of the plain, and the function of their forts was at least in part to prevent irruptions from the hills beyond. Old Carlisle and Papcastle were probably largely agricultural, while Caermote may also have been industrial, looking in part to the fells for its prosperity as well as to the lowlands.

Old Carlisle (OLENACVM)

(a) Stukeley, *Iter Boreale*, 54. (1725):

From the north-east entrance two Roman roads depart; one full north,

[1] E.g. Wolsty Hall, Old Brampton, Jacob's Gill.

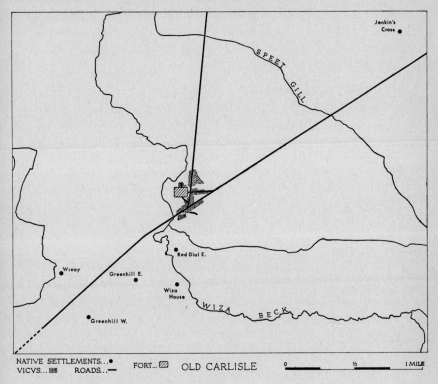

Fig. 9

as far as we could see, paved with coggles; on each side of it are the square plots of houses: the other road marches north-east, paved in like manner; it passes over two great moors, and there it is very apparent: we travelled along it to Carlisle.

(*b*) Horsley, *Britannia Romana*, 112. (1732):

The river *Wiza* runs on the south and the west sides of the station, about half a mile from it,[1] and the descent to the river is steep; yet the outbuildings have been on all sides here, as well as at *Old Penreth*.

(*c*) George Smith (1755), in Hutchinson, *Cumberland*, II, 407:

. . . the *Alae Auxiliariae* appear, by many scattered ruins, to have been encamped eastward a long way . . . there are no remains of buildings

---

[1] The Wiza Beck now runs slightly over 100 yards from the west side of the fort and its tributary from the east less than a quarter of a mile from the south rampart. There is no independent evidence of extra-mural buildings west of the fort.

besides the fort, of which the wall is here and there still to be seen, and some wretched huts, which seem to have been cobbled up by private soldiers, merely to shelter them from the weather; for the remains of them are of very bad stone, . . .

(*d*) Hutchinson, *Cumberland*, II, 400. (1794):

The remains of the station are very extensive, foundations of innumerable buildings being scattered over many acres, as well within the vallum as on every hand without, except to the westward, where the ground descends precipitately to the brook Wiza.

(*e*) The Bishop of Cloyne, in Lysons, *Magna Britannia*, IV, cxlii f. (1816):

The fort was of an oblong figure, 500 feet by 400; and buildings of a large vicus are round it, especially on each side of the road.

(*f*) Hodgson, *Northumberland*, II, iii, 235, n. *u*. (1840):

I am indebted to Mr. Matthews . . . for an accurate plan of the station and its suburbs, the windings of the Wiza round it, the antient roads that lead each way from it, and the present highway past it. . . .[1] With the plan Mr. Matthews further informed me, that '. . . . The remains of the vicus are chiefly to be seen on the south and south-east sides of it'.

Old Carlisle is in several senses a rarity. More is known structurally about the *vicus* than about the fort; and not only has there been recent excavation on the site but also epigraphy provides direct evidence of its internal organization. Inscriptions (81–5) are sufficient to prove the presence of civilians, including two veterans (81, 82), unusual in this region. (80) supplies the vital evidence that the inhabitants had banded themselves together under at least one *magister* and were probably able to have a common fund for public work. Most important of all, this inscription is closely dated to the reign of Gordian III (238–44).

The early antiquaries were impressed by the extent and survival of fort and *vicus* alike. As early as Stukeley they had a good idea of the road system. Most of the latest evidence on this has recently

---

[1] Matthews' plan was found in 1958 by Professor Birley among the Hodgson manuscripts in the Black Gate, Newcastle upon Tyne, as in 1951 he had hoped might occur *CW* (2), LI, 27). Its publication would be of considerable interest.

been published by Mr R. L. Bellhouse[1] and I have adopted his discoveries on my map (Fig. 9), adding the short roads to the south and north gates (both of which are visible on aerial photographs),[2] the latter having previously been noted by Hodgson.[3] I have also added from another aerial photograph a road branching south-east from the main Carlisle–Papcastle highway. I think this must be the road to Old Penrith mentioned by Smith[4] and believed probable by Birley[5] whose discussion of the site is the most recent detailed appreciation and the most satisfactory treatment of the antiquarian sources.

The evidence of the antiquaries on structural remains corresponds to the indications of the aerial photographs. It is clear that the bulk of the *vicus* concentrated on the roads, not on the fort itself. At the south-east corner of the fort the photographs seem to show that the ditch system cuts the road to the north-east, but on examination on the ground it is not certain whether the road runs along the top of the upcast or is obliterated by it. Excavation is required here.

The short spur of road from the north gate is flanked by houses and ends on the edge of a ravine. Post-Roman landslip is probable, but in view of the road north from the east side it is unlikely that this street ran far. I suspect it leads to a bath-house. Further structures lie east of this street, between it and the northeast road.

This road towards the coast was the focus of considerable development, noted by Stukeley (*a*) and visible from the air. East of these houses and between them and the modern road to Wigton a large quantity of Roman material, including tiles, slates and building stones, was observed by Harold Duff and mentioned in print by Collingwood.[6] This material ended in a line 'of roughly squared sandstone' approximately parallel with the modern road and about 40 yards south-west of it (in parcels 1558, 1561). A mixture of charcoal and tiles near the centre of the larger field (1558) suggested a

---

[1] *CW* (2), LVI, 41 ff.   [2] Cambridge, DS, 58; DS, 60; Newcastle, 6/A/30.
[3] *Northumberland*, II, iii, 235.   [4] Hutchinson, *Cumberland*, II, 408.
[5] *CW* (2), LI, 36.   [6] *CW* (2), XXVIII, 104.

hypocaust. The position makes a bath-house improbable but indicates some large residential building, perhaps a *mansio*.

Further houses, all apparently of the strip type, flank the road east as far as the junction at Sunnybank with the highway (cf. Smith (*c*)). South of the fort none appear around the gate, but there is again a solid row of houses on each side of the north-east and main roads. South of the main road and on the edge of the ravine of the Wiza Beck lies a particularly large structure or structures (cf. Cloyne (*e*), Hodgson(*f*)). East of this excavations were carried out by Mr Bellhouse in 1956.[1] In the area examined three periods appeared, divided by two destructions by fire. In each period the same features were present: stone houses facing the road, backed by further houses constructed of wattle and daub. Provisional assessment of the pottery indicates occupation in the second and third centuries. There was no securely stratified pottery associated with the re-occupation after the second fire. The topsoil contained fourth-century pottery but none was found dating after 367 and the same was true of surface finds in the adjacent ploughed field. Small finds included unstratified a pipeclay Venus (cf. Lysons' report[2] of what sounds like another, found together with a leather sandal in 'a well about six feet deep near this station') a bronze steel-yard-weight of Romano-provincial workmanship (pl. IV a) perhaps with affinities with work in other Celtic provinces of the empire,[3] a simple silver 'crossbow' brooch (? third century) and a fragment of samian (Dr. 18/31) with the graffito TARVTI(.).[4] Among the slates were two incised slabs.[5]

The evidence available suggests a *vicus* starting in the second century, perhaps largely in timber, destroyed at least partly during that century or the next, re-built, organized with a *magister* by the reign of Gordian III, destroyed again (almost certainly in 296) and re-built for the last time in the early fourth century. If the buildings in the area excavated are representative, the settlement was structurally most impressive in the latest period.

---

[1] *JRS*, XLVII, 203. [*CW* (2), LIX, 15 ff.]   [2] *Cumberland*, CLXXXVI.
[3] *JRS*, XLVII, pl. XV, 2.   [4] *JRS*, XLVII, 233, no. 35.
[5] *JRS*, XLVII, 203: their interpretation remains uncertain.

There is no archaeological evidence for occupation in the settlement after A.D. 367. There seems no way of assessing the value or significance of the report by Nennius of the construction by Vortigern of a castle of refuge, located by a gloss of uncertain date as at Old Carlisle.[1] Collingwood's alternative suggestions, indicating periods four centuries apart to which the Nennian reference may refer, inspire no confidence in any conclusions that may be drawn from this material and are a deterrent to attempts to follow any continuity of occupation into the fog of the Dark Ages.

The surrounding countryside

The function of these *vici* as trading settlements has long been inferred. The steelyard-weight is one sign of such activity. Yet the emphasis has been on their trade with the troops, with the traveller and with the barbarian beyond the frontier. At Old Carlisle aerial photography has made it possible to see the fort and vicus in relation to its immediate countryside, not with reference to military strategy and tactics but as a centre for the native population. The map (Fig. 9) shows the position of the native sites known in the area.[2] None of the sites shown here has been excavated, but there is no reason to doubt their Roman date. The precise location of the farms around the fort has been determined by the hillocks and low ridges of glacial origin which are a prominent feature of this unemphatic landscape. Yet here and elsewhere in this western part of the frontier region it is very noticeable that the native settlements tend to concentrate on the Roman roads, lying like Roman villas on a convenient spot within a short distance of the highway. Here this exceptionally heavy concentration of sites is most probably explained by the coincidence of unusually good land and the factors of the security offered by the presence of the fort, the market facilities of the *vicus* and possibly some system of direct purchase of food supplies by the garrison.

[1] *The Antiquary*, XLI, 409 f.; cf. *CW* (2), XXVIII, 110 ff.; LI, 16 f.
[2] [Cf. *CW* (2), LIX, 1 ff.]

Papcastle (DERVENTIO)

(*a*) Stukeley, *Iter Boreale*, 51. (1725):

The famous font, now at Bridekirk, was taken up at this place, in the pasture south of the south-east angle of the city, by the lane called Moorwent. In the same place lately they found a subterraneous vault, floored with freestone.... The name of the Boroughs includes both closes where the old city, or rather *castrum*, stood; for they find stones and slates with iron pins in them, coins, and all other matters of antiquity, upon the whole spot below the *castrum*, towards the water side.... On the side of the hill are many pretty springs: at one of them we drank a bottle of wine, to the memory of the founders; then poured some of the red juice into the fountainhead, to the Nymph of the place.

(*b*) Routh, Jr, letter to Roger Gale, *Surtees Soc.* 76, 106 f. (1742):

As to the ruins at Papcastle, I made as particular enquiry as I could of the man in whose grounds they were discovered, and of some of his neighbours who were present at the finding of them; the close in which they lay is a little to the southward of the fort, on the declivity of the hill towards the river, and is bounded on the west by a narrow lane, probably the Via Militaris continued, and is usually shown to strangers as a place the most remarkable here for finding of Roman coins.

These are the largest ruins ever known to be discovered in these parts; for they mett with three walls, besides the pavement; the first, layd E and W, was covered with earth nigh a foot high; parallel to it, at the distance of about 7 yards, they found a second; between those two, about 2 yards deep (the highth of the walls*) they came to a pavement curiously laid with large flags, ¾ of a yard square, and 2 or 3 inches thick, as I measured them; but, imagining money must have been hid there, they covered it again till night, when they tore it all up, as far as they had opened it. It was composed of flags of different thicknesse, under the thinner was found a coarse strong cement, which has caused all those to be broken in the taking up, whereas the thicker are pretty intire. Part of the wall stood upon the floor, and the edge was secured by a fine red cement, 2 inches thick, which they suppose was intended to keep the floor drye. They imagin they were at a corner of the building, the 3d wall standing at right angles with the first and second, and parallel to the stony lane, upon which was an old hedge.[1]

Upon the floor they found a sort of a stone trough, or rather the base

---

[1] From the structural details it is probable that this building was a bath-house.

of a pillar, about a foot high, the hollowed part square, and about 2 inches deep.

In digging likewise they mett with a small earthen vessel, which I procured, of the fine red clay, beautifully smooth,§ with letters imprest upon the bottom, but so defaced as not to be intelligible; the people call it a salt-seller, from its shape. Some years ago this man's father, who found these ruins, dug up a conduit. . . .

* These walls were six yards broad, and well cemented. [R. Gale]
§ A patera. [R. Gale]

(*c*) Bishop of Cloyne, in Lysons, *Magna Britannia*, IV, clxxxix. (1816):
Many coins and other Roman Antiquities have been lately found near the station at Papcastle, in digging the foundations of a house for Thomas Knight, Esquire.

(*d*) *Ibid.* cxlii. (1816):
. . . part of the ancient wall is still visible in the lane on the road-side going towards Wigton.[1] Coins and other antiquities have been frequently discovered on the bank sloping from the fort to the south-west, the usual situation of the *vicus*.

Extra-mural development is known to have occurred south and east of this fort.[2] The antiquaries limit their attention to the slopes to the south, where they suggest in vague terms an extensive area producing Roman finds (*a*, *d*), but the only clear indication of a structure that can be extracted from their accounts is the building, almost certainly a bath-house, described by Routh (*b*), and stated by R. G. Collingwood to have lain 'in the field between the village and the river now known as Sibby'.[3] Stukeley's structures outside the south-east angle clearly formed part of the waterworks of the fort.

The only modern excavation outside the fort revealed a fragmentary building outside the east gate, on the south side of the entrance.[4] It lay a mere 10 feet from the rampart, which has aroused suspicion of an official though civil purpose, and caused it to be compared with building VII in the Housesteads *vicus*. These

[1] The wall is perhaps part of the same structure as that reported by Routh.
[2] [See now *CW* (2), LXIII, 96 ff.]   [3] *CW* (2), XIII, 132.   [4] *Ibid.* 137 f.

suspicions are in both cases reasonable but so far unconfirmed. The pottery from this building was not satisfactorily published, but the report[1] implies that none of the samian was dated earlier than the late second century by Bushe-Fox. Indications of another building were noted eastwards, on the opposite side of the modern road, possibly to be associated with the blackened grain and samian found here from time to time.

The oddest feature of the site is the reported find of 'raw clay ... made up into Samian shapes' found alongside a Roman well at Derwent Lodge.[2] The clay is said to be foreign to the district and no satisfactory explanation has yet been offered. Perhaps these were sherds softened by soil, as occasionally happens.

[I did not feel that the sum of the evidence was entirely conclusive, but the discovery in 1962 of a tombstone (93 a) recording a man with no military associations, a woman (?) and a girl has clinched the argument for the existence of a *vicus*.]

Caermote

Few things are certain about Caermote, but the nature of the civil occupation is less uncertain than most. The military features were not to any great extent clarified by the excavations of Robinson in the eighties of the last century[3] and Haverfield in 1902,[4] but the latter at least succeeded in establishing the Roman character of the site. Examination of their reports suggests that an earth and timber fort was succeeded by a fortlet situated in its north-west corner. The latter also possessed an earth rampart but *may* have had stone buildings. The larger enclosure may have been a temporary camp (pieces of 'sewn leather'[5] suggest tents), but the double ditches and very substantial rampart surely point to something more permanent for the smaller one.

Extra-mural structures seem to be confined to the area north of the forts and east of the road which runs through the centre of the larger fort. Without further excavation it is quite impossible to say with which fort these extra-mural buildings are to be associated. It

---

[1] *CW* (2), XIII, 139.   [2] *Ibid.* 133.   [3] *CW* (1), VI, 191 ff.
[4] *CW* (2), III, 331 ff.   [5] *Ibid.* 334.

is difficult to discover from the two reports whether there were two stone structures here or one divided into two rooms. The plan drawn after Robinson's excavations suggests the former. Chancellor Ferguson reports:

> The buildings, be they Roman or not, have been roofed with lead, and have been destroyed by fire. Mr. Robinson took out over three stones of lead that had run into the soil, and more yet remains. Quantities of iron nails, in a decomposed condition, were also found, and much charcoal.[1]

There is no need to follow this writer in assuming a roof of lead. It seems clear that this was an industrial establishment. It may, as Professor Birley has suggested, have received material from mines on the north side of the Skiddaw range, but such mining in the Roman period has yet to be proved and the destination of the road in each direction from Caermote is still uncertain. That it was an official depot for the collection of the products of mines is unlikely, for it is most improbable that the authorities would have left so valuable a commodity as lead in bulk in an extra-mural building if it were government property. Moreover the roughness of the structure was emphasized by both excavators.

Ferguson also notes:

> At B and C the soil has been disturbed: on being dug into it was found to be full of half-made or decayed fragments of brick, probably the debris of brick-making.

'B' appears to be the site of the eastern of the two buildings, 'C' a pair of banks some 50 yards north of this point. Chancellor Ferguson may well have been right in his interpretation.

It is, of course, possible that these industrial activities were military and placed outside the timber fort for safety—or even that this was an important official industrial establishment under the protection of a specially constructed fortlet. But the scale of the place as at present known argues against the latter, while the typical strip-type building shown on the earlier plan and its characteristic

[1] *CW* (I), VI 193.

location give no reason for failing to record this site as at least a 'probable'.

THE LAKES

Roman occupation of the Lake District follows the characteristic pattern for control of a mountain area. The total absence of Roman material from the central part of the district suggests that it remained dangerous and hostile for a long time, while the extensive system of forts belies any idea that it was unpopulated. According to the usual scheme the district was isolated by a ring of roads, with forts at the mouths of the main valley entrances into the hills. Rebellious communication between the Lakes and the northern Pennines was prevented by the forts and signal stations of the Eden–Stainmore road. Movement south along the coast out of the Shap Fells or sea-borne incursions from Morecambe Bay were kept in check by the fort at Watercrook.

Ambleside (GALAVA)

Ambleside[1] is one of the most attractively sited of Roman forts. It lies on the floor where two deep valleys converge on to the head of Windemere. Northwards is the natural route into the centre of the Lake District and westwards through Langdale the road to Hardknot and the sea at Ravenglass. This line of forts not only watched for disturbance in the mountains, it also prevented raiding southwards into Cartmel and Furness Plain, areas which had been prosperous in the pre-Roman period (to judge from the distribution of bronze implements)[2] and where the prevalence of Roman material implies a degree of Romanization considerably in advance of that in the mountain districts.

The fort itself occupies almost all of a small platform between the lake and two rocky knolls. The latter, which reach turret height, must have presented some inconvenience for the look-outs and the placing of the fort here must indicate an overriding desire for closeness to the shore. This may have been partly defensive, partly for convenience of water-supply, but perhaps also for ease of patrolling

---

[1] [Was the retired centurion (cf. (111)) of the 1962 inscription (*JRS*, LIII, 160, no. 4) resident in the fort?] [2] *CW* (2), XXXIII, 182 ff.

the lake by boat, watching the hills on either side and controlling the route by water to the sea.

There is not much space north of the fort for a civil settlement due to the knolls mentioned, and it is difficult to imagine that the troops refrained from erecting shrines to the Genius Loci or the Nymphs on these ideal spots.

R. G. Collingwood's trial holes north of the fort in 1920 revealed a road and, to the east of it, floors over an area '200 feet north and south by something like 30 to 60 feet east and west, becoming broader where the rocks give more room, to northwards'.[1] This establishes the existence of extra-mural structures but reveals little of their nature. The area is too large to be accounted for by a bath-house alone. Where datable the pottery was second and third century but unfortunately was not reported in detail. Some sort of civil occupation seems certain, but its nature is quite indeterminate.

Ravenglass (GLANNAVENTA)

At Ravenglass there is sufficient evidence to indicate the presence of extra-mural structures north of the fort. From personal observation M. C. Fair and R. G. Collingwood reported pottery and other unspecified Roman material north of the fort[2] scattered over 'some three or four acres'.[3] The only structural remains, apart from the bath-house which still stands outside the north-east angle of the fort,[4] were tiles from a hypocaust, slates, floor tesserae and samian, revealed in a slip of the sea-face, 'from the area north of the fort'[5] —perhaps from the same building as that also reported by Miss Fair, saying 'structural remains, including tiles, like those from Muncaster, and pottery are to be seen some 500 yds. N of the fort and W of the railway line, which doubtless formed part of the Annexe, and traces of roads which run east from it'.[6] There is no evidence

---

[1] CW (2), XXI, 13; cf. CW (2), LV, 318 f. [and JRS, LIV, 156—add. note Jan. 1965].

[2] CW (2), XXIV, 249; XXV, 374 f.

[3] Collingwood, Roman Eskdale, 44; Finds over a considerable area are also suggested by William Jackson's note of field names: 'Castle Meadow, Castle Field, Stone Warron, Stone Acre, Broad Walls, Walls Field, Walls Close, Black Stones, &c.' (CW (1), III, 21). These names are not recorded on the Ordnance maps and it would be of considerable interest if a local historian could locate them.

[4] CW (1), III, 23 ff.   [5] CW (2), XXV, 374 f.   [6] JRS, XXXIV, 79.

for an annexe,[1] and these remains suggest an elaborate building which, as it cannot be the bath-house, is quite likely (as Professor Birley has suggested to me) to have been a *mansio* rather than a private house.

The quantity of material north of the fort and the considerable area over which it is scattered permits us to record a probable *vicus* here, but excavation is needed before certainty can be reached, as there *might* have been a *mansio*, temples and tombs sufficient to account for the surface finds. Excavation has however now been carried out on the second-century Muncaster tilery (Park House, Muncaster)[2] but it remains uncertain whether it was civil or military, though the former is perhaps more likely.

Watercrook (ALAVNA)

(*a*) Machell, MSS II, 82 f.=*CW* (2), VIII, 98 f. (seventeenth century):

Near the N. corner at 70 yards distance are lately discovered the foundations of som old outer Roman buildings 2 or 3 joynd in . . . abrest extending lengthwards to the S.W. 3 rooms on a floor of 5 yards square, and fronting and flanking with the N. East side of the great Romane fort, where several fragments of Roman Antiquities have bin discovered. In the first Roome wh lyeth NE was an Oven floored as they informed me of bricks of 1 ft. diameter and 3 inches thick, on which was impressed a Lyons-paw, as true and exact as if a Lyon had trod on the clay before it was baked. But the arching was made on the concave with their brick or tiles fixed one to another and on the convex with Roman cement wh so incorporated the whol mass together that they could [not] procure one single tile of whole and entire but broke them in pieces. Near the oven mouth 3 large flags . . . one upon another and the Lowest had this inscription the face turned downe wards.[3]

(*b*) Horsley, *Britannia Romana*, 484. (1832):

The town, I believe, has chiefly stood between the fort and the water on the west side; for here they still plow up cement and stones. These are of free stone, such as the *Romans* always made use of . . .

---

[1] *CW* (2), XXVIII, 357 f.   [2] See *CW* (2), LVIII, 30 [and now LX, 1 ff.; LXI, 47 ff.].

[3] Machell does not give the text of the inscription, but R. G. Collingwood suggested that it was CIL, VII, 292, which was re-used as a flagstone (*CW* (2), XXX, 99) = (111). This re-use of a probably third-century tombstone would suggest that at least one phase of the life of the building lay in the fourth century.

At this site there is sufficient evidence to prove the presence of civilians but insufficient for a *vicus*. The chief evidence is the inscription (111). The dedicators, freedmen, are certainly civil, but the exact status of the deceased at death is most uncertain, and there is some reason to suspect that he was engaged in official business, military or civil. If this were so, he and his men are unlikely to have been *vicani*. The structural evidence on this site is not easy to interpret. The most important is the report of Machell in the later seventeenth century (*a*). The structure he describes lying 70 yards north or north-west of the fort is distinct from the bath-house convincingly identified some 60 or 70 yards south of the fort.[1] The structure seems to be three-roomed, of an overall dimension of 45 by 15 feet and possessed of an hypocaust. This last feature renders it improbable that it was an ordinary *vicus* house as its size might suggest. Its position might indicate that it was part of a bath-house of a different period to the other, or perhaps a *mansio*. Horsley's observations do not add a great deal (*b*) for R. G. Collingwood has pointed out that he may be referring to the same structure as Machell.[2] It is unfortunate that as the fort lies with its *corners* to the four points of the compass it is extremely difficult to follow the directions given by the antiquaries. Moreover, Machell's 'fronting and flanking with the N. East side of the great Romane fort' is particularly obscure, for Collingwood notes that 70 yards from the northeast side would put the site into the river.

One further item is of particular interest, the discovery of a kiln, possibly a pottery, on the far side of the river. However, it is at present uncertain whether it was military or civil, and as it has been discussed by Professor Birley[3] I shall not go into its details.

THE ROAD TO THE SOUTH

If a Roman traveller had left Carlisle by its southern gate, intending to journey to London, he would first have passed between the tombs of the city cemetery and into a broad valley bordered by hills. To the east the Pennines rise abruptly from the valley floor, to the west is Inglewood Forest and the fells. The road follows the

---

[1] *CW* (2), xxx, 102 ff.   [2] *Ibid.* 104.   [3] See *CW* (2), LVII, 13 ff.

western edge of the valley, and by the time it has reached Old Penrith, the first station of consequence, it is separated from the main vale of the Eden by the moderate heights of the Lazonby Fells. This is excellent agricultural land, and Romano-British enclosures are reasonably common. At Brougham the traveller could make his choice, whether to turn left through the Stainmore pass to take the eastern route to the south or continue straight on for one of the alternative western routes.

THE WESTERN ROUTE

The road south over Shap would have led the traveller through country wild in terrain but perhaps less dangerous from hostile tribesmen and bandits than that over Stainmore. In the thirty-five miles through the hills from Brougham to Overborough (Burrow-in-Lonsdale) there is only one intermediate fort, Low Borrow Bridge, and no minor posts at all. Instead there is a cluster of native sites of an unusual type, grouped around the road in the Lyvennet valley near Crosby Ravensworth.[1] The chief of these is Ewe Close (pl. VI), which is actually on the road, but there are at least seven others and probably more. They are quite unlike the native farms further north, which normally consisted of a simple ditched enclosure, possibly associated with very large fields. Here the settlements comprise stone huts attached to groups of small sub-rectangular enclosures, the whole settlement presenting in most of the instances an irregular outline. The general appearance in fact resembles a broken honeycomb.

The distinctive appearance of these settlements strongly suggests a different people from those around Carlisle, and R. G. Collingwood pointed out that Ewe Close itself has every appearance of being the seat of some local chieftain. It is a difficult question whether or not to call it a village. It is certainly not a Romanized settlement, but rather the most important of a group of purely native settlements, a very primitive form of village among farms. Collingwood also pointed out that there was good reason to suppose that this group was in existence when the Roman road was

[1] *CW* (2), XXXIII, 201 ff.

first built and that the route was deliberately and at some inconvenience taken through it. This might indicate a military desire for surveillance by patrols, but the absence of army posts in this district is marked. The nature of the group suggests a distinct clan or sub-tribe of the Brigantes, and these special circumstances imply that it was friendly from the early days of the Roman occupation. Its chieftain was perhaps one of those Brigantians who were loyal to Queen Cartimandua and the alliance with Rome.

From Low Borrow Bridge to Overborough the valley gradually opens out and the River Lune turns gradually away westwards into the coastal plain at Lancaster and on to the sea. The main road continues due south from Overborough and after five miles begins to climb up into the Forest of Bowland and passes out of the frontier region.

Old Penrith (VOREDA)

(a) *Anonymous*, Harleian MSS 473, *Certaine verie rare Observations of Cumberland* . . . (Richardson, *Reprints of Rare Tracts* . . . , VII, 8) (before 1574):

Within ij myle of New Perith there is a place called Plomton with a park, and in the side of it, there appear the ruynes of an old town of a myle compas about, of the countrey called Old Perith, and digging up ther, they fownde stones fayr of every sorte. . . .[1]

(b) Horsley, *Britannia Romana*, 111 f. (1732):

The remains of the out-buildings here continue very considerable, . . . On the west side there is a descent, as usual, towards the river, and great ruins of a town. The ruins of buildings also on the other sides, particularly on the east and south, are very remarkable . . . I was informed, that the pavement of the military way was sometimes found to be above the foundations of the houses, at a part that lies between the station and *Carlisle*; which looks as if that part of the way had been laid anew, after the town, or part of it, had been in ruins.[2]

(c) Hutchinson, *Cumberland*, I, 479. (1794):

. . . its situation is close to the grand Roman road, leading to the wall,

---

[1] Birley has shown that the information in this passage came from Edward Threlkeld on the occasion of a visit to him by the author on 2 September 1574 (*CW* (2), XLVII, 168 f.).

[2] This account (which clearly distinguishes between the fort and *vicus*) is repeated *verbatim* by Warburton (*Vallum Romanum*, 114 f.).

and whose remains, before it was interrupted and covered by the turn-pike road, were very visible.

(d) *Ibid.* 490. (1794):

On opening a large cairn, west of the station, about four years ago, the remains of columns were recovered, No. 9 in the plate.—The foun-dations of houses, and hearth stones much burnt, were found.—In the same ground, several pieces of red pottery were turned up with the plow; the bottoms of some vases had the potters' marks, No. 10 in the plate.[1]

(e) Gough, *Camden* (2), III, 443 f. (1806):

The remains of the outbuildings and the station are very consider-able ... and great ruins of a town are on the west side next the river ... A military way goes hence towards Keswic, and part of another between this place and Carlisle is found above foundations of the houses.[2]

(f) Bishop of Cloyne, in Lysons, *Magna Britannia*, IV, cxliii. (1816):

The foundations of the houses which formed the *vicus*, are discovered in abundance on the south-west descent to the river, and altars and coins as usual.

(g) *Ibid.* clxxxix. (1816):

A singular capital of a column, ornamented with human busts and acanthus leaves, was found several years ago, at the distance of about 100 yards from the eastern wall of the station.

(h) Jefferson, *Cumberland*, I, 463. (1840):

During a repair of the turnpike-road in 1817, the workmen dis-covered a square well of excellent water, nearly opposite the station, which is supposed to have been of Roman construction; and within a few yards of it they found a sepulchral tablet of stone with a long in-scription, much defaced.

(i) Bruce, *Roman Wall* (1), 359. (1851):

On the outside of the south-east corner of the station, an arched

---

[1] The plate (facing 481) shows two fragments of a column with diameter about 18 inches, one a base, and a stamp on a samian base drawn as vv* ITVII.

[2] Most of Gough's information clearly derives from Horsley.

chamber, or passage, was discovered a few years ago; but it is now filled up with rubbish.[1]

Extensive remains of ancient foundations have been removed from the field on the east of the station; here according to tradition, Old Penrith stood. There are also indications of suburban buildings to the west of the station.

The early antiquaries, the inscriptions, casual extra-mural finds, ground observation and aerial photography each independently attest a *vicus* at Voreda. Threlkeld's estimate of a town 'a myle compas about' was, if anything, conservative (*a*).

West of the fort. Only on the west side can anything now be seen on the ground of the 'great ruins of a town' which so impressed the early antiquaries. And what can be seen are the sad traces of stone-robbing rather than the structures themselves. An aerial photograph[2] shows the despoiled remains of a series of strip-houses along the side, towards the fort, of a road running down the slope from the west gate in a south-westerly direction. Slight traces of another house lie on the opposite side of this road, a considerable way down the slope. Further houses north of the gate cling to the narrow triangle of plateau between the ditch and the steep drop to the river flats.

Disturbance has been in progress at least since the removal of a 'cairn' *c*. 1790, whose precise position unhappily was not noted (*d*). Hutchinson's details suggest a considerable structure, and his 'hearth stones much burnt' prompt the question whether it might not have been the large building showing on an aerial photograph close to the river and which I suspect to be the bath-house of the fort. Mention of ploughing 'in the same ground' strengthens this identification, for the flat space here in the bow of the river is the only place really suitable for that operation.

[1] Any suggestion of civil purpose in the 'arched chamber' can quickly be disposed of. It is clear that it was the arched drain in the fort wall found by Losh in 1812, to whose drawings in *AA* (1), 1, Donations, 2, Professor Birley has drawn attention (*CW* (2), 1, 202 ff.). The whole passage is reproduced by Whellan (*Cumberland and Westmorland*, 577). Both Bruce and Whellan also mention a well found 'some time ago' when lowering the level of the turnpike 'about a quarter of a mile south of the station'. It is not certain whether this is a different well from that of Jefferson (which appears to have been rediscovered in 1935) or an inaccurate locating of the same well.

[2] Cambridge, DM, 56.

More recent disturbance, this time draining, brought up a group of mid-second-century pottery, but once again the position was not precisely recorded.[1]

East of the fort. Horsley, Hutchinson and Bruce all report extensive remains east of the fort. Much destruction seems to have occurred in the eighteenth and early nineteenth centuries, especially during work on the turnpike road. It is probable that the well found in 1817 (*h*) is identical with that found under the modern road in 1935 opposite the north end of the fort.[2]

An aerial photograph shows crop-marks at right-angles to the present road, but they are not sufficiently distinct to indicate whether they represent ancient structures or not. More important in this area are the reports of 1935 and 1942[3] on finds produced in road-levelling. The 1935 site yielded, besides the well, some possibly pre-Hadrianic sherds and a quantity of other pottery that included Hadrianic, Antonine, third- and fourth-century pieces, as well as a little Huntcliff ware. Other finds included the handle of a *patera* of a type manufactured in the first century but which remained long in use and has appeared outside the empire in a context probably to be dated to the second half of the second century.[4] To barbarians and perhaps to the humbler provincials such objects were treasured heirlooms and their occurrence cannot provide more than a *terminus post quem*. A steelyard weight from the same site at Old Penrith is Roman but undatable. It may be compared with that from the *vicus* of Old Carlisle.

In 1942 work on the east side of the modern road produced samian and coarse pottery of second-century date but no associated structures. Some caution has to be applied when considering stray finds on this side of the fort, especially near the south-east angle, since a major drain is known to have left the fort at this point (*i*).

South of the fort. Less evidence exists for extensive extra-mural growth on this side, though Horsley links it with the eastern quarter in density of buildings. Aerial photography shows vague marks

[1] *CW* (2), XXXIV, 217 f.   [2] *CW* (2), XXXVI, 132 ff.   [3] *CW* (2), XLII, 232.
[4] S. Muller, 'Juellinge-fundet', *Nordiske Fortidsminder*, II, i, cited by Wheeler, *Rome Beyond the Imperial Frontiers* (1955), 59 ff.

west of the present road beyond Castlesteads farm and outside the south-west corner of the fort. Otherwise there is only Bruce's report of a probably Roman well on the road a quarter of a mile south.

North of the fort. The aerial photograph shows a row of striphouses at right-angles to the present road and clearly bordering its Roman predecessor. Horsley records reports of foundations under the Roman road on this side of the fort. These were clearly of an earlier period than the road and probably therefore earlier than those now visible.

Burials. M. Cocceius Nonnus (90) was interred 200 yards north of the fort and east of the road, while a further 200 yards on a cremation burial was made in the second century close to Whintonhill.[1] Another cremation of about A.D. 200, was found in the field east of the fort in 1863 or 1864.[2]

It is also worth noting that the Lysons report the discovery, at a point about 100 yards from the east wall, of a capital strongly reminiscent of that with busts found at Cirencester.[3] This may have come from an elaborate building, perhaps most probably a temple or a monumental tomb, but it may have formed part of a single votive column like those in the gigantomachy cults of the Rhineland and the famous 'Jupiter Column' erected by the people of the *canabae* of Mainz under Nero.[4] Such columnar monuments are ancient and widespread (votive capitals in Athens are among the earliest evidence for the Ionic style), but were especially prominent in Roman Germany. Nor were German civilians absent from Old Penrith—the veteran of the *ala Petriana* had retired here instead of returning to his home, the *colonia* of Vetera (87). The dedicators, too, of the weird inscription to the Unseni Fersomari,[5] found about 100 yards north of the fort, were Germans and may have been veterans (the reading of EE, IX, 1124, being uncertain on this point).

Another sacred structure seems to be implied by the stone which

[1] *CW* (2), XLII, 232. [2] *CW* (2), LII, 183.
[3] Richmond, *Roman Britain* (1955), pl. 8. [4] CIL, XIII, 11806.
[5] This name seems quite genuine and not a modern joke.

records its repair and which Professor Birley has demonstrated was found near the river 'a few roods from the south corner'.[1] It is possible that Hutchinson's report (d) refers to this monument. Like the peopled capital the dedication cannot be proved civilian, but the position of these monuments and of the burials gives perhaps a rough indication of the outer limits of the settlement.

The inscriptions

Mention has already been made of at least one veteran—and his presence implies a *vicus* at some time after *c.* A.D. 120 (87). Greca, too, was clearly resident in the *vicus*, even if her father and brother were both soldiers (88). Aicetuos and her daughter Lattio were doubtless in the same position (89), while there is no reason to think that Aurelius' Celtic father, Avo, was sufficiently exalted to qualify for residence in the *praetorium* (92). On the other hand, Hylas, foster-son of a legionary tribune, was undoubtedly so placed (91). The status of M. Cocceius Nonnus (90) and the *quaestorius* (86) is in each case uncertain, but the daughter of the latter was perhaps an inhabitant of the *vicus*.

Summary

Apart from the problem of whether or not the tombstone of M. Cocceius Nonnus indicates a *vicus* so early that it would be un-paralleled in the region, the greatest difficulty in understanding the site is the fact that the position and even the existence of Antonine military occupation is unknown. A third-century garrison is attested,[2] and, as revealed on the aerial photographs, the layout of the existing fort is reminiscent of the Severan plan of High Rochester. The occurrence of the famous five reliefs of deities re-used in the fort wall suggests a Constantian reconstruction after a disaster, as at Risingham,[3] but it is, of course, equally possible that the whole fort is Constantian and of one build: Birley assigns the fort to this period on plan.[4]

It is possible that forts of other periods lay on a different site.

[1] EE, IX, 1226; *CW* (2), LII, 185 f.   [2] CIL, VII, 315.   [3] *CW* (1), XV, 46.
[4] *CW* (2), XLVII, 173 f.

Aerial photography has revealed ditch-systems in the second field to the east, but these seem to represent temporary works, perhaps responsible for the suggestion of pre-Hadrianic occupation in the pottery. Horsley, with remarkable perception of the meaning of stratification, realized that the presence of road-metalling over foundations implied two Roman periods, perhaps with a destruction between. That the earlier period was not an Antonine fort must be disproved by excavation before the existence of a second-century *vicus* can be entirely accepted. But, though its date is uncertain, the existence at Old Penrith of a large settlement of substantial buildings and literate population is proved.

Brougham (BROCAVVM)

Stukeley, *Iter Boreale*, 45 f. (1725):

The square plot of the city is very perfect, on the south side of Brougham Castle; it had a broad ditch round it. ... The high ground by Countess Pillar, where most of the inscriptions were found, seems to have been the site of the city, and this the castle or fort; the Roman road lying between. ...[1]

It is hardly surprising that a settlement should have grown around Brougham, for it is the central point in the military system of the district.[2] Here the main road branches, east into Stainmore, south over Shap, while south-westwards runs the road which forms the southern side of the band which controlled the Lakes.

An aerial photograph shows the buildings of the *vicus* flanking roads from the west and east gates of the fort.[3] The latter road is clearly heading for the Countess' Pillar and the beginning of the straight section eastwards. Across the river the main road can be seen running off north-west for Old Penrith and Carlisle.

It was in that part of the *vicus* where the main road comes in from the east that a coin-hoard of the third quarter of the third century was found in 1910[4] 100 yards from the fort. How much further east the *vicus* stretched is a problem. Stukeley's location is clearly a

---

[1] Stukeley's use of the word 'city' in two senses is confusing, but his sense is that the high ground was the site of the *vicus*.

[2] *CW* (2), XXXII, 124 ff.   [3] Cambridge, DO, 67.   [4] *CW* (2), XI, 209.

guess based on the occurrence of inscriptions in the area of high ground to the north-east. But the inscriptions are tombstones and altars: *prima facie* evidence against houses in that quarter. A single well found under a fallen altar[1] is insufficient proof of the contrary. This cemetery extended into the field north of the Countess' Pillar, the find-spot of (14). The discovery of tiles and dressed stone in the same field can as easily indicate tile-graves, masonry tombs or shrines as houses.[2] In 1958 further confirmation was found by the discovery at NG 545292 of a sandstone foundation and some distance away part of a tombstone, as well as a late third- or early fourth-century inhumation about 30 feet from the first.[3]

The people of this *vicus* are unusual in that all known had single, non-Roman names—Ressona, Annamoris (14), Pluma, Lunaris (15), to which Audagus[4] and Baculo[5] should perhaps be added. The influence of local custom cannot be ruled out, but in any case the indication is of a prosperous native element in the civil population. In this connexion it is worth noting the discovery from the air by Dr St Joseph of a field-system (and, incidentally, a temporary camp) in the second field east of the modern bridge, and of native settlements at Frenchfield (537295), Sceugh Farm (544298), Winderwath (600285) and north-east of Lightwater Bridge (553293)— a grouping reminiscent of Old Carlisle.

The fort was occupied in the third century and also in the period after A.D. 369. The activity of the *vicus* in at least the earlier period would be likely on general grounds and is supported by Hübners' impression that (15) was third-century, and by the coin hoard of that period. Recently the presence of a civil population in the late-Roman period has been powerfully supported by Dr Douglas Simpson's argument for a sub-Roman occupation in the fifth and later centuries.[6]

Overborough (*properly Burrow-in-Lonsdale*) (GALACVM ?)

(*a*) Leland, *Itinerary*, ed. Hearne (3), VII, 51. (*c.* 1539):

Borow now a Vyllage, set in *Linesdale* a vi. Myles beneth the Foote of

---

[1] *CW* (1), I, 63.   [2] *CW* (1), II, 151.   [3] *JRS*, XLIX, 106.   [4] CIL, VII, 295.
[5] LS, 806.   [6] *CW* (2), LVIII, 68 ff.

Dentdale, hath beene by likelyhod sum notable Town. The Plough menne find there yn ering *lapides quadratos*, and many other straung thinges: and this Place is much spoken of of the Inhabitants there.

(*b*) Camden, *Britannia*, (1), 433. (1587):

quo in loco nunc *Over Burrow* est, pertenuis sane rusticorum viculus, quem urbem magnam fuisse, amplosque campos inter *Laccum* & *Lonum* occupasse, & ad extrema deditionis, fame nihil non experta, compulsam nobis memorarunt incolae, quod a maioribus quasi per manus traditum acceperunt. et variis certe priscae vetustatis monumentis, insculptis lapidibus, tessellatis pavimentis, Rom. nummis, & nomine hoc novo quod nobis Burgum denotat, locus iste antiquitatem suam asserit.

The tombstone of Aurelius Pusinnus and his wife Eubia is the only real evidence for a civil population at this site (93). Professor Birley has rightly observed that none of the inscriptions from this site can be shown to have any connexion with military life.[1] But it is equally true that none but the tombstone mentioned can be *proved* to have a civilian association.[2]

The reports of the antiquaries are most unsatisfactory. The idea of a civil settlement originated with Whitaker,[3] but he had no evidence beyond the accounts of Leland and Camden. How flimsy this evidence is will appear from the extracts I have given. Leland says nothing significant, while there is not the slightest reason to think that the *urbem magnam* of Camden was in fact anything other than the complex military works now proved to exist.[4] The story of this *urbs*, Camden says, the locals related as learnt from their forebears, by whom it has been transmitted 'from hand to hand'. To anyone who has had conversation with the present inhabitants of an ancient site, this has all too familiar a ring.

The discovery of Anthony Moorhouse's notes disposes of the idea that his discoveries in 1905 were in any way connected with a *vicus*, for it is clear that he in fact came upon the north-west corner and north wall of the fort.[5] These were obviously the discoveries shown to Villy and remembered by the men on the Burrow estate.[6]

[1] *CW* (2), XLVI, 141. [2] CIL, VII, 290; EE, VII, 946; EE, IX, 1377.
[3] *History of Richmondshire*, II, 260 f. [4] *CW* (2), LIV, 66 ff.
[5] *CW* (2), LIV, 97 ff. [6] *CW* (2), XLVI, 134 f.

What Moorhouse found west of the main road by the excavation in which Mr J. Wilson assisted[1] is uncertain. It was a different site from those described in the Moorhouse papers and I cannot help suspecting that, in the confusion caused by the excavators and Mr Wilson unknowingly talking about different sites, the word 'corner' was put into the latter's mouth, even assuming that he had a precise memory of what he had seen as a boy some forty years earlier.

The wall discovered in 1947[2] lay parallel with the ditches which underlay the stone fort, a probably Constantian station. The wall both overlay a road which was presumably contemporary with the southern (Flavian) ditch, and sealed Trajanic-Hadrianic pottery. North of and close to the wall, burning was discovered associated with samian datable after A.D. 160. The structure appears to be earlier than the second road which, from the pottery evidence presented in the report, is surely Severan. This building might have lain in an annexe, whose northern defences could be represented by the discoveries near the summer-house in 1947, attached to the second-century fort whose clay rampart appeared in 1952–3. The building *may* have served a civil function.

There is nothing to connect Aurelius Pusinnus and his wife with the *praetorium*, and it is probably necessary to postulate a *vicus* in which Eubia at least lived, if not her husband and the other people mentioned above.

STAINMORE

The left-hand road fork at Brougham led into a district of a different complexion from that just described. Here the signs of the Roman army are thick on the ground and Romanized civil life very apparent. The contrast with the friendly but noticeably native area traversed by the southward road serves to underline the paradox that where the terrain was rough and naturally unattractive to civilized civilians, the presence of a hostile native population stimulated the growth of *vici*, because it forced the introduction of large garrisons, while a friendly tribe resulted in the reverse.

Beyond Brougham the road passes close to several farming

[1] *CW* (2), XLVIII, 32 f.   [2] *Ibid.* 23 ff.

settlements very similar to those further north and unlike those on the other road, and it is apparent that we are here still in the general area of the Eden Valley pattern of occupation. However, from Kirkby Thore to Brough-under-Stainmore and on over the top of the pass the road becomes closely guarded by fortlets and signal stations. This intensive military activity explains the presence of *vici* at Brough and Kirkby Thore, in the latter case augmented by the traffic down the Maiden Way from Whitley Castle and the central sector of the Wall.

Kirkby Thore (BRAVONIACVM)

(*a*) Thomas Machel, *Philos. Trans. Abridg'd*, III, 430 ff. (1687):

A Strange Well was lately discover'd . . . in the common Road through *Kirbythore* in *Westmoreland*; 'tis about 10 Yards from the River *Trootbeck*, and as many from the great *Roman Causeway*, which leads to *Carlile*, and goes betwixt it and a place call'd the *Burwens.* . . . It hath been covered with a Plank of Wood . . . about 9 *Inches* thick, in the fashion of a Potlid . . . and above this was Gravel and Pavement about a *Yard* thick. Instead of *Walls*, there were two large *Wooden Vessels*, one upon another, like Hogsheads, or Wine-pipes, with Bung-holes in them. . . .

The Workmen Flattered themselves with the Hopes of some *Treasure*, but they only found some *Old Earthen Vessels* with pieces of *Urnes*, one piece of a *Drinking Glass*, and several *Sandals.* . . .

The *Sandals* were some for *Men*, some for *Women*, and some for *Children*; . . .[1]

(*b*) Gough, *Camden* (2), III, 411 f. (1806):

The main body of it stood in a place called the *Burwens*, on a rising ground at the bank of the rivulet called *Troutbeck*, not far from the river Eden. The square inclosure, called the *High Burwens*, seems to have been the area of it, containing eight score yards in diameter, now ploughed and cultivated, and the outer buildings to have run along the said rivulet, at least as far as to the fulling mill, or further beyond the Roman way, and so up the west side of the high street, about 160 yards, and thence again in a straight line to the west angle of the said area. In all these places

---

[1] Machel's account also gives a detailed description of five pieces of decorated samian, but their stratigraphical relation to the other objects is naturally not recorded. One of the women's shoes had a decorative trailer of leather attached to the top of the heel-grip.

have been found conduits under ground, vaults, pavements, tiles, and slates with iron nails in them, foundations of walls both of brick and stone, coins, altars, urns and other earthen vessels.[1]

Both in epigraphy and structures the evidence here is small in quantity but interesting in nature. The lady recorded on the extra-ordinary tombstone (69) was the daughter of a standard-bearer, whose monumental mason made a brave attempt at a memorial of the 'funeral banquet' type. The connexion with the army of the other lady, Antonia Stratonice (68), is less certain, but it is difficult to resist speculating whether she had any association with the *numerus equitum Stratonicianorum*, a third-century unit recorded at Brougham, the next fort up the road.

A further piece of evidence is provided by Machel's account of the well found near the Trout Beck, which contained, among other things, women's and children's shoes. This indicates the presence of civilians as at Bar Hill and Whitley Castle, but unlike those sites the other evidence here shows that some civilians at least were resident in an extra-mural settlement.

Industry is represented by bronze-smiths, whose presence is attested by lumps of fused ore and whose products are similar to those from Brough-under-Stainmore.[2] The workshop is like those at Brough and Stanwix to be dated around the middle of the second century, and Kirkby Thore consequently falls into the group of *vici* existing, if in primitive form, at that period.

Structurally the *vicus* is represented only by the rather vague description of Gough, which suggests a settlement south-west and west in the triangle between the Trout Beck, main Roman road and the fort. An earthwork, or rather the rounded corner of an earthwork, fills the angle between the modern main road and a lane at a point 1400 feet west of the west corner of the fort. [The existence of this bank has long suggested that the civil settlement may have had defences, and excavation by Miss Dorothy Charlesworth has now revealed that it did indeed possess substantial walls and extended over at least 30 acres.[3] It seems likely that it will have to

---

[1] It is not clear which finds came from inside the fort and which from without, but it is clear that at the least there were stone buildings over a considerable area outside.

[2] *RCHM Westmorland*, xxxix ff.   [3] [See Charlesworth, *CW* (2), LXIV (forthcoming).]

be transferred to the category of *town* in view of its unusual development, which was perhaps due to its key position in the road system.]

Brough-under-Stainmore (VERTERAE)

The civil activity at Brough-under-Stainmore contains features of unusual interest. Professor Richmond has suggested that an agent of the provincial procurator was stationed here, charged with the reception of special dues or products collected over a wide area by military units, including consignments from the mines near Whitley Castle.[1] Richmond is inclined to date the operations of this office to the third century; and on general grounds of the use of the army in administration this dating seems reasonable. It is the other side of the third-century picture to that revealed at Risingham, where the procurator assisted the military.[2]

The single civil inscription from this site, the tombstone of the boy Hermes (13), has been brought into association with this activity by R. G. Collingwood's reasonable suggestion that the person responsible might have been a Greek clerk in the office. He was, at any rate, remarkably literate.

A sign of different, and apparently earlier, civilians is the large collection of bronze products, deriving from a local workshop.[3] Like the Stanwix and Kirkby Thore workshops this producer seems to have been working in the middle and later second century and to have been making a variety of objects, some for military use and some for civil. The latter include rings suitable for children.[4]

One outstanding question remains unanswered: in what caravanserai lay 'all the traffic concentrated for the long and lonely crossing of the Pennines, carefully guarded by its convoy-station at Maiden Castle' (Richmond)?

5. THE NORTH-EAST

Descending eastwards from the Stainmore Pass the road passes first through Bowes, where the only extra-mural building known

[1] *CW* (2), XXXVI, 104 ff.   [2] CIL, VII, 1003.
[3] Partly catalogued by H. S. Cowper (*CW* (2), III, 70 ff.) and R. G. Collingwood (*CW* (2), XXXI, 81 ff.); cf. *CW* (2), LVIII, 50.
[4] *CW* (2), XXXI, 82, nos. 10, 12.

is the bath-house whose remains are still visible south of the modern cemetery, and out into the broad valley of the Tees and its tributaries. Greta Bridge and Piercebridge are at first sight part of the peaceful region of York, a land of villas, small towns and agriculture. But a glance at the military map will reveal the true position. These two forts, with the dependent fortlet of Carkin Moor, are the first for fifty miles to the traveller coming north. When Dere Street and the Stainmore road part at Scotch Corner each becomes fortified, fulfilling the dual functions of guarded through-route and of a *limes* controlling the flanking hills. It is not surprising to find a *beneficiarius consularis* at Greta Bridge to scrutinize the traffic entering the frontier region by this route from the provincial capital, and a massive fourth-century fort at the Tees crossing at Piercebridge. Physically, too, the frontier region properly starts here, for immediately past Scotch Corner on either road we begin to meet the hills, gentle at first and then increasingly fierce.

The two roads north across the Tees are somewhat different in character. Dere Street is clearly an essentially military road, the main artery on the east and the line which controlled the Pennines from this side. The easternmost road, which is one of the continuations of Ermine Street and eventually becomes the Wreken Dike, is for most of its length without military posts. Only at Chester-le-Street does it run into the frontier system. In fact it may be more accurate to see the roads from Chester-le-Street to Newcastle and South Shields as branches of Dere Street, fanning out from Binchester. This would leave the Tees–Chester-le-Street road as a mainly civil route, serving the agricultural lands of eastern County Durham. This region of Tees and Wear corresponds to the Cumberland Plain and the Eden Valley and most probably served the military market in a similar way. The farms of this area are less well known than those of the west, largely due to the density of modern settlement. Nevertheless, sites such as Esh[1] and North Dunslawholm (Horsley) in the valley of the Tyne[2] attest the presence of the sub-rectangular farm [though they may be like West Brandon

[1] NZ 193431.   [2] NZ 088676.

purely Iron-Age].[1] Though it has not yet been proved that the density of these farms is as great in the east, there is an indication that in one respect this area was more advanced in the presence of two villas, one certain at Old Durham and one possible at Holme House, near Piercebridge.

Greta Bridge (MAGLONA ?)

(a) Horsley, *Britannia Romana*, 486. (1732):

The fort itself has not reached within the park, but the military way has gone through it, and crossed the *Greta* a little below the present bridge, nearer to *Morton*, and falls in again with the high road, at an house a little south from *Gretabridge*. It leaves the fort about a furlong or two on the southwest side. The *Roman* town seems to have been of a much larger extent, and to have reached as far as *Rookby* and *Morton*. The *Kirk-croft*, which lies between *Rookby hall* and the river *Greta*, near its confluence with the *Teese*, is full of old buildings and ruins.

(b) *Ibid.* 485 (on the provenance of CIL, VII, 280). (1732):

... this altar was found on the bank of the river, hard by the yet remaining foundations of two houses or buildings near the water. My landlord gave them the name of *chapel* and *parsonage*. That which he called the *parsonage*, had stood close by the bank of the river, about two hundred yards below the union of the *Teese* and *Greta*. Its length was parallel to the bank or course of the river, and measured about seven yards, its breadth about five. The foundation stones of the side wall next the river, were wrought out, and carried away by him. Some part of the foundation of the other side was yet remaining. The building had been of square stones, and most probably Roman. He farther assured me, that a great many very fine stones had been got out of the ruins of this and the neighbouring building, which he called the *chapel*, and is about forty or fifty yards south from the other, and has not stood so near to the river. It is about nineteen or twenty yards long, and eight broad. The altar now at *Morton* was found (as I have hinted before) a few yards to the north or north-west of the former building. These must be the buildings, which have been mistaken for cells of the *Nymphs*; for I was well assured by others (and I made some search myself) that there were no artificial cavities in any of the rocks.

[1] [*AA* (4), XI, 1 ff.]

Greta Bridge was a site of some importance in the organization of the area, for it was the first large military station for the west-bound traveller after leaving Dere Street near Scotch Corner, and may also have had some control over upper Teesdale. From the inscriptions alone there is sufficient evidence to establish a *vicus*, for they record not only two women (55, 57) and a girl (56) but also a veteran (57). Horsley's cautious observations suggest that this *vicus* flanked the Roman road in Rokeby park, north of the fort, and ran down to the Greta and perhaps the Tees (*a*).

Mortham

Three-quarters of a mile north-east of the fort and on the right bank of the Tees about 200 yards east of its junction with the Greta[1] Horsley reported two structures and the provenance of a fragment of two inscriptions by *beneficiarii consularis* (*b*).[2] It is probable that a dedication to a nymph by one Neinbrica and her (or his) daughter (54) also came from the same spot, in view of the association of this place with nymphs in the local beliefs of the eighteenth century (*b*). The nature of the buildings is uncertain, but if Roman it may be that Horsley's landlord was not far wrong in identifying in them a sacred site.

Piercebridge (MAGIS ?)

Horsley, *Britannia Romana*, 486. (1732):

An aqueduct (if I am not mistaken) has gone just through the present town, and the foundations of houses every where appear, especially when the earth is in any way opened, or even well watered with rain; and after a shower the coins are also discovered, and gathered up in abundance. A large stone coffin was also found here, and other antiquities. . . . This station and town have been on the north side of the *Teese*, but there is another rivulet on the north side of the station. . . .

As I went from *Durham* to *Piercebridge*, I saw two seeming tumuli, one a mile from the town on the left, the other near the entrance to the town on the right.[3] The military way from *Binchester* to this place is very visible

---

[1] NZ 086451.   [2] CIL, VII, 280.

[3] The tumuli north of Piercebridge seem now to be lost. They were (if Roman) probably associated with the large cemetery near the railway. Two tumuli are known south of the river in the grounds of Cliffe Hall. Taken with the tombstone of Acilius (94) and perhaps the unidentified ancient site recorded at the turn to the Hall (*AJ*, VI, map facing 213) they suggest a corresponding cemetery flanking Dere Street to the south.

near *Piercebridge*. My landlord called it the *broad way*. He also told me of a bridge, some of the wood of which was still remaining. There was an elevation very visible beyond this bridge (which was over the rivulet) but I took this to be rather the continuance of the military way, than any part of the ramparts of the station. The way points directly to the *Tofts*, the field in which the station has probably been, and from whence the coins have the name of *Toft-pieces*.

The presence of civilians at Piercebridge is firmly established by the tombstone erected by Aurelia (Fad)illa in memory of her husband Aurelius Acilius, an *ordinatus* (94), and by the burial of a woman aged twenty-five to thirty, discovered in 1933 about 60 yards downstream of the present bridge on the northern bank of the Tees. This lady's bones were enclosed in a lead coffin within a stone cist and their Roman date was confirmed by the presence of a glass unguent bottle.[1]

The aerial photographs make it possible to go a stage further and prove a *vicus*.[2] The prominent track of Dere Street had long been noted running north to south in the field known at the Tofts. Stukeley[3] had seen it as a great stone bank in the eighteenth century. By 1849 it was reduced to a crop-mark,[4] and as such it has remained to the present day.[5] The branch road running from Dere Street to the probable site of the east gate of the fort was also observed in 1933.[6] But the complete evidence for a *vicus*—the loop-roads with the strip-houses—was unknown until it was seen from the air (pl. I).[7]

This discovery makes clear the significance of the interest shown by the early antiquaries in the Tofts. Horsley thought the fort probably lay here, and though his wording is ambiguous it is at least possible that the foundations he reports were the strip-houses of the aerial photographs.

Nothing is known of civil structures on the other sides of the fort. To the south there was little room between fort and river. On the west an inhumation was reported in 1903 100 yards from the

---

[1] *DN*, VII, ii, 242 f.   [2] Pl. I; and my own photographs.   [3] *Iter Boreale*, 72.
[4] MacLauchlan, *AJ*, VI, 218.   [5] E.g. 1915: *DN*, VII, ii, 240; 1933: *ibid.*; cf. pl. I.
[6] *PSAN* (4), VI, 235.
[7] In pl. I the fort lies just off the left-hand edge of the photograph.

gate.[1] North and north-east a considerable cemetery was found during railway construction in 1855-6. This lay between points '200 paces to the east, and about 120 paces west' of Dere Street,[2] partly under the coal depot. This cemetery seems to have been preponderantly inhumation, though a few cremations are reported. Further burials were discovered in 1956 during gravel digging west and south of this site. In December 1956 I myself observed here bones scattered by the mechanical grab. I have also observed the aqueduct in this quarry. Between this cemetery and the fort, a distance of some 200-300 yards, a large quantity of miscellaneous Roman material has been turned up by the same gravel diggings and is the subject of a report by Mr G. H. Richardson of Piercebridge.[3] None of it can be proved to represent civilian activity. The northern limit of the *vicus* may well have been the Dyance Beck where it crosses the Tofts and where the timbers of a second bridge seem to have been visible in Horsley's day.

Despite the solid evidence for a *vicus*, Piercebridge presents unusual problems. Plentiful second-century pottery among the chance finds proves Roman occupation from the time of Hadrian, and the tombstone of Acilius ought to indicate the presence of a unit in the third century. Yet the known fort was a new and very large structure of the Constantian age.[4] So far there is no sign of the whereabouts of an earlier fort. There is direct evidence for the date of the *vicus*, and something more can be inferred.

Direct evidence for the dating of the *vicus* was obtained in excavation in 1939.[5] The road from the east gate of the fort to Dere Street was examined at a point about 150 feet from the fort. Both this road and a *vicus* building on its north side were found to have two periods of construction, the first early fourth-century and almost certainly contemporary with the foundation of the existing fort. The pottery from the second period is said to have been clearly later in type and it may represent a Theodosian reconstruction. A second house, south of the road, was found slightly to overlie the road-gutter of the second period and must therefore be contempor-

---

[1] E. Wooler, *The Roman Fort at Piercebridge*, 179 f.   [2] *Ibid.* 171 ff.
[3] *DN*, XI, 165 ff.   [4] *DN*, VII, ii, 274 ff.   [5] *DN*, IX, ii, 129 ff.

ary or later than that. This evidence is the latest yet from a *vicus* in the region, and may suggest that here at least there was no movement of families into the fort in 369.

Something also can be deduced about other parts of the *vicus*. Dere Street north of the bridge[1] was found to have been reconstructed at least once,[2] but no indication of date was discovered, nor the relation of the road periods to the buildings, one of which seems to have been touched by the excavators.[3] It is, however, safe to assume that the original road was at latest Agricolan. The branches are a different matter. That running eastwards from Dere Street near the centre of the *vicus* is at present undatable, but since the street leading to the east gate of the fort is early fourth-century, the north–south loops on the west side of Dere Street which are clearly subsidiary to this entrance road are Constantian or later. The same applies to the strip-houses that face on to them. The second row of buildings south of the entrance road lies on a different alignment and may therefore be of different date, though they may preserve the line of a loop or by-pass to the south gate. On present evidence, therefore, it is impossible to prove the existence of a *vicus* earlier than *c.* 300, and the probability is that it developed when the great Constantian fort was built.

Holme House

Approximately 1,000 yards south-east of the Roman bridge a crop-mark was recorded by Dr St Joseph.[4] This revealed a rectangular, ditched enclosure with slightly rounded corners and a single entrance. An avenue or drove bounded by further ditches seems to lead to the entrance. This crop-mark is reminiscent of the enclosure surrounding the villa at Ditchley, though no internal buildings are visible. The hint of a villa is strengthened by Mr G. H. Richardson's report of the finding of Roman pottery and *tesserae* on the site, and the Ordnance Survey records it as a 'substantial building'. General circumstances are strongly in favour of its being a villa. Its position a short distance off a main road and not far from

---

[1] *DN*, VII, ii, 240 ff.; *PSAN* (4), VI, 235 ff.   [2] *DN*, VII, ii, 244 ff.   [3] *Ibid*. 246.
[4] Cambridge, DU, 84; JX, 75–7.

a civil centre is typical. The land is good, a point emphasized by the bronze statuette of a ploughman and team found at Piercebridge,[1] and is associated more with the peaceful area south than the frontier region proper. The size of the native population it could support is attested by the siting of the Brigantian fortifications at Stanwick, two and a half miles away. But it will require the discovery of domestic buildings to make the identification certain: the enclosure could be a temple precinct.

Binchester (VINOVIA)

(*a*) Horsley, *Britannia Romana*, 399. (1732):

The out-buildings, as usual, have been between the station and the river, or to the south-west of the station.[2]

(*b*) Hutchinson, *Durham*, III, 348, quoting 'Mr. Gyll's MS'. (1794):

That in building a bridge over the river Gaunless, in the park at Bishop Auckland, in the year 1757, was found a Roman urn of greyish clay, filled with ashes, earth and the remains of human bones: I saw it in the custody of the Bishop of Durham. The place where this urn was found was about a quarter of a mile from Binchester; where several other urns and pieces of pottery have been discovered.[3]

Binchester is one of the rare sites at which a civil settlement is attested chiefly by excavation. However, before considering the finds made by Proud and Hooppell in 1877 and subsequent seasons south-east of the fort, it will be as well to note that the one direct report by an early antiquary, Horsley, locates the extra-mural buildings not on this side but south-west. It is probable, too, that the 'exceeding fair bridge of one arch upon Were' recorded by Leland was that which must have carried Dere Street across the river west of the fort, where the road is clearly visible from the air.

---

[1] *BM Guide to the Antiquities of Roman Britain* (1958), 54, no. 13.

[2] Horsley's phrasing is a little obscure, for it is not clear whether he is suggesting alternatives (working on probabilities) or describing the same spot from observation in different terms. The latter is probably the correct interpretation (and the expression 'as usual' no more than yet another use of one of his favourite phrases when talking about the situation of extra-mural structures.)

[3] This passage also has one obscurity, for it is not clear whether in the last clause Gyll is referring to the place where the cremation was found or to Binchester itself. If the former, it is additional evidence for a cemetery in this area.

The nineteenth-century excavations[1] revealed Dere Street proceeding south-east from the fort until eventually lost in landslip 150 yards from the defences. On the south-west side of the road stood a close-packed row of houses, of which the nearest lay about 200 feet from the fort. This building was thought to be a square structure, with sides of about 35 feet, but the plan suggests that it was part of a strip-house. The remaining six were all strip-houses, of which only one ('U') had any internal partition observable. This building measured 91 feet by 25 feet 8 inches, and stood to ten courses of masonry.[2] Hooppell most creditably recognized three structural periods in this part of the site. His illustrations permit some modification of interpretation. It is clear that building 'U' is structurally later than the earliest road-drain observed, but earlier than the second.[3] Thresholds at the topmost level show that the buildings continued in use for a very considerable period. Five rubbish pits excavated on the cliff edge behind the houses in 1929 by James MacIntyre produced Flavian pottery[4] but emphatically do not prove a Flavian *vicus*. Further Flavian pottery was reported in 1927 to have been found close to a possibly Roman wall near the water's edge south of the strip-houses[5] and was observed on the bank in 1958 in the course of revetting operations.[6] The slope was probably the rubbish-dump of the Flavian fort.

The houses were found to be provided each with a pair of square bases for pillars at the street end, indicating open fronts. Hooppell's plate[7] suggests that these bases were raised to the level of the latest period road observed, architectural fragments being incorporated in the reconstruction.

On the opposite side of Dere Street and 50 feet from it, part of a bath-house was discovered, at a point approximately 200 feet from the fort.[8] This showed signs of two phases, as well as a wall from a later building apparently unconnected with the bath.

[1] Which were exhaustively and frequently published by Hooppell—the fullest account being his three articles 'Vinovia', *JBAA*, XLIII, 111 ff., 299 ff.; XLVI, 253 ff.

[2] *JBAA*, XLIII, 120 ff.   [3] *Ibid.* plate facing 121.   [4] Steer, thesis, 135 ff.

[5] *PSAN* (4), III, 135.

[6] Seen by J. P. Gillam, W. Dodds and myself, 4 July 1958, and the pottery, which was associated with soft burnt clay (not from a kiln), removed to Corbridge.

[7] *JBAA*, XLVI, facing 254.   [8] *JBAA*, XLIII, 304 ff.

A masonry-lined well was found in the same excavations approximately 575 feet south-east of the fort, apparently just north of Dere Street which was lost at about this point.[1]

Two most important inscriptions come from this site recording *beneficiarii consularis* and suggestive of considerable civil activity (CIL, VII, 424; EE, IX, 1133). Both are dedicated (by different *beneficiarii*) to the Matres Ollototae, and the find-spot and circumstances of discovery of the latter are known. It was found about 80 yards north-east of Dere Street east of the fort, and was unweathered.[2] There is therefore strong reason for supposing that there was a shrine to these curious deities near this spot, patronized by the incumbents of the beneficiary station.

One cemetery is known from reports of cremations half a mile south-east of the fort within the bishop's park, close to the point where Dere Street must have crossed the Gaunless, an eastern tributary of the Wear. The first cremation was found in 1757 (*b*), the second (whose precise location is uncertain) was uncovered in digging for sewage works between November 1937 and May 1938.[3] The pot containing the latter was dated to *c*. A.D. 300. Masonry also seems to have been struck on this occasion and the details supplied to Dr K. A. Steer suggested the possibility of a circular tomb.[4] This roadside cemetery probably marks the limit to which ribbon-development is likely to have spread.

Lanchester (LONGOVICIVM)

[(*a*) Hodgson, *AA* (1), I, 119. (1822):

The extensive ruins of the station at Lanchester, and especially of its suburbs, show that it was once a place of considerable importance.

---

[1] *JBAA*, XLIII, 114; XLVI, second plate facing 254.   [2] *The Reliquary* (2), V, 3.
[3] Steer, thesis, 173.

[4] Another, better known, interment is recorded by the tombstone of a cavalry decurion, (CIL, VII, 429), seen in 1819 a quarter of a mile on the opposite side of the fort, used in a footpath near the Bell Burn (*AA* (1), I, 142). Mr Orkney Skene was not the first to see it (contrary to general belief), for Samuel Lysons had reported it as early as 1813 as found several years previously (*Reliquiae Britannico-Romanae*, I, iv, pl. III, fig. 3) without recording the provenance. It is therefore uncertain whether or not its use in the footpath was subsequent to the original discovery and it may have been found and first read in quite a different place.

(b) *Ibid.* 120 f. (1822):

When the ruins of a great part of the station at Lanchester, and especially of its suburb, were raised about forty years ago, the great numbers of hearths, cinders and slaking troughs that were found, and that resembled those of our own smitheries, induced the neighbouring people to conclude that the Romans were 'a tribe of smiths.'

Hodgson's report was brought to my notice by Professor Birley and it seems very likely that it represents a *vicus*. Nevertheless confirmatory evidence that this industrial activity was not directly military would be welcome.]

Ebchester (VINDOMORA)

The evidence on this site is restricted to the observations of Christopher Hunter who, however, took some pains to come to an independent opinion on the basis of his own inspection of the site, satisfying himself 'so far as to reduce my Mind from the vulgar Opinion, that this has never been more than a Place nam'd from that Pious Virgin St. *Ebba*, which is all Mr. *Cambden* says of it'. He observed that 'Here have been Suburbs towards the West, South, and perhaps East, of a considerable Extent; but towards the North the Wall has stood upon the Top of a steep Bank, under which runs the River *Derwent*. . . .'[1]

It seems unlikely that a bath-house and perhaps a few military temples or shrines should account entirely for such obviously substantial surface indications. On the other hand, a large *mansio* could be responsible for considerable surface indications and with the military extra-mural buildings together present such an appearance. As at Ambleside it is necessary to record the near-certainty of civil activity, but without further details it is impossible to add the site to the list of *vici*.

Chester-le-Street (CONCANGIVM)

The evidence for civil occupation at Chester-le-Street is most unsatisfactory. The inscription mentioning the military *territorium*

[1] *Philos. Trans. Abridg'd*, v, ii, 44.

will be discussed later: it implies that before A.D. 216 the area had
been under an authority other than the army, but it does not reveal
the identity of that authority or prove that its centre was a civil
town at Chester-le-Street.

For finds on the site it is necessary chiefly to rely on the observations of Canon F. H. Jackson, rector 1919–35, as recorded by Dr
Steer in his unpublished thesis. Steer plotted the finds, together
with earlier discoveries, demonstrating Roman occupation over a
wide area. But until it is proved that military occupation was at all
times restricted to one area, that the forts of all periods lay on one
site, there is bound to be considerable doubt as to which of the
finds are genuinely extra-mural.

Of the finds, those of coins and pottery reveal nothing of civil
significance by themselves. The occurrence of five altars[1] north of
the fort suggests a group of shrines on the slope towards the river.
The last of these altars was recovered in 1886 in a well found outside the north-west angle. However, though none are specifically
military, there is no way of distinguishing whether they were dedicated by civilians or privately by soldiers.

On the south, Steer very reasonably made a cautious equation of
the circular or apsidal structure found west of St Cuthbert's Road
with the hypocausted 'villa' of 1856 which contained a building
inscription of *legio II Augusta*,[2] interpreting it as the fort bath-house
(cf. the 'villa' at Carrawburgh). The discovery of 2½ cwt of iron in
the 'villa' suggests that, like the baths of Llantwit Major[3] the building was at some period converted to industrial uses. It is not impossible that the curved structure was itself an industrial installation.
The building of 1886, if not a bath-house (and its position away
from the river injects some doubt into the identification), may have
been a *mansio*. In this connexion the stoke-hole or furnace added to
the Benwell *mansio* may be recalled.

A short stretch of road observed by the Canon as running north-
north-east of the curved structure must represent either a branch
road or a *vicus* street. The discovery of the bridge of the main road

---

[1] CIL, VII, 452-4; EE, VII, 984-5.   [2] CIL, VII, 455; PSAN (1), I, 121 f.
[3] *Arch. Camb.* CII, ii, 117 f.

in 1930–1 at a point north of the north-west corner of the fort makes it most unlikely that the road here noted was a by-pass loop round the fort. Somewhere south of the fort there must have been a road-junction, a fact that doubtless explains the concentration of finds in this quarter, apparently between the two roads. The discovery of burials about 90 yards south of the fort, in the plot south of the Rectory and west of St Cuthbert's Road, suggests that this was chiefly cemetery rather than an area of civil dwellings. The foundations reported in the Rectory grounds themselves could represent a tomb or temple.[1]

The most interesting—and for this purpose significant—feature of the site is the distribution of culverts outside the area of the fort. That found east of the branch road probably served the 'villa'; that south-east of the modern bridge may have been the outlet of the main drain of the fort. Two others, however, ran north–south on the west side of the fort (in Osborne Road and between it and Front Street), seem to have no connexion with it and are most easily explained as draining a civil quarter, like those at Chesters.

None of this is, taken separately, convincing evidence for a *vicus*, but in sum it is enough to make its existence a probability. [This is now much strengthened by finds in 1963 (*JRS*, LIV, 156)—additional note, Jan. 1965.]

Old Durham

The Roman site at Old Durham lies east of the city of Durham on the north bank of the Sherburn House Beck, approximately 700 yards upstream from its junction with the Wear. Three rescue excavations were carried out, in 1941–3, 1948 and 1951, on the fragments of a complex site revealed in the course of gravel-digging.[2] The site as excavated extended over an area of a little less than a quarter of an acre, and occupation was proved from the early second century (if not the first) to the fourth. It ended in destruction by fire, and there was no sign of activity after A.D. 367. The details of the site are fully set out in the three reports,

---

[1] [They have now been proved to be a temple—information from Mr Eric Parsons.]
[2] *AA* (4), XXII, 1 ff.; XXIX, 203 ff.; XXXI, 116 ff.

and it is here only necessary to summarize and comment on the facts discovered.

Chronologically three of the phases are precisely placed: an early Antonine ditch, a Severan pit, and a small bath-house of non-military type[1] in use in the earlier fourth century.[2] East of the bath-house was burnt material from another stone structure, also associated with fourth-century pottery.

Into this framework several other features must be fitted. In the ditch, over the Antonine primary silt and under the rakings from the fourth-century stokehole, was a quantity of broken dressed stone from a demolished building, and the structure of the bath-house itself contained a broken roofing-tile. This establishes the existence of at least one stone building destroyed before the fourth century. North of the bath-house, at a distance of about 57 yards, lay two circular stone structures, perhaps threshing-floors. These were not themselves datable, but one overlay a pair of foundation trenches, and a patch of builders' lime associated with later second-century pottery.[3]

It seems reasonable to identify the site as a villa on the basis of the bath-house and the circular floors. There is a high probability that an associated dwelling-house of some pretensions existed nearby (lost in gravel-digging?), of which the fourth-century debris east of the baths may be a trace. It seems most unlikely that the bath-house either stood alone or that its owners themselves lived in a native farmstead of the common (and extremely primitive) northern type.[4] Indeed, it has been proved that a building of Roman type had already stood on the site before the baths were built. What has not been proved is that there were ever any non-Roman structures in the settlement. The ditch can as well be the

---

[1] *AA* (4), XXII, 16.

[2] All the pottery reported is fourth century, except two fragments of second-century samian, one from the hypocaust and one from the destruction debris. These sherds are probably to be treated as strays.

[3] Both the filling of the ditch with broken stone and the preparation of the lime may represent Severan clearing and building operations, since it is difficult to see how the ditch, if it remained open in the third century, could have avoided acquiring some third-century material, in view of the occupation in that century attested by the pit.

[4] The bath-house was sufficiently lavish to possess window-glass and painted wall-plaster, *AA* (4), XXII, 10.

boundary of a villa as of a native homestead, and the single native pot from its primary silt the relic of native servants or labourers, or a stray from earlier and perhaps totally unconnected native occupation.[1]

To summarize, it is certain that there was on this site a Roman civil settlement of a type as yet not certainly paralleled in the region, that this was demolished twice, the second time almost certainly in the general disasters of A.D. 367, and that occupation was continuous from the early Antonine period. The site has proved one fact of prime importance—that the region could support not only urban settlements on the Roman pattern but also the life of a Roman country estate. It is a testimony to the efficiency of the frontier system that such a development could occur at a spot not under the immediate protection of a garrison. The suggestion that it began at the time of the Antonine advance into Scotland, when this area ceased for a while to be close to the frontier, is consistent with the evidence from the site and convincing,[2] but it is equally clear that the reversal of the Antonine policy did not cause the site to be abandoned. On the contrary, the place was sufficiently attractive to bring prosperous Roman civilians back after successive disasters. But the most interesting question of all remains unanswered, for the evidence is insufficient to prove whether the thoroughly Roman aspect of the site was the result of Romanization of the local native population or whether the owners of this establishment were, in origin at least, Romans from elsewhere in Britain or abroad.

6. SCOTLAND AND THE ANTONINE WALL

North of a line approximating to the present Anglo-Scottish border, evidence for civil activity of any kind becomes extremely scanty. As yet no extra-mural structural evidence has appeared which could not indicate military buildings, and of the [four][3] civil inscriptions only one certainly indicates a *vicus* (26), evidence which

---

[1] There is some indication that this pot may be first century—*AA* (4), XXII, 15—but this native pottery is as yet difficult to date precisely (cf. *AA* (4), XXXV, 172 f.).
[2] *AA* (4), XXII, 16 f.   [3] [See (112).]

appears meagre indeed when compared to the 108 civil inscriptions and the abundant structural material of more southerly areas.

The clue to the explanation of this striking difference is provided by the line of demarcation, which in fact represents the northern frontier of the empire as adopted by Caracalla. Most of Scotland, unlike northern England, was under permanent Roman occupation only for a few years at the end of the first century and the comparatively short period of sixty to seventy years in the second century and early third, of which but little was free from alarm and disaster. It is therefore not surprising that so high a proportion of the known settlements lie in England.

There have, however, recently been some surprises on the Antonine Wall. Even the outlines of its history are by no means absolutely certain. It is just possible that the timber buildings observed outside the Agricolan fort of Easter Happrew represent a first-century *vicus*,[1] but since this is as yet unparalleled on the British frontier and moreover only one of the group of three buildings resembles a normal strip-house, it is perhaps more likely that these were builder's huts like those at Birdoswald. Further south the first civil settlements were appearing in the second century, and it would be reasonable to expect a scatter of civil material along the Antonine Wall. This in fact is what is found. Mumrills, Carriden, Auchendavy, Bar Hill and Balmuildy[2] have each produced signs of civilians but only at Carriden is there direct proof of a *vicus*. Professor Richmond has recently suggested that the scatter of material —sherds, hearths and indeterminate timber structures—recorded outside both fort and annexe on several sites (notably Bar Hill and Cadder) represents early *vici*.[3] There seems a strong possibility that he is right, but the theory requires the test of the spade.

ANNEXES

Bar Hill raises by implication the biggest problem in the study of civil occupation on these Scottish sites, the question of the use of the annexes to forts which are so common here and comparatively rare elsewhere. These are normally rectangular enclosures attached to

[1] *JRS*, XLVII, 201 f.   [2] [And Westerwood, see (112).]   [3] *PSAS*, XC, 5 f.

one side of the fort, protected by defences similar to the main rampart and ditches and often cover a considerable area. The whole problem is still very obscure, but so far there is little positive evidence to support the view that they contained civil settlements. Discussion of these fortified enclosures has long been influenced (not to say bedevilled) by Arrian's account of his inspection at the Phasis where he ordered an extra ditch to be dug to include the harbour and the civil settlement.[1] This was clearly a special case: the primary purpose was protection for the shipping and it need have no relevance to the problem of the relatively common annexes of the northern part of our region. The indeterminate discoveries in the Duntocher annexe[2]—cobbling, ash, pits, trace of hearth or furnace, scattered small finds—are typical of what is generally known of Scottish annexes.[3] Nowhere yet have the most characteristic of the buildings of the *vicus* unequivocally occurred, the long rectangular houses of stone or timber presenting their narrow fronts to the street. The only unequivocally identifiable building that occasionally occurs inside the annexe is the wholly official bath-house.[4] Nothing demands civil use: the available evidence points to the military. Protected enclosures for army stores, hard-standing for vehicles (i.e. cobbling), lines for pack-horses, tented accommodation for troops in transit or attached irregulars and open space for such operations as smithying which constituted a serious fire risk (particularly to timber buildings)—all these were vital to the functioning of the unit as an efficient force. They are precisely the sort of activities which would leave the traces noted, traces which do not correspond to those found in attested *vici*.[5] The excavations at Zugmantel showed that even a timber *vicus* leaves a characteristic pattern.[6] They show too that the problem could be settled finally by

---

[1] *Periplus*, IX. [2] Robertson, *Duntocher*, 61 ff.

[3] Cf. Caerhun, Rough Castle, etc.

[4] E.g. Old Kilpatrick, Balmuildy. The real problem is that there has been so little large-scale excavation as yet in the annexes. Opinions must therefore be tentative.

[5] At Milton beads and a single lead loom weight were found in an apparently late-Flavian annexe (*Trans. Dumfr. & Gall.* (3), XXVIII, 202, 210), but the former are not uncommon (? as souvenirs or even barbaric male adornment) and the latter may have been scrap metal.

[6] *Saalburg-Jhb.* X, 50 ff., 55 ff.

the total excavation of an annexe with the techniques at present available, for even if there were a civil settlement, trenches and trial holes would never make any sense of so irregular a site. At Duntocher the annexe was designed in layout and structure as an integral part of the military station and enclosed an area considerably in excess of the fort proper. This was at a date when extensive civil occupation is unlikely in the area, let alone by deliberate official design.

It is of course perfectly possible, and indeed probable, that the annexes at times acted as makeshift *mansiones*. Even if senior officials and officers in transit stayed with the commandant, doubtless their retinues were often housed in tents or other temporary accommodation. The annexes to road posts, as at Antonine Chew Green, almost certainly fulfilled this purpose. But this does not mean that they ever enclosed permanent *vici*.

The annexes of the Antonine Wall and its area correspond in function to the space between the Vallum and Hadrian's Wall (which was in fact an elongated annexe) and like many of the features of the Scottish wall are a version of the earlier works which was more economical to construct and operate. The idea had already appeared long before in Scotland on Agricolan sites, when a large civil dependent and Romanized population is even less credible. In fact, far from being intended to enclose civilians without official connexions, the annexes were specifically designed to keep them out.

This view is based on the tenuous evidence at present available, but it can only be reversed if proof of prolonged and unmistakeably civilian occupation is produced in an annexe. New material can come to light at any time.

Balmuildy

[Horsley, *Britannia, Romana*, 167. (1732):

The fort at *Bemulie* stands on the south side of the river *Kelvin*, and at the west of end of the village. And here the ruins of the *Roman* town or outbuildings are very remarkable. Several subterranean vaults have been discovered, and *Roman* antiquities discovered here. . . .

This report, brought to my notice by Professor Birley, is rather surprising, for it suggests much more substantial extra-mural buildings than have yet been noted on any other Antonine Wall site. I should like to be quite certain that it represents more than can be accounted for by official extra-mural buildings and perhaps soldiers' shrines and tombs, but must record Balmuildy as a 'probable'.]

Auchendavy

Civilians are recorded on two tombstones which came from the otherwise military cemetery (1, 2). This cemetery lay somewhere east of the fort, for certain of the stones are said to have come from a position close to the Antonine Wall and near to Shirva. The name Shirva is incorporated in the names of several places in the three-quarters of a mile between Auchendavy and Shirva proper. On general probability I suspect that it was in the neighbourhood of Shirva Dyke cottage. There is no sign of a separate cemetery for civilians, for (2) was found not far from a group of tombstones which included at least one military.[1] Two tombstones of the 'funerary banquet' type from this cemetery may also represent civilians, since the deceased are shown in civil dress.[2] Unfortunately as these bear no inscriptions it is impossible to prove the status of the dead.

On inscription (2), the memorial of Salmanes, the eastern names, lack of military ranks and the youth of the deceased combine to suggest most strongly that the two Salmanes were civilians. But it is quite impossible to prove that they were traders as has been suggested.[3] The names of the freedmen recorded on (60) and (97) also originated in the eastern part of the Roman world, and it is feasible that Salmanes and his son, like Eutychus (60) and probably Theodotus (97), were in the service of a fort-commandant.

On the status of the lady Verecunda no evidence is available (1). Something, however, can be deduced about another woman who may have lived at this site. This is the slave, later sentenced to penal servitude, whom Birley[4] has conjectured was at Auchendavy in the service of M. Cocceius Firmus, centurion of *legio II Augusta*

---

[1] *RWS* (2), 435 ff.   [2] *Ibid.* pl. LV.   [3] *Ibid.* 439.
[4] *PSAS*, LXX, 363 ff.

and dedicator of the well-known series of altars.[1] Professor Birley's argument is most ingenious, but to accept it does not mean acceptance of a civil settlement. There is very good reason to believe that M. Cocceius Firmus was at least acting commandant of the fort.[2] In other words, if the woman was resident at Auchendavy she was a servant in the *praetorium*.

Bar Hill

The presence of civilians on the Antonine Wall at this site was revealed in the excavations of the fort in 1902–5 by the discovery of shoes which from size and style must have been worn by women and children. It is unfortunate that no statistical analysis was published of the three to four hundred items of footwear of all types found on the site. Thus it is not clear what proportion was in fact attributable to women and children (as distinct from youths), though it was stated that there were 'heaps'.[3] But soldiers' boots were certainly the most numerous category.[4] For the same reason it is now impossible to discover the exact provenance of the non-military shoes, since it is merely reported that footwear came from rubbish pits 1, 2, 8, 9; from the well in the court of the *principia* ('2 boots'); and from the ditches—all of the Antonine fort.

Sir George Macdonald appears to have been somewhat unhappy about the implications of the evidence. His original reaction was that these civilians 'cannot, of course, have dwelt within the gates; that would have been a grave breach of military law'.[5] He spoke again of the 'dwelling-houses in the annexe or annexes that must have lain outside the main ramparts',[6] but later in the same work thought the fact that 'the shoes of women and children occurred so constantly in the pits and ditches of the fort itself, and not of any annexe, tends to raise doubts as to whether in the more distant outposts the exclusion of all save soldiers from the *castella* was rigidly insisted upon.'[7] He did not draw the conclusion which seems inevitable, that these civilians were resident in the fort but quite properly, as members of the commandant's household. In the

[1] CIL, VII, 1111–15.   [2] RWS (2), 431.   [3] PSAS, XL, 533.   [4] Ibid. 508.
[5] Ibid. 533.   [6] RWS (2), 281.   [7] Ibid. 452.

space of half-a-century the *familiae* of successive commanding officers could wear out quite a large number of shoes.

Traces of 'fireplaces' and pottery found north-east of the fort[1] may indicate an annexe, an extra-mural bath-house to this or the Agricolan fort, or (from the position close to the Military Way) a cremation cemetery. They are no proof of a civil settlement, whose existence there is little reason to suspect.

Westerwood [see (112)]

Mumrills

Excavation in 1958 produced material in quantities which give some hope that considerable progress is about to be made in the study of the annexes and of the Antonine Wall as a whole. The 'Agricolan camp' was found to be an annexe to the Antonine fort. Inside the annexe the fort ditch had been filled and later Antonine occupation of an uncertain character carried on over it.[2] The pottery suggested a date of *c.* A.D. 160 and included an intriguing and undoubtedly civil object, a baby's feeding bottle. Whether this genuinely originated from a civilian resident in the annexe or was rubbish from the commandant's household or dropped from luggage in transit remains unanswerable.

The position for this site at the time of writing therefore is that one civilian is recorded at Mumrills, and we can safely postulate at least one woman in charge of the baby; and that occupation of some sort is recorded in the annexe. It is to be hoped that the final results will provide firm evidence on the nature of this activity.

Carriden (VELVNIA)

This site became of great interest to the student of civil settlements when the altar erected by the *vicani consistentes* was discovered east of the fort in 1956 (26). The text and the constitutional significance are discussed elsewhere. The most important fact is that it is the first unequivocal evidence for a *vicus* on the Forth–Clyde line. It is therefore all the more surprising that it records a communal organization.

---

[1] *PSAS*, XL, 534.   [2] *JRS*, L, 91.

M

Dietrich Hafemann has pointed out that Carriden, apparently lying at the eastern end of the Antonine Military Way, was the probable port of supply for the Wall.[1] This implies unusual traffic of a sort peculiarly attractive to civilian merchants and likely to require the presence of government officials. As yet there is evidence of actual occupation at Carriden only in the second century[2] and the *vicus* must be *provisionally* assigned to that period. It is not impossible that extensive civil occupation appeared here under these special circumstances and not elsewhere in Antonine Scotland. However it would not be surprising if third-century occupation were found at Carriden, for a port on the Firth of Forth would have been extremely useful if not essential to the campaigning armies of the Severi. This would be true irrespective of whether the Antonine Wall was re-occupied as a whole or not. Nevertheless, until very recently the cautious historian would have had to say that the outside dates for this site were A.D. 140 and A.D. 211; but the discovery of a significant quantity of *fourth*-century pottery at Cramond changes the picture.[3] It now seems more likely that these coastal sites were held well after the abandonment of the Antonine Wall as a system—if not continuously, at least by successive commanders campaigning into Scotland. There can be no doubt that the history of Roman Scotland has much still to reveal nor that the present series of investigations is likely to produce big changes in thinking on this subject.[4]

SOUTH OF THE ANTONINE WALL

Newstead (TRIMONTIVM)

One further site has produced evidence of early civil activity, though of an entirely different kind. Newstead lies at a strategic point on the road north where it is about to enter the Lammermuir hills through which it must pass before reaching the Antonine Wall, and it also controls the place where the Tweed emerges from the hills to the west into the broad rich vale of the Merse. Yet there is

---

[1] *Beiträge zur Siedlungsgeographie des römischen Britanniens*, I, 162 f.
[2] *JRS*, XXXVII, 166; *PSAS*, LXXXIII, 167 ff.
[3] *JRS*, LII, 163.   [4] See e.g. *JRS*, L, 84 ff.

absolutely no sign of a *vicus*. It is difficult to explain this other than by recourse to date. Once again, the occupation seems to have come to an end too early for the growth of a substantial *vicus*. The civilians here were of a different sort. The clue lies in the obvious importance of the site as an administrative centre and as a staging post. It is difficult to identify the large, villa-like structure which lay immediately to the west of the baths other than as a *mansio*. Its excavator, James Curle, hesitatingly associated it with the bath-complex.[1] Indeed, its occupants probably made use of these baths in the early, larger state of that structure. Unfortunately only the cobble foundations of the *mansio* survived and the plan recovered appears fragmentary. The main rooms lie around a central court like those of an officer's house. Irregularities on the south side and the presence of a dividing wall across the court suggest alterations and additions.

The easternmost end of the building is overlain by the boundary mound surrounding the small bath-house now identified as early Antonine.[2] Uncertain is its relationship to pit LVII (which produced material from the Agricolan and Late Domitianic-Trajanic demolition periods). The cobbled foundations suggest the structure is to be associated with the part-timbered buildings of the Late Domitianic period rather than the wholly timber Agricolan phase. This would place the life of the building between *c*. A.D. 86 and *c*. 100.

There is unfortunately no record of the relation of the drain from the baths to the eastern projection of the *mansio* which it crosses on its way to the river. The possibility of a structural link with the baths is interesting, and it will be remembered that south of the Saalburg another courtyard house lay similarly close to a bath-house, at a comparable distance from fort and road, and at precisely the same point in relation to the *porta praetoria*.

Up to this point everything has suggested that Roman civil occupation in Scotland ended with the close of the second century. But is this necessarily true? A re-occupation of military sites in Scotland during the campaigns of the Severi has long been a sub-

---

[1] *Newstead*, 93, fig. 7, and 98.   [2] *PSAS*, LXXXIV, 23.

ject of speculation and controversy. On general grounds it seems difficult to see how these campaigns could have been carried out without holding at least the supply ports on the east coast, and the evidence of transhipments at South Shields strongly suggests that something of the sort was the case. In view of the general lack of evidence for second-century *vici* in the area, it seems worth excavating the one known, but undated, *vicus* in the light of this situation.

CHAPTER IV

CIVIL ARCHITECTURE IN THE FRONTIER REGION

Architecture may perhaps at first sight seem a grandiose term to apply to the structures of the *vicus*, and yet they represent a revolution in the way of life of the region that cannot be overestimated. The simple but Romanized houses of the *vicani* and the complex official buildings introduced the local population for the first time to the essential principles of Western architecture. This is hardly less of a revolution in standards of life and thought than the idea of urban life itself, the most important principle embodied in the *vicus* and an essential characteristic of it, however simple its form.

To talk of town-planning in connexion with the average *vicus* is rather misleading, for nothing is clearer than that these settlements normally had none. Most *vici* grew up as ribbon-development along the roads leading away from the gates of a fort.[1] Occasionally a back-lane developed into a secondary street.[2] By-pass loops round forts often attracted houses[3] and sometimes the concentration on roads due to possible trade from passers-by led to the main focus of development being the roads themselves rather than the fort.[4] Some tendency towards development along the outer edge of the fort ditches away from the main roads is also observable.[5] Sometimes, too, there was considerable development around the bath-house,[6] including a *mansio*.[7]

Two other general principles can be observed. There was (as Horsley noted time and time again) an understandable preference for the more pleasant spots—often a sheltered slope towards a

---

[1] E.g. Brougham, Maryport, Binchester, Beckfoot.
[2] E.g. Housesteads, Piercebridge and probably Chesterholm.
[3] E.g. Chesters, Housesteads.   [4] E.g. Old Carlisle, Piercebridge.
[5] E.g. Greatchesters, Carrawburgh, Chesterholm.   [6] E.g. Carrawburgh, Chesters.
[7] Chesters, Newstead, cf. Saalburg.

river[1]—and a general avoidance of areas in use as cemeteries whose desecration was forbidden by law.[2] The existence of a cemetery in an area is *prima facie* evidence against the probability of a *vicus* on that piece of ground, and in the case of cemeteries lying some distance away from a fort the supposition can reasonably be made that they are not early and may be avoiding a civil settlement immediately outside the defences, whose outer limits they thus define.[3] Sometimes early cemeteries went out of use, perhaps forgotten after a break in occupation, and the *vicus* spread over them, but so far Maryport is the only certain example of this in the region.

Temples and shrines also often lie on the outskirts,[4] sometimes in association with the cemeteries.[5] Since the majority of these seem to have been erected by soldiers, there may have been a definite order preventing their erection immediately outside the fort.

The largely haphazard nature of the development of extra-mural settlements is slightly mitigated by the one example of an attempt at planning on a grid-system,[6] and by two important instances of official activity or common action by the *vicani* with official permission. At Chesters a system of drains serving the houses of the *vicus* joins a main drain from the fort on its way down to the river. The construction of such public drains in the *vicus* in itself may indicate a communal organization, and the connexion to the military system cannot have been made without official permission. It is, of course, possible that these drains were put in by the army, concerned for the welfare of troops living out after the Severan reforms. But in any case the proof of practical official interest in the *vicus* holds good. The second example occurs at Housesteads, where the front end of house VIII is paved in one piece with

---

[1] E.g. Wallsend, Benwell, Netherby, Papcastle, etc.

[2] This seldom prevented the re-use of tombstones for building material (e.g. nos. 24, 53 etc.) though this often seems to be subsequent to a disaster when the site had been wrecked and removal of broken tombstones could be justified, carried out perhaps by a new unit with a change of civil population, circumstances when the feeling for the tombs of ancestors might be weaker than usual.

[3] E.g. Chesterholm, Maryport ('Serpent Stone' cemetery), etc.

[4] E.g. Carrawburgh.

[5] E.g. Maryport, Benwell. The household shrine at Housesteads is so far unparalleled.

[6] Corbridge—a site exceptional in many other ways.

the street. This must either again represent official action on behalf of the *vicus* or possibly some liability on the part of the householder for the upkeep of the road in front of his property. It is therefore clear that though the siting of houses and even the line of the streets was in general uncontrolled, there was an organization to deal with the basic public utilities of the *vicus*. This is of the utmost importance, for it is of the essence of town life and classes the *vici* however humbly within the urban Mediterranean form of society.

1. HOUSES AND SHOPS

The private dwelling of the *vicanus* is by far the commonest extramural structure. In its normal form it is the so-called 'strip-house', of which over 175 examples are known in the region.[1] This long, narrow, rectangular building is the most characteristic civil building and its presence is certain evidence for a *vicus*. The identification is confirmed by the fact that on all the sites, except Beckfoot and Binchester, there is other conclusive evidence for a *vicus*. The building varies in size normally from *c.* 35 by *c.* 17 feet to *c.* 60 by *c.* 25 feet, most commonly being *c.* 50 by *c.* 20 feet. A few monsters are known, particularly at Binchester where the largest strip-house measured 125 by 45 feet and the smallest 75 by 25 feet. Occasionally the shape is more nearly square, ranging from 25 by 18 feet to 50 by 45 feet.[2]

These houses are normally placed end-on to the street, though a very few lie with long axis parallel to it.[3] The entrance is usually at the front but a number possess doors in one long side.[4] Many have a front portion open to the street and some of these possessed a single central post[5] with signs that the front could be closed with double doors or shutters,[6] while others may have had an open

[1] They have been noted at Housesteads, Binchester, Chesters, Chesterholm, Piercebridge, Brougham, Beckfoot, Benwell, Maryport, Greatchesters, Old Carlisle, Old Penrith, Corbridge and Carrawburgh (*probable*).

[2] E.g. Housesteads, buildings X, XVI, XXII, XXVI, XXVII; and the most westerly house at Binchester.

[3] E.g. Piercebridge, centre of Pl. XXXIV.

[4] E.g. Benwell, building A; Maryport; Housesteads, buildings VII, the annexe to III, and perhaps XXV.

[5] E.g. Housesteads VIII.   [6] Benwell, C.

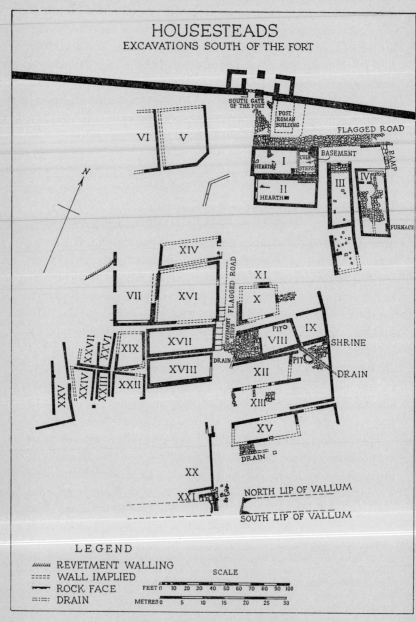

Fig. 10 *Typical* vicus *buildings*

veranda.[1] Internal partitions are not very often recorded,[2] but they may often have been of flimsy material. Cellars are rare in the British *vici*[3] unlike their German counterparts.[4] There is every reason to think that these open-fronted structures were used as shops and taverns, though there is as yet no certain example in the region of counters as at Pompeii and Herculaneum (and recently restored in the 'Römerhaus' at Augst).

The great majority of the *vicus* houses recorded on the British frontier have been of stone, but this may partly be due to accidents of preservation and excavation. All those in timber at present known were subsequently rebuilt in stone,[5] and many more may exist under stone houses. No timber houses have yet been found and excavated in sufficiently good condition to learn anything in detail of their arrangements, but the closeness of the timber structures excavated at Xanten[6] to the British stone strip-houses suggests that the timber houses here were very similar.

The origins of the strip-house, which is very frequent both elsewhere in Britain[7] and abroad[8] have much exercised continental scholars.[9] Yet it seems unnecessary to go further than the obvious dictates of convenience to explain the shape of these houses. Street-frontage in any tightly packed urban context is almost always sought after and expensive, especially when trade is a major interest. Thus whether the setting be a Roman *vicus*, a medieval town or a modern Italian city the buildings assume the same shape—open shop at the front, workroom or store and living quarters behind or above, with perhaps a yard at the back served by a lane parallel to the street.[10] This pattern of building can hardly help evolving under

[1] Though the twin pillar-bases at Binchester are perhaps due to the unusual width of the buildings.
[2] E.g. Housesteads IV.   [3] Housesteads I.   [4] E.g. Butzbach, Zugmantel, etc.
[5] Benwell, Old Carlisle, Housesteads.
[6] An excellent restored drawing of one is published in *Bonn. Jhb.* 152, 82, Abb. 2.
[7] E.g. Brecon Gaer, Nash-Williams, *Roman Frontier in Wales*, 135, fig. 58; Caerleon, *JRS*, XLV, 121, fig. 6; and a Flavian example, Prestatyn, *Arch. Camb.* XCII, 212 ff. and fig. 4.
[8] E.g. Saalburg, cf. *AA* (4), XII, 259, pl. XXIV (cellars only excavated); Butzbach, *Saalburg-Jhb.* XIV, 15, Abb. 3; Vechten, *Jaarverslag van de Vereeniging voor Terpenonderzoek*, XXIX–XXXII, 33.
[9] E.g. Swoboda, *Carnuntum* (2), 168 ff.
[10] There is yet no certain proof in the British *vici* of a second storey; but cf. in Dacia on Trajan's Column (Cichorius, LXXXIX).

these particular circumstances and is both natural and convenient.

There is one other form of house which conforms to the same requirements and which occurs once in the region. This is the large 'double-fronted' house which has a narrow entrance passage on to the street, flanked by a pair of small shops. The Constantian house on site XX at Corbridge is of this type.

2. OFFICIAL RESIDENCES: 'MANSIONES'

In the region there are several large extra-mural stone houses which are quite unlike the normal strip-houses of the *vicus*. They lie at Newstead, Benwell, Corbridge and Chesters (with possibles at Ravenglass, Old Carlisle and Watercrook).[1] For the purpose of comparison another structure of this class has been included in the discussion which follows, excavated at Brecon Gaer.[2]

Dating

The individual dating of these structures has been discussed above. It may conveniently be summarized here: Newstead, *c.* A.D. 86 to *c.* 100; Brecon, 100/125 to *c.* 140 (Phase I may be Flavian); Benwell, Severan, closing date unknown; Corbridge, Antonine or Severan to ?367; Chesters, unknown.

Plans (see Figs. 6, 7, 8)

The plan at Newstead is similar to those of such large military houses as the *praetoria* of auxiliary forts or the tribunes' houses in fortresses, in which the rooms are ranged round a central colonnaded court. The surviving portion of the first phase at Brecon may represent such another court. The second phase at Brecon, however, reveals far more drastic alterations than seem to have occurred at Newstead.

Benwell was a straightforward 'barn-building', slightly modified in the second state. Corbridge commenced with a plan similar to that of a winged corridor-villa but was very considerably modi-

---

[1] The timber building observed north of the fort at Birrens by Dr St Joseph is now thought by him not to fall within this group, *JRS*, XLI, 57.

[2] *YC*, XXXVII, 60 ff.

fied in the later phases. At Chesters the plan visible from the air is too fragmentary to provide detailed information, but appears to be similar to a villa of the type in which a number of connected buildings are grouped around a large courtyard.

Though the basic plans differ they are in each case of a pattern well-known in Britain. Seeming irregularities are due to additions made without regard for the original design, after the common fashion of owners of large houses in Roman Britain and elsewhere. No clear trend or development in design appears. The only point to be noted is that plans which were adopted for country houses further south in Britain seem chronologically to have replaced the enclosed courtyard house as the model for these structures. The courtyard house was a natural design for a site surrounded by streets and other buildings.[1] The Mediterranean town house turned in on itself, but transplanted to the northern provinces it no longer needed to keep out the sun, though privacy was still valued and it was desirable to exclude the noise and dirt of the street. This was as true in a fort as in a town. It was natural for the army engineers building the earlier of these structures to adopt the plan of the officer's house which they knew so well. But it must have become obvious that when sited well clear of the fort (and at first with comparatively little civil settlement nearby) advantage could be taken of patterns which admitted more light and air, suitable to the climate of the region.

The identification of this class of building as *mansiones*, or lodgings for official travellers, was suggested tentatively by Jacobi,[2] more firmly adopted by Wheeler discussing Brecon and powerfully supported by Birley,[3] who pointed out that there is a reference to such establishments on ILS, 231, which records the construction of *praetoria* in A.D. 60–1 on the military roads in Thrace, the work being carried out by the procurator of the province on the orders of the emperor.

It is possible to supplement and amplify the arguments in support of the identification. Several features indicate that the

---

[1] Cf., for example, houses VII S and XV S at Caerwent or house XIV 1 at Silchester.
[2] *Das Römerkastell Saalburg*, 117 ff.   [3] *AA* (4), XII, 224 f.

surviving buildings were constructed to the order of the government. Legionary tiles were used at Brecon, Corbridge and the Saalburg '*Kaufhaus*'. Moreover, at Newstead, Brecon and the courtyard house at the Saalburg (and possibly Chesters) it appears that these buildings were in each case at some time part of the same structural scheme as the external bath-house of the fort.

But these are not the only reasons for accepting the identification. These houses are quite unlike the others in the *vicus*. Scale of construction, complexity of fittings and decoration suggest the official. Few private persons in this region are likely to have had both the ability and inclination to build such a house at Newstead in the first century; or at Corbridge could have afforded to construct a private monumental fountain in the third century and employ a wall-painter five times on the same room in the fourth.

The location of the known buildings in the region suggests siting related to administration and commerce—the road junction and river crossing at Corbridge; the navigable waters of Benwell; the North Tyne crossing, sheltered valley and native centre of Warden at Chesters; the natural hub of administration at Newstead. Could they be the stations of the *beneficiarii consularis*? Unfortunately the distribution of inscriptions recording the presence of these officials does not touch that of the buildings at any point. Moreover, the *beneficiarii* proliferated in the third century. Yet two of the four datable British *mansiones* are of the late first century or first half of the second. Moreover, a *beneficiarius* was of comparatively low rank and unlikely to command so lavish a residence.

Epigraphy gives little direct help in suggesting alternatives. Other than the carrying out of some special work, the normal occasions for the private erection of inscriptions were religious dedications and the burial of relatives. Both are far more likely where the persons in question were in residence in the particular place for some considerable time. If officials were stationed at these sites there ought to be some epigraphic trace. There is none. Moreover, there is notably little trace of occupation material reported from the excavated buildings, and at Corbridge the contrast with the relatively abundant finds of pottery on other parts of the site excited comment from the excavators. In other words the buildings were not much lived in, as might be expected if, like Judges' Lodgings, they provided occasional, though generous, accommodation for important visitors. The need for such accommodation is obvious, since even if military officers might be lodged in the commandant's house some provision must have been required for civil officials, not least the staff of the *procurator provinciae* who belonged to a branch of the administration different and independent from that of the governor and his military subordinates.

3. BATHS

A bath-house was a standard piece of equipment in a permanent military establishment, and the fact that it was often, but by no means invariably,[1] situated outside the defences merely indicates military convenience and safety. The bath-house cannot properly be considered part of the *vicus*. There is therefore no cause to discuss the bath-houses in detail here, but I wish to draw attention to one point and to suggest some possible explanations which have a bearing on the life of the *vicus*. Many bath-houses possess a large *apodyterium*, or undressing-room,[2] and it has recently been proved in the case of two on Hadrian's Wall that this was a Severan addition.[3] It appears that these rooms were an innovation in the Severan period, at the very time when troops were being permitted to live out and *vici* were growing fast. It is possible that civilians were now admitted to the baths, but unlikely in view of the fact that such *apodyteria* occur in bath-houses inside forts and that there are remarkably few objects from baths which can definitely be associated with women—and surely no place would be more likely to collect lost feminine trinkets and toilet articles. An alternative explanation is that the bath-house became a club for soldiers where they might meet their colleagues, many of whom no longer lived with them in the barracks, an object which might well receive official support on

---

[1] E.g. Halton Chesters, Bewcastle.

[2] E.g. Benwell, Halton Chesters, Chesters, Carrawburgh, Greatchesters, Bewcastle.

[3] Bewcastle, *JRS*, XLVII, 204 f.; Chesters, as yet unpublished survey (December 1956) by J. P. Gillam and others.

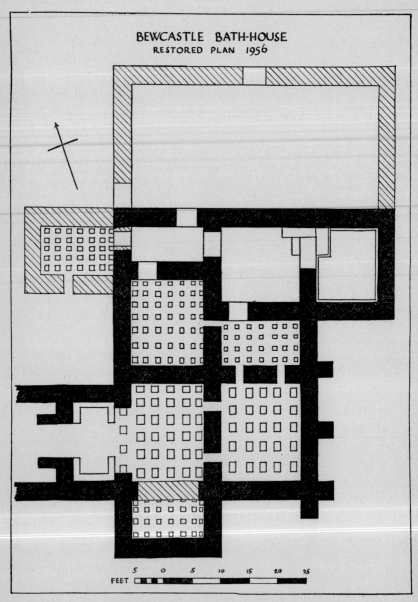

BEWCASTLE BATH-HOUSE
RESTORED PLAN 1956

FEET

Fig. 11 *Typical military bath-house (Bewcastle)—solid: Hadrianic; shaded: Severan and later. Excavated and drawn by J. P. Gillam.*

174

behalf of unit morale. There is, moreover, a matter of convenience, for while it is easy and normal for those living in College to walk to the bath-house in dressing-gown and slippers, it is considered inconvenient, if not decidedly odd, to come in from lodgings in the town in the same garb. A squad of men could be marched from its barracks wearing the minimum of clothing, but it must have been considerably more difficult to arrange such matters when men lived out and may have proceeded to the baths independently from their homes, perhaps on their way to the fort wearing uniform which would have to be left somewhere while bathing. There is of course the difficulty in this suggestion that not all bath-houses have *apodyteria* where *vici* are known (e.g. Netherby) and vice versa (e.g. Bewcastle). I do not wish to press the suggestion but hope that it is at least worth consideration when the problems of bath-houses are being considered.

4. TEMPLES AND SHRINES

It may legitimately be doubted whether a section on temples can justifiably be included in a discussion of the structures of the *vicus*, for it has proved impossible to associate a single civil dedication or other proof of civilian worship with any of the temples of which identifiable structural remains exist in the region. Where the patrons of such temples are known they are in every case either military (whether acting officially or privately) or of uncertain status. It is therefore obviously impossible to infer a civil settlement from the presence of a temple outside a fort, and sites on which there is no corroborative evidence for a *vicus* have been omitted from consideration. Yet it is certain that some civil or partly civil temples existed, for such an unweathered altar as that of Diodora at Corbridge (39) cannot have stood out-of-doors and is too elaborate to have formed part of the furniture of a wayside shrine, quite apart from its having been served by a regular group of priestesses.[1]

---

[1] The communal dedication at Carriden (26) is also unweathered, but like other inscriptions in that area it may have been deliberately buried after a comparatively short period. The association of the imperial family in the dedications at Chesterholm (32) and Old Carlisle (80) raises the possibility that they were erected in some primarily official place.

Nevertheless, the occurrence of this altar at Corbridge is perhaps symptomatic. The building of a temple implies the presence of either a rich benefactor or a considerable and prosperous community of worshippers of a particular deity, neither of which is likely to have often been found in the *vici*, and is perhaps only to be sought at Corbridge and Carlisle. It is therefore reasonable to suppose that the majority of civil sacred structures were small shrines similar to that of the *genii cucullati* at Housesteads. Any substantial temple found outside a fort is *prima facie* more likely to have been erected by the relatively numerous and well-paid soldiery than by the *vicani*.

Despite these facts, the temples of the military must, like the bathhouses, have been conspicuous objects among the extra-mural buildings and it has already been observed that there is good reason to think that they and their associated cemeteries played an important part in determining the siting of civil houses. It is therefore useful to note the position and dating of such temples when considering a particular *vicus*, but their structure does not require detailed analysis here.

CHAPTER V

THE CIVIL SETTLEMENT AND THE IMPERIAL SYSTEM

1. THE RIGHTS AND DUTIES OF THE 'VICANI'

To a considerable extent the public and private status of a Roman citizen depended upon residence and origin. Liability to his *patria* remained with a man though he moved his home (*domicilium*) elsewhere. He was also liable for duties imposed by his parent's home town, even though he himself was not born there. This however, did not absolve a person from duties in his actual place of residence. Several authorities underline the responsibilities of an *incola*.[1] He must submit to local jurisdiction in both places and perform any public duties required of him. It was even recognized that a man could have a *domicilium* in more than one place at a time.[2] Again, rights and duties could be assumed if a man, not possessing a residence in a certain place, nevertheless carried on a business there.[3] Office implied duties[4] and full *munera et honores* could fall on a man in several communities at once. These included the sometimes expensive right to take part in the public life of the community. People were liable not only to submit themselves to the jurisdiction of the local magistrates and to pay local taxes but, under the heading of *munera*, to take on duties of a minor but often troublesome and expensive sort: supervising the upkeep of roads, providing the remounts for the Imperial Post and entertaining visiting officials. It

[1] *Dig.* L, i, 29; *Cod. Just.* x, xxxix, 1.
[2] *Dig.* L, i, 6. Any disputes as to whether or not a man was an *incola* (and therefore liable for public duties) went before the provincial governor (*Dig.* L, i, 37, claimed to be based on a rescript of Hadrian).
[3] Ulpian, *Dig.* v, i, 19, 2. Only on the basis of membership of more than one community can we explain such inscriptions as CIL, XIII, 7222, or III, 10305, recording citizens of one township who held office in another community. Indeed in the case of the latter inscription it has even been suggested that the man's father belonged to a third community.
[4] Cf. *Cod. Just.* x, xxxix, 3.

177

N

seems likely, for instance, that the conduct and upkeep of the *mansio* for official visitors was a charge on the local *civitas* rather than the army—doubtless on the *vicani* when there was a *vicus* at the particular station. It was therefore of particular importance for the purposes of census, taxation and public duties—all of which were closely interconnected—to determine to which communities a person belonged. It was, furthermore, important to discover in which province he dwelt, both in matters of private law and to determine whether a particular provincial governor had jurisdiction over him.[1]

Soldiers settling in the *vicus* were presumably excused from public duties which theoretically might otherwise be incurred. Their colleagues who had similarly settled in chartered towns near to their stations were apparently exempted from the duties normally arising from domicile.[2] This, however, did not extend to the families of the latter, who *legibus patriae suae et provinciae oboedire debent*. It is likely that the families in the *vicus* were similarly bound.

Before A.D. 212 there will have been many free men in the *vici* who were not Roman citizens. Most of these in the British frontier region must have been *peregrini*, for there is no evidence for large-scale grants of Latin status. It is clear that they were not without legal recognition. The special provisions to regulate the relation between veterans and their wives is but one example of the processes which led to vast extensions of the law. Local custom, which had regulated the affairs of the natives, came gradually to influence the law and even to produce provincial variants. In practice it must have been only in those processes requiring the strict forms of the civil law (e.g. manumission) that there would have been much distinction between citizen and peregrine. However, there were certain duties and taxes which the peregrine escaped. But there was one privilege that the citizen possessed, perhaps the most prized— the right of appeal to Caesar.

---

[1] Cf. *Cod. Just* VII, xxxiii, 12; Buckland (1921), 250, n. 3.   [2] Cf. *Dig.* L. iv, 3.

2. THE INTERNAL ORGANIZATION OF THE 'VICUS'

Deferring until later the problems of what corporate status the *vicus* might have had, and though at this stage in the argument the legal relationship of the *vicani* to the *vicus* and to other authorities remains unexplained, it will be as well to put on record the fact that there was a communal organization in the *vicus*, that the *vicus* did exist as a group of people rather than a mere inanimate huddle of houses. In Britain the evidence is contained in the four communal inscriptions already mentioned which mention *vikanorum magistri* (80), two examples of single *curam agentes* (26, 32) and one record of a *decretum vicanorum* (65). The *vicani* were therefore capable of considering themselves as a group, possessed a *magister* or *magistri*, passed resolutions and appointed persons to carry them out. There is no sign of a regular committee or *ordo*, and the Housesteads inscription is positive evidence of the contrary, that decisions were taken by the *vicani* meeting as a whole.[1] There is no evidence for officers other than the *magistri* and the *curam agentes* appointed for a specific piece of work.[2]

Despite their simple organization the *vicani* were able to raise money, administer funds and hold land.[3] Without money and plots of ground they could not have erected monuments. Money could be raised in the ancient world by public subscription, private donation, fees for office and taxation. The first two methods are perhaps the most likely in a *vicus*, and the Old Carlisle inscription may be evidence for the first (if Haverfield's ingenious restoration of the last line be correct),[4] and the whole organization may have similarly been on a nominally voluntary basis, a point to which I shall later return.

---

[1] Contrast legionary *canabae*, where *decuriones* are known (e.g. CIL, XIII, 6733, A.D. 276).

[2] Though aediles are known in *canabae* as early as the reign of Hadrian, CIL, III, 6166; and are found in a *vicus* as far north as Brough-on-Humber, while a quaestor is known in *canabae* (CIL, XIII, 7222) and a *vicus* in the Dobrudja (*AE*, 1924, no. 144), and even slave clubs had the full range of officers (ILS, 7353).

[3] *Canabae* could certainly hold common funds and even called them 'public' (e.g. Apulum, ILS, 9106: *conscribti et c.R. consistentes kan. leg. . . . ex pec. publ*).

[4] *aere collato a vikanis d.d.*

3. THE CONSTITUTIONAL POSITION OF THE CIVIL SETTLEMENTS

We can now come to grips with the central problem, the position of the civil settlements in the imperial system. It must be admitted from the outset that there is yet no certain answer to many of the facets of the problem and that what follows is an attempt to marshal the evidence and suggest some possibilities. The essential fact upon which this investigation must hang is that a *vicus* of any kind, be it ward of a city, hamlet on an estate, country village or town at the gates of a military station, was always a dependent part of some larger organization. Ulpian summarizes the position admirably: 'qui ex vico ortus est, eam patriam intellegitur habere, cui rei publicae vicus ille respondet'—the man who comes from a *vicus* is considered a citizen of the local government unit to which that *vicus* answers'.[1] Our object must therefore be to discover the *respublica* of which the frontier *vici* can have formed part. It is easy to assume the whole region to have been under 'military government', extremely difficult to find parallel or constitutional basis or even how it can have worked in practice. Who can have collected the taxes, carried out the census and provided local courts if there were no civil authority? Somehow we have to find that authority.

It is necessary to go back to the early days of the Roman conquest to see how the situation reigning in the heyday of the *vicus* can have arisen. First, however, let us take a look at what happened on another frontier that presents perhaps the classic instance of constitutional development unhindered by the setbacks and complications of Britain. On the Upper German frontier part of the conquered territory was administered in Flavian times as an imperial estate under a procurator.[2] Under Trajan, doubtless in view of advancing Romanization, the area was re-organized with native *civitates* formed into Roman units of local government. We notice that the alternative forms of government, direct and indirect, are represented by the imperial estate and the *civitas* respectively.

[1] *Dig.* L, i, 30.   [2] *ORL*, LI (1936), 39.

Was there a third possibility, that the army itself sometimes fulfilled the functions of a civil authority? Except for the limited and special instance of the military *territorium* (of which more shortly) the weight of legal *theory* is against it. Considerable tracts were clearly within this military *territorium*, but is is most improbable that the whole region formed one vast formal military district. The problems of taxation and registration of the very considerable civilian population would have been a tremendous burden on a garrison fully occupied with more purely military matters, quite apart from the constitutional difficulties. Evidence for the status even of legionary *canabae* is admittedly scanty, but such as there is suggests that these civil settlements did not legally lie within the *territorium legionis*. When *legio II Adiutrix* carried out work on a bath-house lying within the *canabae* at Aquincum under Severus Alexander it felt it necessary to record the fact that the piece of ground upon which it stood was *territorio legionis*, presumably implying that the surrounding land was not.[1]

This does not imply that the local military commanders were without any control over the *vici* at their gates or the natives of the surrounding countryside. In time of emergency they could certainly act swiftly and drastically. The legionary legates at Vetera in A.D. 69 did not hesitate to loot and raze the *canabae* at the approach of the enemy. But there were better precedents than the arbitrary actions of military commanders in wartime. Ordinary *civitates stipendiariae* had no rights against an officer with delegated *imperium*, and the exercise of supervision over local authorities by military officers is recorded in several places during the second century.[2] How little, then, is the theoretical independence of *civitates* on the heavily garrisoned and barbarous fringes of the Roman world likely to have been respected. Even in Italy difficult areas were on occasion placed under the direct supervision of officers detached for this special duty, *centuriones regionarii*.[3]

How then do these ideas apply to Britain? The frontier region

---

[1] CIL, III, 10489.   [2] *Hermes* (1894), 502; Misenum, A.D. 159; Ravenna (*Not. Dign*).
[3] E.g. Környe, A.D. 210 (*Act. Arch. Acad. Hung*. III, 198); the Frisii to A.D. 28 (*Tac. Ann.* IV, 72); cf. Ribchester, *JRS*, XXXV, 25.

presents a number of difficulties both from the scarcity of any sort of constitutional evidence and from its varied nature and history. Before the coming of the Romans the region was divided between several native states: the Brigantes of Yorkshire, Westmorland, Cumberland and County Durham, the Votadini of Northumberland, the Selgovae of the Central Lowlands of Scotland, the Novantae of Galloway, the Damnonii of the Forth–Clyde Isthmus and the Venicones of Strathmore and Fife. Of these tribes only the Brigantes, Votadini and Damnonii concern us directly here, since the civil settlements under review are confined to these lands, the majority being in Brigantian territory.

It seems reasonably certain that Rome's original policy in Britain had been to occupy the south, the frontier of which was to be secured by a treaty with the Brigantes as a buffer state against the wild and unprofitable peoples of the north. The fall of the pro-Roman queen Cartimandua and the success of her spurned husband Venutius in rallying the Brigantes to the anti-Roman cause forced a radical change of policy under the Flavians, which led to a series of campaigns aimed at the total subjugation of Britain. Eventually the excessive expenditure of money and tying up of large numbers of troops caused Domitian and his successors, with extensive and growing military commitments elsewhere, to modify this aim and settle for the establishment of a frontier including the Brigantes, and at times some of their northern neighbours, but not attempting to embrace the peoples beyond the Forth–Clyde line. Except for the campaigns of Septimius Severus in the far north, the history of the region in the Roman period is the history of the various attempts to find the most satisfactory frontier line.

A constitutional consequence of the Flavian annexation of Brigantia seems to have been the recognition of the Brigantes as a Roman *civitas* with a centre at Aldborough (Isurium Brigantum). There is considerable obscurity about the extent of this *civitas*. Stamped pigs of lead from the mines of Derbyshire and dedications to Dea Brigantia as far north as Birrens bear witness to the extent of Brigantian influence but tell us little about the area of the *civitas* as constituted under Roman rule.[1] However, it seems to be generally agreed that the Brigantes as a people, and at least at first as a *civitas*, occupied the whole of the frontier region as far north as Hadrian's Wall and most probably also a district beyond its western end including Annandale and Eskdale. The outpost forts of Birrens, Netherby and Bewcastle may well have been intended to watch over the outlying wing of this dangerous tribe.

It has more than once been suggested that a primary function of the Wall was to cut the Brigantes of the Pennines off from their brothers further north. But this does not *necessarily* imply that the Brigantes north of the Wall were outside the *civitas*.[2] Roman physical frontiers were not *per se* legal or administrative boundaries: the imperial estate on the Upper German frontier extended on both sides of the *limes*. Frontier works were situated according to strategic and tactical convenience and the Tyne–Solway line was an obvious one for any military architect to choose. The outpost forts show that physical occupation by the army went north of this line, and there is no reason to suppose that the civil authority should not have done likewise. I can give no credence to the theory that the Vallum formed the civil boundary of the province, which would be quite without parallel: if a visible line were really needed as a barrier whether for legal or customs control purposes the Wall would have provided an admirable one.

The Brigantes of the hills certainly needed watching. The most reasonable explanation of the Vallum is as a barrier to prevent casual raiders on the equipment and animals kept outside the forts from bearing their loot back to the wild Pennine country to the south, where the Roman government had also found it necessary to keep their forts garrisoned. However loyal the surviving pro-Roman nobles of Aldborough and their descendants may have been, the tribesmen of the hills remained their unruly selves. Brigantia had always been a federation of clans rather than a single unit and

---

[1] These pigs are much quoted as evidence for the size of Brigantia, but is there any reason why a Brigantian-owned enterprise should not have operated in a neighbouring territory?

[2] I am inclined to think that Spartianus' *murum . . . duxit qui barbaros Romanosque divideret* (*Vita Hadriani*, 11) refers to the practical and general purpose and has no relevance to this minor legal and administrative problem.

Venutius had drawn on allies from the north. It is indeed likely that the hillmen resented the authority of Aldborough quite as much as the presence of the Roman army, even as they had rejected the sovereignty of their pro-Roman queen.

Traces of the subdivisions among the Brigantes remained under Rome. From Beltingham comes an altar (4) dedicated by the *curia Textoverdorum* which seems to represent a clan gathering for religious purposes.[1] At cantonal and provincial level official religious functions were so allied with political that we may have here a trace of a system of *pagi* or 'rural district' subdivisions of the canton. Place-names with the *corio-* suffix perhaps represent the same thing.[2]

Before the late-Roman period nothing is known of the status of the more northerly tribes, except that it appears from archaeological evidence that the tribes of south-west Scotland were thoroughly subdued, their hill-top fortresses being taken and destroyed, while the Votadini were allowed to remain in occupation of their tribal centre at Traprain Law. The latter possibly had a semi-independent status like that of Cogidumnus of Chichester, *rex et legatus Augusti*. This tradition of friendship towards Rome on the part of the Votadini survived throughout the Roman military occupation of the north and even beyond.

By A.D. 100 Roman occupation of all territories north of Brigantia had for the time being ceased, though there is reason to believe that Rome continued to consider these people as Roman subjects. But this was to be but a temporary cessation. Under the Antonines a determined attempt was made to secure at least the Lowlands of Scotland. At this point it becomes necessary to discuss an enigmatic but crucial statement by Pausanias, the second-century Greek topographer:[3] 'He [Antoninus Pius] also deprived the Brigantes of the greater part of their territory because they too had

---

[1] C. E. Stevens, *AA* (4), XI, 142 ff.

[2] Corielopocarium (*Rav.* 142) perhaps=Corstopitum (*It. ant.* 464, 3); cf. Coritiotar (*Rav.* 77) certainly in S. Scotland and perhaps a centre of the Votadini, as Coria Otadinorum (Ptol. II, iii, 10); and Corda (*Rav.* 71)=Korda (Ptol. II, iii, 8) among the Selgovae: *corio* meaning 'host' (Holder, I, 1126).

[3] VIII, xliii, 3.

attempted an incursion under arms, into the Genounian district whose people were subjects of Rome.' Pausanias is summarizing the events of the emperor's reign and emphasizing that he never conducted any wars of his own volition but punished unprovoked aggression. Birley, in a most stimulating article,[1] has advanced the theory that this records an attack by 'Free Brigantes' of the region beyond the Wall, perhaps against the Votadini, and the defeat of the aggressors in the campaign of Lollius Urbicus which led to the re-occupation of south Scotland and the construction of the Antonine Wall. Birley points out that Antoninus' salutation as *imperator* in A.D. 142 was the only one of his reign and deduces from this that this must be the war to which Pausanias refers. But there is more than one objection to this theory. The very concept of 'Free Brigantes' has several weaknesses. We have noted the presence of Roman military units in Brigantian territory beyond the Wall and doubted whether this district lay outside the *civitas*. Antoninus' action supports these doubts. If the raid was indeed carried out by transmural tribesmen—and this seems quite likely—the confisca-tion of the *greater* part of the territory of the Brigantes only makes sense if the *civitas* was responsible for these people.

Can this punitive action have been taken by Lollius Urbicus? I do not think so. If the Brigantes as a whole had proved disloyal and dangerous the Pennine forts and the Wall ought to have been strengthened under Lollius Urbicus, yet the opposite happened. The barrier of the Vallum was erased and the doors removed from the mile-castle gateways. Freedom of movement took the place of close military surveillance. This does not in the least look like a tri-bal area just punished for armed misbehaviour. It seems better to re-turn to the theory first propounded by Haverfield who associated the action of Antoninus with the military reconstruction in the Wall region epigraphically attested for A.D. 158 under the governor Julius Verus.[2] There is the sharpest contrast between the liberal policy of the early years of Antoninus' reign and the repressive military control of the period from 158. Under the next emperor the governor Calpurnius Agricola was obliged to strengthen the

---

[1] *Dumfr. & Gall.* (3), XXIX, 46 ff.   [2] *PSAS*, XXXVIII, 54 ff.

Roman hold on the Pennines, while two decades later still Ulpius Marcellus was forced to abandon Scotland, concentrate his forces on the Hadrianic frontier and restore the Wall and Vallum to full effectiveness.

The main objection to Haverfield's theory was that as Pausanias said that Antoninus Pius carried out no aggressive wars, the war of 142 must therefore be the campaign against the Brigantes. Yet in no sense can the re-occupation of Scotland *up to the Forth–Clyde isthmus* be considered merely as a punitive measure against the Brigantes, not even in the mouth of the most partisan Roman apologist. Pausanias' defence of the emperor would be better justified on the grounds that territory that had once been conquered by Rome was really Roman and that the occupation of Lowland Scotland was simply a military reshuffle within the bounds of the Empire. The *salutatio imperatoria* of Antoninus Pius would not necessarily preclude such an argument, since it is clear that the Romans were quite capable of double-think on this sort of matter. But I am more inclined to think that the war of 142 really was an external war, and that the fact that the Genounians are referred to as 'subjects of Rome' refers the incident in which they were involved to the period when the whole area south of the Antonine Wall was already conquered and absorbed into the province.

The date of the punishment of the Brigantes may be in doubt but its reality is not. Yet its nature has been little discussed. Pausanias' precise meaning contains no element of doubt. Our translation needs a slight modification to bring out the full force of the verb of action—Pausanias says quite clearly that the emperor took away most of the territory of the Brigantes *for himself* (ἀπετέμετο). The use of the middle mood of ἀποτέμνω is unmistakeable. This can only imply that an imperial estate was established, the land became the property of the emperor and its revenue passed to him. Pausanias gives us no clue to the part of Brigantia taken over, but it seems likely that the Brigantes retained the Yorkshire kernel of their ancient kingdom. The reconstruction of military sites by Julius Verus and Calpurnius Agricola strongly suggests that the territory the Brigantes lost was in fact the frontier region that they had shown themselves unfit to govern. The consequence of this for our investigation is that it now becomes a probability that the earliest civil settlements, including the growing town of Carlisle, lay in the Antonine period within an imperial estate, the direct possession of the emperor and under the control of his procurators.

The administration of the area began to worry the government some time before the Severi came on the scene. This is suggested by the appearance of a *beneficiarius consularis* near Catterick in the reign of Commodus at a spot only a few miles south of the frontier region proper and, be it noted, in a region that can hardly at any time have been outside the *civitas* of the Brigantes. The murder of Commodus in A.D. 193 brought much greater problems. In the desperate struggle for the throne that followed the governor of Britain, D. Clodius Albinus, was one of the principal contestants. Temporarily in alliance with the strongest of the pretenders, L. Septimius Severus, while the latter disposed of the third, C. Pescennius Niger, Albinus was created 'Caesar' and held Britain, Gaul and Spain. For four years he waited and prepared for the eventual struggle. Finally, he withdrew the army of Britain from its stations to challenge Severus at Lyons in 197, where he met defeat and death.

The sudden growth of *vici* under the Severan dispensation brought new problems, but the government's answer seems to have been an extension of the *beneficiarius consularis* system rather than the encouragement of local administrations. The Severi seem to have concentrated their attention on the expression of the military might of the dynasty represented by the new depot-town of Corbridge. If we are looking for an explanation for a third-century decline in the cities and villas of Britain, in everything except the military-dependent *vici*, in such strong contrast to the glory of Severus' own home town of Lepcis under his generosity, it is worth remembering that before the economic and political chaos of the middle third century set in Britain was already in an unfavourable position unique in the empire. Britain had fought enthusiastically[1] for her pretender and it would be surprising if under the conqueror there were a flowering of prosperity and free

[1] In contrast to the situation a century later in the war between Allectus and Constantius.

political life among the leading citizens, the very people to whom the defence of the realm had been delegated by Albinus. We should therefore expect to find a decline in public life in Britain more acute than in most provinces and this accords well with present archaeological evidence. The Severi here reserved their support for the development of the new army of Britain and all that appertained to it. The frontier *vici* flourished under the new conditions for the troops: prosperity was to go hand in hand with political nonentity. It would be entirely in accordance with the temper of the later Roman Empire for the civil settlements to come more and more under the immediate control of the army, irrespective of what the theoretical constitutional position might be.[1] It would be all the easier if the region were already an Imperial estate, since the distinction between the Emperor's property and that of the State was almost defunct in the third century and later, while the Emperor and the army together were coming to be the State for all practical purposes.

4. THE MILITARY 'TERRITORIUM'

From time to time I have mentioned the military *territorium* and we have seen how careful the Romans were to define it from the surrounding land. In so heavily garrisoned a region as the British frontier it is obviously important to be clear what this *territorium* comprised and its place in the system. The military *territorium* seems to have included the various sorts of land under the direct control of the army: the ground on which military installations were built, practice ranges and land set aside for the direct supply of forage, hides, timber and other commodities for feeding and equipping the troops.[2] It certainly included the *agri vacui et militum usui sepositi* from which civilian settlement was entirely barred[3] and which were represented in Britain by the area between Hadrian's Wall and the Vallum and perhaps by other areas as well.

But in what respect do these lands differ from a private citizen's

---

[1] [Cf. the delegation of certain civil functions (apparently contrary to strict legality) to a military unit in respect of the immediate neighbourhood of the station, as demonstrated in fourth-century Egypt (van Berchem, in Bell (ed.), *The Abinnaeus Archive*, 18 f.).]

[2] The responsibility of the *conductores faenarii* and *pequarii* in the legions.

[3] Tac. *Ann.* XIII, 54; cf. *AA* (4), XXXVIII, 24 f.

estate? The clue is in the term used. The jurist Paulus, writing in the early third century, links the concepts of *iurisdictio* and *potestas* with *territorium*,[1] and it is worth noting that there are instances where the boundaries of the *territoria* of *civitates* run with those of the army, implying equivalent status.[2] The basic meaning of *territorium* is 'lands or territory under a particular authority',[3] the area within which an officer's writ runs.[4] The reason for the use of the term for the military lands is clear. The army is the Roman people both in itself and as represented by the governor (or rather the emperor as proconsul for whom the governor is legate) and within its *territorium* an army unit is a locally sovereign Roman *respublica* in just the same way as a *civitas* or *municipium*.

Territoria legionum are recorded in many parts of the empire, but it is notable that the term is never linked with the name of an auxiliary unit. *Prata*, a word without the overtone of autonomous authority, is used in connexion with both legions and *auxilia*.[5] It is therefore clear that land was in fact allotted to auxiliary units but it seems likely that the final authority over the whole military territory lay normally with the legate of the nearest legion. This derives from the fact that the *auxilia* were both in theory and in practice auxiliaries to the legions and perhaps reflects an origin in the days when the legions could be contrasted as citizen bodies with the wholly peregrine *auxilia* and be considered as the Roman *Quirites* in their military array—in fact as *respublicae* equivalent to *coloniae*.

Considerable amounts of land in the British frontier region must have lain within the military *territorium*, under the authority of the legion at York and outside the control of any *civitas* or imperial estate. Any civilians there must have come directly under military control, but the care taken in defining military *territoria* elsewhere—for example the plots for bath-houses—and the rigid exclusion of civilians from the zone beyond the Vallum suggest that the authorities did their best to avoid the problem by keeping civilians out.

---

[1] *Dig.* II, i, 20.   [2] *ILS*, 5969; EE, VIII, p. 408, 131.

[3] Pomponius, *Dig.* L, xvi, 239, 8: '*Territorium*' *est universitas agronum intra fines cuiusque civitatis.*

[4] *Ibid. quod. magistratus eius loci intra eos fines terrendi, id est submovendi ius habent.*

[5] E.g. ILS, 2454, 2455, 5969.

5. THE PLACE OF THE 'VICUS'

What in the final assessment was the place of the *vicus* in the system? Was it in any sense a local government unit? From the practical point of view there is remarkably little recorded that the *vici* actually did as corporate bodies but our knowledge is limited by our reliance of necessity on inscriptions, by their nature only likely to record a limited range of events. From these the *vicani consistentes* would seem to be restricted to erecting religious and honorific monuments. Yet a glance at the official epigraphic output of, say, the Greek cities under the Empire will reveal that even from *respublicae* of the highest type the balance of inscriptions is very heavily tilted in this direction.

But can the *vici* be compared with the *civitates* in any sense? Residence in a *vicus* certainly qualified a man for citizenship of the *respublica* within which it lay. But a person dwelling out in the countryside had equal rights. A *vicus* on an estate could be little more than a common chattel, treated as any other private landed property. It may be argued that the *vici* had *magistri* and passed *decreta* and so must have been public bodies. But it was not necessary for a body to be a chartered citizen corporation to develop the symptoms we have noted, officers, titles and constitution approximating to the municipal type and based ultimately on that of the Roman republic.

The Roman government was always highly suspicious of attempts to combine, seeing criminal conspiracies in the most innocent tradesmen's guilds and religious groups. But certain private associations were permitted to exist when their purposes were open and their loyalty was beyond question. In the provinces they might even be encouraged as a medium for Romanization. At the bottom of the scale were the *collegia*, who nevertheless had their funds,[1] their *magistri* and their quaestors. Even slave associations could possess decurions, aediles and quaestors.[2] Rather higher came such organizations as that in the imperial estate in Upper Germany which was able to record work done *ex decreto ordinis saltus Sumelo-*

----

[1] ILS, 7244; ILS, 7291.   [2] ILS, 7353.

cennensis.[1] There is no doubt, however, that in this case real control was in the hands of the *procurator saltus* and his staff. Perhaps closest to the *vici* were the *conventus* of Romans resident in a foreign place. From there some of the *canabae* and *vici* themselves originated. It is significant that, unlike the *civitates* and other *respublicae* but like very many of these associations, the *vicani* named their chief officers *magistri*. Yet they were something more than just Chambers of Commerce or Residents' Associations. In Roman eyes the *vicani* in a *civitas* were members of a city state or similar organization and the rural *vicus* was, like the Attic deme, as much part of that state as the *vicus* or ward of the town. Possibly the nearest modern analogy in status and function is the parish council. But we must not be lured by this analogy into the idea that they were organs of local democracy. To the imperial government all local government units were bodies upon which burdens could be laid, not representatives of popular opinion: to the people of the region they were the means by which the more wealthy members of the community were encouraged or compelled to undertake personal and financial public duties in return for honours and social prestige. The decay in local government in the empire is in fact marked by a growing unwillingness on the part of the upper classes to shoulder the increasing public burdens put upon them, until membership of a local council became little more than an ill-disguised form of taxation. At the same time its active functions and political influence were whittled away by the ever-growing octopus of the central administration. It is an odd paradox that it was only in periods of chaos that the local organizations regained any political importance, and even then they were more likely to fall under some *tyrannus*, whether military adventurer or local magnate, than to become little republics even of the most oligarchical kind. Let it be said with the maximum of emphasis that local government in the Roman empire was organized essentially for the benefit and convenience of its masters, occasionally in a paternalistic manner for the welfare of the local population, but never for the encouragement of political expression and popular liberty.

[1] CIL, XIII, 6365.

6. THE THIRD CENTURY:
REVOLUTION AND PROSPERITY

The Severan age in Britain was not to be so politically and socially colourless as might be expected from the picture of decay presented by historians concerned chiefly with the South or mesmerized by the classical age of the Roman army in the Flavian, Hadrianic and Antonine periods. On the contrary, it was a period in which bold re-modelling of the military and political structure of Britain was followed in our area by a leap forward in prosperity. We have seen how the living-out of soldiers and the abolition of the Vallum produced a vast growth of *vici*: the local administration had to be re-fashioned to deal with the problems posed by this massive half-military, half-civil development. What happened to the organization in the face of these changes? There is no doubt that under the Severi the region remained theoretically under civil administration—even if under increasing supervision by officers of the government—and an inscription of A.D. 212 from Chester-le-Street recording the re-definition of an area of military *territorium* on the re-occupation of that fort supports the existence of non-military authority at that time (since the ground in question had clearly passed from military to some form of civil jurisdiction).[1] The question is whether the Severi retained the dispositions of their predecessors.

One of the most extraordinary phenomena of the early third century in our area is the emergence of a powerful cult of the goddess Brigantia.[2] The dating is not in doubt and is most striking in view of the discrediting of the Brigantes and the drastic reduction of their *civitas* only fifty years previously. From the political angle there are a number of important features about this cult. First, four of the seven known dedications come from the frontier region,[3] secondly one of these was by a procurator for the health of the emperor and the imperial house[4] and, thirdly, the well-known representation of the goddess from Birrens shows her with the

---

[1] EE, VII, 986.   [2] *AJ*, XCVII, 36 ff.   [3] ILS, 4717, 9318; CIL, VII, 1062, 875.
[4] CIL, VII, 875.

mural crown, as tutelary deity of a city or *civitas*.[1] I think it is possible that Septimius Severus restored the honour of the Brigantes by returning to them their lost northern territory, which in turn would mean the dissolution of the imperial estate. The greater part of the region would once more be Brigantian, but with this difference, that now the central government through its political agents took a much closer interest in the everyday workings of the civil administration and the *decuriones* were reduced to the position of unpaid and often unwilling servants of the State.

The changes of the early third century in our region are a symptom of the close interest of the Severi in this province on the periphery of the empire. They took its problems so seriously that from A.D. 208 to 211 they attended to them in person. For four years the effective capital of the Roman world lay at York while the victor of Lugdunum did not spend his last years nursing his gout in the well-earned luxury of a Sullan retirement but in the rigours of campaigning and reconstruction, restoring peace and security to the land which had produced his last rival for the imperial throne.

At York itself the *canabae legionis* found themselves suddenly a metropolis and by A.D. 237 they were a *colonia*.[2] Such grants were standard Severan policy elsewhere, but the British legions had hardly earned such a favour from this emperor, and in this case the presence of the imperial court was probably the cause. The *canabae* can hardly have failed to expand under such an unusual stimulus, while the legionary legate must have been far too harassed to cope with the problems of civil administration.[3] [It is possible that the former imperial lands were not returned to the Aldborough *civitas* but formed the endowment of the new *colonia*, and the *civitas* could have been attached to it.]

On gaining control of Britain the Severan government had been faced by the problems of reconstruction, securing the country from external attack and assuring the loyalty of army and people. Peace was the first essential, to allow the work of reconstruction

---

[1] CIL, VII, 1062.   [2] *JRS*, XI, 102.

[3] The third- and fourth-century occupation is concentrated south and west of the Ouse, abandoning an area settled in the second century north-west of the fortress. This perhaps implies a planned development in the third century, possibly with colonial status in mind.

O

to go ahead. Towards the external enemies of the north the policy of the Severi was direct. First Danegeld was paid to keep the tribes quiet while the Wall was repaired and a new system of forward defence designed and constructed. Meanwhile bases were built and supplies brought up in preparation for the second stage, massive retaliation. Three campaigns secured the greatest military success of Roman arms in Scotland and gave the frontier its longest period of peace.

The problem of internal security was more difficult but the answer was subtle. The Antonine occupation of southern Scotland had foundered upon the unreliability of the Pennine and Northumbrian tribesmen, and in conformity with the by then traditional policy of exclusion and repression the Vallum was reconditioned late in the second century. Yet by the end of that century there are signs that the situation was changing. The proliferation of unwalled *vici* along the Wall so fast so early in the third century implies a considerable degree both of Romanization and of friendliness on the part of the local population. The first *vici* had already appeared and the inhabitants of the native settlements, who had for a long time been using Roman products, must by now have begun to appreciate the benefits of security, the profitable market and the prospects of a well-paid career for their sons and solid husbands for their daughters offered by the Roman army. The Severan government, with a boldness and insight worthy of an Agricola, decided on integration rather than repression. The Vallum was swept away, military regulations drastically revised to permit soldiers to establish regular families and their unions with native women officially recognized. This is the Agricolan policy of peace through urbanization in a new guise. Moreover, the *Constitutio Antoniniana*, whatever its immediate purpose, underlined the fact that the concept of Roman and native was obsolete, that there were no longer two peoples in the eyes of the government. It is significant that in the frontier region there is no evidence that the local population ever again caused trouble to the authorities.

The most pressing problem of loyalty, however, was not posed by the civilians. Severus, survivor of a multilateral civil war, was

acutely conscious of the threat to the central government of powerful governors and independently minded provincial armies. Britain had produced a formidable rival for the imperial throne and
the British army had been willing to leave its province and fight
ferociously for its choice. The government had now to secure the
personal loyalty of the individual soldier to the Severan house and
to make it less easy for governors to collect great armies without
authority. With the troops Severus started with an advantage, for
he had been decisively victorious and the Roman army was inclined to trust a soldier-emperor. Moreover, his military vigour
showed no signs of slackening and he certainly had no intention of
allowing the army of Britain idleness in which to nurse grievances
and foment mutiny. This was the reverse of the coin with which he
solicited the loyalty of the soldiers. The attractive obverse, tradi-
tionally consisting of donations and increases of pay, was further
decorated by the ingenious Severus. Few Augusti can have been
more popular with their troops than the emperor who encouraged
them to live with their families and conferred respectability on
their wives and children. In Britain the army remained loyal
throughout the tenure of the throne by the Severi and elsewhere
the policy was successful while the founder of the dynasty lived.
But the effect went deeper than mere personal gratitude to the
emperor, for it bound the troops to their stations as nothing before
had done. Over a century earlier Tacitus records the unwillingness of a garrison to leave its friends and relations for service in a
strange land and uninviting climate,[1] but now to leave the frontier
in support of a pretender meant leaving unprotected their own
homes and personal property.

The problem of the over-great commander was common to
the frontier provinces of the empire. In similar circumstances the
Flavians had abolished the two-legion fortresses, to avoid undue
concentration of forces in one spot. The Severi carried the process
a stage further to limit the total legionary forces at the disposal of
any one governor to a maximum of two legions. This process was
initiated by Severus and completed at the latest by Caracalla. In

[1] *Hist.* II, 80.

Britain the problem was not urgent while the emperors themselves were in the country but it must have become acute when Caracalla was making his final dispositions before leaving in A.D. 211. The division of Britain into two provinces cannot be much later than this date.[1] But the foundations for the new system had already been laid, doubtless with the eventual departure of the imperial family from Britain in mind.

From Flavian times the main garrison of Britain had lain in the north, but its food seems largely to have been supplied from the enormous agricultural reservoir created by the development of the Fens in the early second century. While the army of the north remained dependent on the south for its food, he who controlled the South could ultimately dictate the policy. However, in the Cumberland Plain at least it seems probable that by the end of the second century the farms were reasonably productive, and the new government took steps to hasten the process throughout the area. The massive frontier defences on the line of the later Anglo-Scottish border secured the fertile valleys between the Cheviot and the Wall, while the new port at South Shields, and the base at Corbridge and the construction of the Military Way made supply of the Wall by sea from the Plain of York much easier. Moreover, the expanding *vici* and the friendlier relations with the local population must have stimulated agriculture and made the arrangement of local supply of produce far easier than requisitions from the sullen and secretive natives of an earlier age.

The net result of these developments was to produce a startling contrast between North and South in the third century. Based largely on the archaeological evidence of the South the accepted picture of the third century has been of decay in town and countryside alike. Villas were abandoned, towns decaying and public works in disrepair. The age of violence and inflation, the punishment of revolt, lay heavy on the civil life of the country. Yet we have seen the very opposite happening in the North. The new army of Britain was favoured and public and private development shot

---

[1] The problem of the precise dating of the two provinces is outside the immediate scope of this book.

forward. If Britannia Superior was on the downgrade the balance was redressed by the rapidly growing prosperity of at least a major part of the sister province. Indeed the contrast is so acute that it poses the question whether, in view of the peace secured by the success of the Severan frontier policy, the factors of inflation and intermittent political severance from the capital of the empire are sufficient to explain the decay in the region that the frontier was designed to protect. This is particularly true in view of the contrast presented by the succeeding century, when the South so markedly recovered in face of much more difficult external conditions. But this is a question lying beyond the scope of the present inquiry.

The success of the Severan re-planning seems to have been rapid, for by A.D. 220 at the latest the province had been divided somewhere south of Lincoln. Lincoln, York and the frontier region fell into the Lower Province. The consular governor of Britannia Superior lost the immediate command of the northern army and that day-to-day contact with its personnel so valuable for fomenting rebellion, while the praetorian legate was perhaps kept in hand by the presence in his area of the *beneficiarii consularis*[1] of the Upper Province who could report the state of affairs to their consular master.

The Severan policy was more successful militarily than politically. The frontier system was not broken by direct assault while properly manned for a century and a half and the military machine retained its efficiency and readiness for action. Unfortunately, the ever-increasing ties of family and sentiment between the army of Britain and the local population can only have served to strengthen its sense of independence and in the course of the third century it successively supported the *imperium Galliarum*, a revolt under Probus,[2] and the pretensions of Carausius. When it came to a direct clash with the forces of the continental government the northern troops obeyed the orders of Carausius' murderer and successor Allectus, even if unenthusiastically. This miscalculation cost them their homes.

Considerable obscurity still surrounds these events in 296. It

---

[1] The exact function of these relatively minor officials remains uncertain.
[2] Zosimus, I, 66, 2.

looks as if the regular troops failed to support Allectus when it came to battle,[1] with the customary fickleness of Roman armies in civil conflict, but we need not accept without reserve the declaration of Constantius Chlorus' panegyrist that the conquering representative of the government in Rome was received with joy by the provincials—unless it was by the unhappy civilians of the South who had had too much of rapacious military usurpers and prowling armies.

7. THE FOURTH CENTURY AND AFTER

The northern barbarians had once again wrecked the frontier region, but Constantius had an easier task than Severus a century earlier, for he was able to use an undamaged army to reconstruct its own stations and homes. The identity of the re-occupying force and the need for rapid restoration must constitute a great deal of the reason why in an age of revolution in military thinking the British frontier received no more than minor modifications at a time when there was opportunity for reconstruction on new lines. Thus the pattern of military dispositions and civil settlement remains much the same in the earlier fourth century as it was in the third.

The origins of the much discussed features of certain parts of the frontiers of the Roman empire in the late period may well lie in the existence of irregular units of peasant milita in the third century. Yet I suspect that the farmer-soldiers commonly supposed to be typical of the frontier forces of the fourth century are no more than a phenomenon of a few localities with peculiar problems. The general evidence runs in the opposite direction. Diocletian and his successors certainly reformed the military system, replacing the old provincial legions by new, possibly smaller legions relying upon recent advances in military architecture, developments in cavalry and the increased use of artillery instead of sheer weight of infantry. Manpower was short in the late Empire, mechanical and architectural ingenuity was not. In fact the forts and walled towns of this age are strongly reminiscent of the castles and cities of the Middle

[1] Eumenius, *Pan. Constant. Caes.*, 16 f.

Ages, where again the engineer was called in to permit comparatively small forces of trained men to undertake the operations of defence. Moreover, there were strong political advantages for the central government in reducing the size of the major frontier units and developing a central élite and highly mobile reserve under their immediate control. There is, however, remarkably little evidence that the frontier forces became peasant soldiers. The Theodosian Code records arrangements for the payment of *annonae* to garrisons in kind, implying that they were not supporting themselves on the land.[1] Again, provisions in the late legal sources for allotments of frontier land are to *gentiles* (barbarians) or veterans, not to serving troops.

On the northern frontier of Britain there is no evidence for major changes even on the purely military side before A.D. 369 at the earliest. Until at least 367 the frontier forts continued to be held by units of the old type and the picture must have looked much as it had in the Severan age. There were no great legions lying right on the frontier to be reduced in size, and the enemy and his habits remained as they had long been.

After the Great Pict War, when nearly all the *vici* disappear and there is some archaeological evidence for increased and different accommodation in the forts, the frontier may have come closer to the system of walled towns and castles on the continental *limes*. But the ordinary Roman civil population was probably confined to the few walled towns and those *vici* which revived in particularly well-protected spots. An entirely new class, possibly imported from outside the region, was perhaps now living inside the frontier forts, a class having no connexion with the former *vicani*. There is no evidence that the latter survived to move into the forts themselves, and it is legally improbable that the trading element should have been allowed to do so. The army remained strictly differentiated from the civilians, as it had always been. The difference between this age and the earlier Empire is that the army was now one of a number of rigid divisions in the State, a class out of which it was extremely difficult for an individual to pass. It is entirely in

[1] *Cod. Theod.* VII, iv.

keeping with late-Roman thinking that the frontier force should
be a class tied to its posts and the hereditary principle was sufficient
to include the families of soldiers in the classification. In certain
cases it was to become a capital offence[1] for persons of *privata con-
dicio* to take over *terra limitanea* allotted to *castellani milites*.[2] The new
system was not a fusion of military and civil but an adaptation of
the system which existed on the British frontier under Severus,
with the simple alteration that instead of more married soldiers
going out of the fort to live with their families, the families themselves now came in. The probable result was that both troops and
dependants were more widely separated from ordinary civilians
than ever before, probably for the first time with a frontier region
separated off as *terra limitanea*, a situation in keeping with the theoretical rigidity of the age.

This situation was short-lived. The withdrawal of troops by
Magnus Maximus in A.D. 383 must have meant the disappearance
of their attached civil tail of families, for even if the women and
children did not accompany the expeditionary force they cannot
have stayed long after its defeat abroad. The Theodosian system
had thus lasted for little more than a dozen years. Nevertheless, the
fact that Corbridge lived when the Wall forts were abandoned is
strong evidence that the towns were not left entirely alone. If, as
seems very possible, Maximus made arrangements by which the
frontier was entrusted to friendly tribes from north of the Wall,[3]
they probably took over the *terra limitanea*. It is clear from the
Theodosian Code (VII, xv, 1) that such *gentiles* could occupy such
territory on the same basis as the *castellani milites* whom they may
in this case have replaced. The position of the towns as enclaves in
the military zone will thus have remained substantially the same
after 383 as between 369 and that date. And so they must have remained till the final collapse of the Roman provincial government
robbed such legal distinctions of the authority which only the
ultimate power of Rome to enforce them could give. Though

[1] *Cod. Theod.* VII, xv, 2; A.D. 423.
[2] Cf. Richmond, *Roman and Native in North Britain*, 125; cf. also the military zones of
the earlier empire, e.g. the Vallum zone. Some civilians had clearly been infiltrating.
[3] Richmond, *Roman and Native in North Britain*, 128 ff.

some life may have survived in the settlements, the people can no longer be considered as civilian members of the Roman empire and pass at this point out of the field of this inquiry and into the Dark Ages.

POSTSCRIPT

I might well have begun this book with some comments on the neglect of the British frontier in most general works about provincial life and on the bare mention which its civil population is lucky to receive. I have preferred to let the facts speak for themselves. If they have not spoken eloquently the fault is mine, for perhaps the most interesting thing to emerge in the course of the investigation is that the Romanized element in the civil population of the region is much more than a slight handful of hangers-on clinging to the army. It was an important factor in the life of the region, both by reason of its numbers and from its importance to the army. Probably even more than the army it became the means by which the local population was involved in the cosmopolitan life of the Roman world. The settlements are no longer for us vague in form but take their place as societies within the Roman system with a distinctive structure and status which can be studied and classified like any other.

An attempt has been made to understand the constitutional basis of authority over the civilians, and something has been deduced of the status of the different groups. There can be no doubt that this is the most important aspect, for the existence of a constitutional background fundamentally separates British society in the Roman period from the prehistoric world. In this age, though the material culture of many changed but little, the people were for the first time subjected to the greatest of the benefits which Rome conferred on her empire, the institution which in future ages was not only to regulate but make possible both personal liberty and the proper ordering of society—the rule of law.

If there is any justification for the neglect of the region by historians of the empire it can only be that so much of the information has lain buried in unpublished sources or in local periodicals inaccessible to continental scholars, who have hitherto been the most interested in the problems of civilian life on the frontiers. For this reason alone it has seemed profitable to assemble the scattered evidence, and, though I cannot hope that conclusions which I have reached in the discussion will be accepted as more than one man's present views on the problems, I like to think that as a *corpus* of material for future study this book may be of some value.

In view of this aim it would hardly be proper if I left the subject without suggesting some of the ways in which the work may profitably be continued. The main problems are now reasonably clear. On the constitutional side the basic task is to learn more about the methods by which the *vici* were administered. Further information is greatly to be desired on the exact definition of the epigraphically attested *territorium legionis*, the detailed functions of frontier *civitates* and imperial estates and the precise application of these concepts to Britain. It would also be useful to know whether the presence of peregrines in office in *vici* in the Dobrudja represents a regular practice in the provinces. How answers to these questions are to be found is not clear, for it would be unreasonable to rely on the discovery of further inscriptions or historical texts, but their existence as problems must be recognized.

More hopeful of solution in that they are suceptible to action are a number of archaeological problems presented by the British material. One of the greatest is to discover the truth about early *vici*. It is essential to discover whether a substantial number of stone *vici* are concealing earlier timber settlements. Apart from the chronological importance of such sites, any information on the details of timber structures would also be of value when considering the timber structures which were constructed on other sites, for example Easter Happrew, Benwell and close to the fort at Housesteads, even at comparatively late dates. There is also an opportunity for further testing the theories on the function of the Vallum as a barrier to civilians in the second century at Chesters, where an Antonine diploma arouses suspicion of a second-century *vicus* and where stone civil buildings are visible straddling the probable course of the Vallum.

Also at Chesters, examination of the interesting drainage system might provide important information on the relation of fort and *vicus*, and excavation of the *mansio* will one day be desirable, for a modern examination of one of these structures is clearly necessary. Site II at Corbridge might also repay re-excavation, if only to check and correct my interpretation. The main civil problem at Corbridge, however, is a full-scale investigation of the town defences. A section just south of the north-east corner should give a clear cut through ditch, wall and bank free from disturbance from earlier excavations. Re-excavation on the north side where the wall overlapped the ditch might provide additional information on the relation of the elements to one another. The north and south gates, too, require re-excavation, the suspected east gate needs proving, and the whole problem of the western extent of the town is as yet hardly touched. At Carlisle there is less hope of learning much, but there is some chance that sections through the medieval wall would reveal the defences around which St Cuthbert perambulated.

Much else remains to be done. At least one annexe will have to be subjected to complete excavation before the disputed nature of these can finally be settled. It will also be necessary to have far more information on the relative dates at which *vici* and forts were finally abandoned to reach certainty on a general movement of civilians into forts after the war of 367. Excavation is also the answer on the sites where the extra-mural indications are extensive but their precise significance uncertain (for example Ambleside, Ebchester and Papcastle). In conclusion I should refer to one of the commonest problems of all, such sites as Risingham at which a civil settlement is epigraphically attested but where structures are so far unknown. In these cases fieldwork on the ground and in the air must come before excavation can be economically used. In the end it must be used, for though aerial survey can now provide in many instances a plan (and more plans can be drawn than yet have been attempted) and sometimes even indicate the chronological relationship of elements in the plan, we have not yet reached such a state of knowledge on symptomatic features of plan that we can date these structures on style alone. Nor is it ever likely to be possible to ascertain the presence or absence of earlier features below without use of the pick and shovel.

I have made much use in this book of the work of the antiquaries of the past and have come to appreciate them as scholars and as people. It would be idle to suggest that here is a vital field for historiography, but time spent on study of their methods of approach and their ideas is not wasted, especially in so far as these reflect on the intellectual climate of their own times.

There is, moreover, a moral in the example of the antiquaries of the sixteenth to the eighteenth centuries. These were men of wide interests who never forgot that the particular sites they were studying represented the classical culture of the Greco-Roman world which they admired and to which they turned for inspiration, and it was this that gave the material remains their significance. With the nineteenth and the twentieth centuries the specialist archaeologist and the purely local historian became more and more prominent. Nor did the earlier antiquaries in the main confine themselves to one period. Nowadays when studying a particular age it is easy to dismiss the remains of other periods as a nuisance or worse: even to the point of deliberate destruction. It is indeed a serious question whether intense study of some intrinsically worthless class of object to the exclusion of other things is not bad for the soul. In fact, in the intellectual pursuit of knowledge we may end by far the poorer and possibly in a lower state of culture than the people we are supposed to be studying. The complexity of modern knowledge may be such that the Renaissance polymath is no longer feasible, but just a little of his spirit is certainly needed: that universal interest in the works of man and nature and the sense that the remains of the past are worth preserving and studying both as products of the human spirit and for their contribution actual and potential to the present.

I am not arguing for an indiscriminate passion for antiquity. The proper approach must necessarily involve us in the difficult business of making judgements of value on the subjects we choose to study. I am well aware that this present book may come under just this class of indictment and can only hope I have provided sufficient evidence for it to defend itself. If the verdict shall go against it, I can only plead in mitigation that at least I recognize that such judgements must be made in every case.

APPENDIX

INSCRIPTIONS AND SCULPTURES
RELATING TO CIVILIANS

This appendix lists the inscriptions and sculptures which provide evidence for the presence of civilians in the frontier region or can be associated with them. All pieces for which there is definite evidence of civil associations have been included. The catalogue includes all inscriptions which mention women, children, men under fourteen years of age or over sixty, veterans and any other persons or groups specifically civilian. I have also listed men whose profession makes it almost certain that they were civilians (e.g. 11, 43) but omitted as indeterminate all those inscriptions which have no distinguishing mark of civilian status or military rank. Many of these must be civil, but there is no means of knowing which. Imperial officials are also omitted—being part of the governmental system and not properly of the civil population—but have been discussed earlier where appropriate. I have included women, children, and servants from the households of military officers, since they are as much civilian as the families of other ranks, though they cannot, of course, be used as evidence for a *vicus* at a particular place.

The arrangement is alphabetical by modern place-names. The items are listed under the Roman site to which they are attributed, except for one (4) whose Roman location is completely uncertain. The form of the entries is largely self-explanatory. When known, the present location of a piece and its museum catalogue number (if any) are given in the title.[1] The headnote includes the provenance and a brief description. The lists of references are not intended to be exhaustive but to give the most important publications. At the foot of each entry the appropriate reference numbers are given in

---

[1] I am grateful to Mr R. P. Wright, Dr David Smith and Mr Robert Hogg for information about the present location of certain stones.

brackets where the item has been included in the major epigraphic collections.

[*Ambleside*: see *JRS*, LIII, 160, no. 4]

1. *Auchendavy* (Glasgow, Hunterian Museum)
Tombstone, found 'a little east from' Shirva. Fragment 2, bearing the third line of the inscription, was not discovered until after Gordon and Horsley had reported on the stone. It records the death of a woman.

D * M * | VEREC | VNDAE

D(is) M(anibus) Verecundae

Gordon, pl. 66, fig. 3; Horsley, 199; Macdonald, *RWS* (2), 439, no. 60 and pl. LXXVI, 3 (CIL, VII, 1120).

2. *Auchendavy* (Glasgow, Hunterian Museum)
Found with (1) 'near Shervy' (Gordon), presumably from the fort cemetery. Tombstone: at the top is a rough gable; above the inscribed panel is a rosette-flanked laurel wreath. The rosettes surmount palm branches. The vertical margins of the inscribed panel are decorated with a cable ornament. The execution is crude.

D * M * | SALMANES | VIX * ANN * XV | SALMANES | POSVIT

D(is) M(anibus). Salmanes vix(it) ann(os) xv. Salmanes posuit

Birley (*Roman Britain and the Roman Army*, 82) points out that the names are probably oriental. He therefore thinks that the erector (whom he considers probably to be the father of the deceased) was most likely a trader.

Gordon, pl. 66, fig. 2; Horsley, 199; Macdonald, *RWS* (2), 438, no. 59 (CIL, VII, 1119).

3. *Beckfoot*
Graffito on a grey cooking pot of the early fourth century which contained a cremation. Found in 1952 by Mr and Mrs K. Watson of Stanwix at a position 200 yards south of the south-west corner of the fort. It is not clear on which side of the road from the south gate

it lay. Other cremations were discovered on the west side of the road in 1948 (*CW* (2), XLIX, 32 ff.) and 1954 (*CW* (2), LIV, 51 ff.), 400 yards from the south-west corner at the cliff-edge.

ṾROCATAE

Vrocatae

The name is that of a woman. Mr Wright suggests that a stem *brocco*—, a badger, is the basis of the name. Vrocata may have been the deceased or a former owner of the pot.

JRS, XLIII, 131, no. 21.

4. *Beltingham* (Newcastle Museum,[1] Black Gate Cat. no. 50)

Altar, noted in Beltingham churchyard in 1835. It is possible that, like CIL, VII, 715, it came there from Chesterholm. Height 32 in.; breadth 18 in.

ḌEAE | SAṬṬADAE | CVRIA TEX | TOVERDŌRVM | V * S * L * M *

Deae Sattadae (?), curia Textoverdorum v(otum) s(olvit) l(ibens) m(erito)

This inscription is fully discussed by C. E. Stevens in *AA* (4), XI, 138 ff. The goddess is otherwise unknown. Mr Stevens convincingly argues for *curia* referring not to a local senate but, as the Celtic *corie*, to a local subdivision of the tribe equivalent to a *pagus*. Thus the Textoverdi are perhaps a *pagus* of the Brigantes.

Hodgson, II, iii, 198 (CIL, VII, 712; LS, 255; EE, IX, p. 593).

5. *Benwell*

Sherd of samian, form 33, stamped PROBVS F, found in excavations in 1938 near the Vallum crossing. It bears a graffito done after firing and presumably indicating the owner. The sherd is Antonine.

AV[.]SINA

Av[e]sina (?).

The suggestion is that of R. G. Collingwood, but it is pointed out that that name is elsewhere unknown (*JRS*, XXX, 188).

---

[1] [*Museum of Antiquities of the University of Newcastle upon Tyne and of the Society of Antiquaries of Newcastle upon Tyne.*]

P

6. *Birdoswald*

This stone was noted on a dairy at Birdoswald in 1785 (Brand). Tombstone.

D M | AVRELI | CONCOR | DI VIXIT | ANN ∗ VN | V̂Ṃ [   ] D ∗ V (?) | FIL ∗ ÂVR | IVLIANI | TRIB

D(is) M(anibus) Aureli Concordi. vixit ann(um) un[um, m(enses) . . ,] d(ies) v(?), fil(ius) Aur(eli) Iuliani trib(uni)

If, as it seems reasonable to assume, the father is the commandant of the fort, it becomes apparent from this stone that this is one of the cases where the commandant had his family living with him, presumably in his house inside the fort.

Brand, *Newcastle*, I, 613 (CIL, VII, 865; LS, 383).

7. *Birdoswald* (Newcastle Museum, Black Gate Cat. no. 165)

Noted in 1752 by F. Swinbow on a wall a short distance west of the fort. The last line has since disappeared. R. G. Collingwood read:

D [| DEC[| DIEB[| ET ∗ BLAE[|]T A X ET |

Perhaps this may be interpreted as:

D(is) [M(anibus).] Dec[ebalus (?) v(ixit)] dieb[us . .] et Blae[sus vixi]t a(nnos) x et [m(enses) . .]

Collingwood suggests from the name Decebalus (?) that the father of the two children was a member of the cohors I Aelia Dacorum in garrison at Birdoswald in the third century and recorded there in the *Notitia*. Blaesus, however, is Latin and is perhaps here a nickname ('lisping').

CIL, VII, 866; LS, 382. Collingwood points out that CIL, VII, 539 (LS, 31) is the same stone as this.)

8. *Birdoswald* (*Harrow's Scar*) (Birdoswald)

Tombstone of a boy, found by I. A. Richmond in excavation at Harrow's Scar milecastle. The stone had been re-used beneath the threshold in the Severan reconstruction of the milecastle. It is therefore pre-Severan. The Severan builders presumably took it

from the cemetery of adjacent Birdoswald. The left-hand part of
the stone is missing. Left *in situ*.

.] M A |]ERENVS |]N II ME II D III

[D(is)] M(anibus). A[urelius S]erenus (?) [vixit a]n(nos) ii,
me(nses) ii, d(ies) iii

CW (2), LIII, 212; *CW* (2), LVI, 26.

9. *Birrens*
'now at Knockhill, near Ecclefechan, in a summerhouse.'—
Macdonald, *PSAS* (3), VI, 145. Pedestal of a statue of Fortuna,
found 'at the station at Burrens' (Pennant).

FORTVNAE P[| SALVTE P CAMPA[| ITALICI PRAEF COH I [|
TVN CELER LIBERTVS | L L M

Fortunae p[ro] salute P(ublii) Campa[ni] Italici, praef(ecti)
coh(ortis) I[I] Tun(grorum), Celer, libertus, l(aetus) l(ibens)
m(erito).

The second cohort of Tungrians is attested at Birrens from A.D. 158
by a building inscription of that date (Macdonald, *Roman Wall in Scotland* (2), 478, n. 1). It seems reasonable to assume that Celer was in the
service of the prefect. He is paralleled by Eutychus, who set up a dedication at High Rochester (60, below) for the safety of the fort commandant
and his wife, and possibly by Theodotus at Risingham (97).

Pennant, *Tour in Scotland*, III, appendix viii, 407 (CIL, VII, 1064; EE,
IX, p. 614).

10. *Birrens* (Dumfries Burgh Museum)
Tombstone, reported as from Birrens by Pennant.

D M | AFVTIANO | BASSI * OR | DINATO * | COH II TVN | FLAVIA *
BAETI | CA CONIVNX | FAC * CVRAVIT

D(is) M(anibus). Afutiano Bassi (filio), ordinato coh(ortis) II
Tun(grorum), Flavia Baetica, coniunx, fac(iendum) curavit

It seems reasonable to follow Sir George Macdonald in supplying the
faint letters in lines 5 and 6 from Pennant's expanded text. The closest

inscription to this in the area is (94), below, from Cliffe south of the river at Piercebridge, where another *ordinatus* received a memorial from his wife. *Ordinati* are known in the third century as centurions of auxiliary cohorts. Here, however, the mention of the unit known to have been at Castlesteads in the third century and the possibly peregrine status of the husband could suggest a second-century date for the inscription. On the other hand, Professor Richmond points out that this unit was too large to have been accommodated at Castlesteads if at full strength (*RW* (11), 198). It is therefore not impossible that a detachment was sent to Birrens at the time when the main part of the regiment lay at Castlesteads (though it is rare that the same unit is found in the region at the same station before and after 196).

Pennant, *Tour in Scotland*, III, appendix viii, 408; *PSAS* (3), VI, 145 f. (CIL, VII, 1078; EE, IX, p. 615).

11. *Bowness-on-Solway* (Carlisle, Tullie House Cat. no. 45)

Votive slab, discovered in 1790 'at Bowness, in Cumberland, very near the western extremity of the Picts' wall, and the most western station thereon'. Rediscovered in 1879. The top is broken but the rest complete. Height 11 in., breadth 17½ in. It contains the following metrical inscription:

] ONIANVS DEDIC[|]ED DATE VT FETVRA QVAE[.]TVS | SVPPLEAT VOTIS FIDEM | AVREIS SACRABO CARMEN | MOX VIRITIM LITTERIS

[. . . .] onianus dedic[o. S]ed date ut fetura quae[s]tus suppleat votis fidem: aureis sacrabo carmen mox viritim litteris

It is obvious that this inscription refers to the type of vow in which someone promises to perform some act in honour of a deity provided that the said deity favour a particular project or give help in some time of need. It is unusual in that it is set up as a written promise in advance. Most of the references to such vows are found on the object dedicated after the event in fulfilment of the vow.

Here the reference seems to be to some trading enterprise, perhaps by sea. Since no gilding survives it is not known whether the vow was carried out.

Hutchinson, *Cumberland*, II, 486 (CIL, VII, 952; EE, III, p. 136; EE, VII, p. 1086).

12. *Bowness-on-Solway* (Carlisle, Tullie House Cat. no. 145)
Fragment of a tombstone of a woman, uninscribed, found
shortly before 1880 in the cemetery of St Michael's church, Bowness. The churchyard lies immediately south of the south-east
corner of the fort. The stone contains the lower part of a grave-
relief representing a standing female figure, draped. Of the figure the
head alone is missing. In her left hand is a bird. A bunch of grapes
is held in her right hand up to which a dog is jumping.
The stone is 19½ in. high and 25 in. broad.

CW (1), IV, 324 f.

13. *Brough-under-Stainmore* (Cambridge, Fitzwilliam Museum)
Tombstone. This stone is a rectangular slab of hard sandstone,
23 in. high and 12½ in. broad. The margins at the sides of the inscribed panel are decorated with a rough, flat representation of
palm branches. Above is a geometric pattern in straight lines. The
lettering is in Greek uncial script. The end of line 2 overlaps the
border.

ΕΚΚΑΙΔΕΚΕΤΗ ΤΙC | ΙΔѠΝ ΤΥΜΒѠ CΚΕΦΘΕΝΤ | ΥΠΟ ΜΟΙΡΗC * ΕΡΜΗ |
ΚΟΜΜΑΓΗΝΟΝ ΕΠΟC | ΦΡΑCΑΤѠ ΤΟΔ ΟΔΕΙΤΗC | ΧΑΙΡΕ CΥ ΠΑΙ ΠΑΡ
ΕΜΟΥ | ΚΗΝΠΕΡ ΘΝΗΤΟΝ ΒΙΟ | ΕΡΠΗC * ѠΚΥΤΑΤ ΕΠ | ΤΗC ΓΑΡ
ΜΕΡΟΠѠΝ ΕΠΙ | ΚΙΜΜΕΡΙѠΝ ΓΗ * ΚΟΥ ΨΕΥ | CΕΙ Α [...] ΓΑΡ Ο ΠΑΙC
ΕΡΜΗC |

Ἑκκαιδεχέτη τις ἰ δὼν τύμβῳ σκεφθέντ' ὑπὸ μοίρης Ἑρμῆ Κομμα-
γηνόν, ἔπος φρασάτω τόδ' ὁδείτης· χαῖρέ συ, παῖ, παρ' ἐμοῦ, κῆνπερ
θνητὸν βίο(ν) ἔρπῃς, ὠκύτατ' ἔπτης γὰρ μερόπων ἐπὶ Κιμμερίων γῆ.
κοὒ ψεύσει ἀ[...] γὰρ ὁ παῖς Ἑρμῆς [.....

The letters are faint and very difficult to read. Of the various suggestions which have been made for restoring the last two lines perhaps
Sandys' suggestion (*Cambridge University Reporter*, 1885, no. 575, 498 f.)
is the most convincing. In the last surviving line he supplied ἀκμῆ, in the
lost final line ἀπόλωλεν. Kaibel (cited in EE, VII, 952) thought that A (α)
could be read at the beginning of the final line, Sandys κμη in the line
before.

This metrical epitaph records the death of a boy from Commagene, perhaps the son of a trader, possibly put up by his father. The reference to the 'land of the Cimmerians' in line 10 is perhaps an allusion to *Odyssey*, XI, 14 ff. The fact that Homer there describes that land as 'shrouded in mist and cloud' suggests that the writer of the epitaph was hinting at the contrast between Britain and Commagene. Perhaps he had read Tacitus (*Agricola*, 12): 'caelum crebris imbribus ac nebulis foedum'. On the other hand, the association of the land of the Cimmerians with the Underworld, being the last place visited by Odysseus before reaching the abode of the dead, suggests that the phrase may merely be a poetic fancy appropriate to an epitaph.

A useful indication of date is supplied by Sandys' observation that the phrase in line 6 is almost exactly paralleled in an inscription of the second century A.D. from Pergamon but does not seem to occur earlier.

The inscription was at first thought to be runic. The fullest discussion is in the *Cambridge University Reporter* (1885), no. 575, 495 ff., on the occasion of the stone being discussed by the Cambridge Antiquarian Society.

(EE, VII, 952.)

14. *Brougham* (Brougham Castle)

Tombstone of a boy; found at Brougham, exact spot uncertain. The deceased is shown standing cloaked.

ANNAMORIS * PATER | ET RESSONA * MATER | F * C

Annamoris, pater, et Ressona, mater, f(aciendum) c(uraverunt)

The name Annamoris does not seem to occur elsewhere. Ressona is also noted by Holder (1177) on CIL, III, 3377, where it is associated with other Celtic names. The parents are almost certainly both native.

(EE, III, 89; LS, 813.)

15. *Brougham* (Brougham Castle)

Tombstone of a woman, found in 1874 near Brougham fort in the field north of the Countess' Pillar.

PLVM[| LVNARIṢ | TITVL * POS | CONIVGI | CARISI | M

Plum[ae] Lunaris titul(um) pos(uit) coniugi caris(s)im(ae)

The first name seems not to be paralleled elsewhere, but Lunaris occurs in the province both as a VIvir of a colony in A.D. 237 and as a votary of

Belatucadrus at Carrawburgh. Hübner thought that the lettering of the inscription indicated a date in the third century.

CW (1), II, 147 ff. (EE, III, 87; LS, 942).

16. *Carlisle* (Carlisle, Tullie House Cat. no. 35)

Slab, probably the base of a relief of the deities, found in English Street in 1861. Height 11½ in., breadth 29 in.

MATRIB * PARC * PRO SALVT | SANCTIAE * GEMINAE

Matrib(us) Parc(is) pro salut(e) Sanctiae Geminae

It appears that the dedicator is conflating the Matres with the Fates of classical mythology.

AA(2), VI, 52. A woodcut is reproduced in the Tullie House Catalogue (CIL, VII, 927; LS, 490).

17. *Carlisle* (Carlisle, Tullie House Cat. no. 83)

Fragment of a tombstone of a woman, found in 1864 in the railway goods yard. There had been a sculptural representation of the deceased, standing, but only the lower part survives. Height 24 in., breadth 29½ in.

D M | ANI * LVCILIE VIX * AN LV

D(is) M(anibus) Ani(ciae?) Lucilie vix(it) an(nos) lv.

Haverfield suggests that the second part of the name may be meant to be Lucilla, though he is sure that an I is to be read on the stone. The I is, in fact, perfectly clear. The association of a cremation with this stone suggests a date in the first two centuries A.D.

Gent. Mag. (3), XIV (1864), 341 (CIL, VII, 930; LS, 496).

18. *Carlisle* (Carlisle, Tullie House Cat. no. 84)

Tombstone of a woman, damaged, found in 1828 in the west city wall near Blackfriars during operations to deepen a vault purchased by a Mr J. Taylor from the corporation.

] M | AVR * SENECITA | V * AN [. .] XX * IVḶ | FORTV[|

[D(is)] M(anibus). Aur(elia) Senecita v(ixit) an(nos) [. .]xx Iul(ius) Fortu[natus (?) (*or* Iul(ia) Fortunata) . . .]

Aurelia Senecita clearly lived more than twenty years. The figure must be xxx or lxx or perhaps lxxx. The first is perhaps the most likely. While it is probable that the person named as (apparently) erector of the monument is her husband, a female relative is not impossible.

Hodgson, II, iii, 221 (CIL, VII, 932; LS, 495; EE, IX, p. 606).

19. *Carlisle* (Newcastle Museum, Black Gate Cat. no. 156)

Tombstone of a woman, found in 1829 'in cutting down Gallow-hill, a mile south of this city'. She is represented as standing, with a flower in her left hand. Pine cones surmount the capitals supporting the arched top of the niche (cf. 68). Height 61½ in., breadth 32½ in.

D * M * AVR * AVRELIA * VIXSIT | ANNOS * XXXXI * VLPIVS
APOLINARIS * CONIVGI * CARISSIME * | POSVIT

D(is) M(anibus). Aur(elia) Aurelia(na ?) vixsit annos xxxxi. Ulpius Apolinaris coniugi carissime posuit.

Hübner's suggestion on expanding the name is wholly reasonable. *PSAL*, XIV, 261; *AA* (1), II, 419. Collingwood dated the lady's hairstyle to the mid-second century. The lettering is curious in that all the O's are diamond-shaped (CIL, VII, 931; LS, 497).

20. *Carlisle* (Carlisle, Tullie House Cat. no. 85)

Tombstone of a Greek, set up by his wife, found in 1892 on Gallows Hill, Carlisle, near the London road. It was re-used as a coffin-lid in a cemetery of wooden coffins. These lay in Roman debris but are not necessarily of Roman date. Haverfield suggested that they were Roman, of the fifth century, since the inscription on style is undoubtedly late. The stone is 21½ in. high and 33 in. broad.

D M | FLAS ANTIGONS PAPIAS | CIVIS GRECVS VIXIT ANNOS | PLVS
MINVS LX QVEM AD | MODVM ACCOMODATAM | FATIS ANIMAM
REVOCAVIT | SEPTIMIA DOM[|

D(is) M(anibus). Fla(viu)s Antigon(u)s Papias, civis Grecus, vixit annos plus minus lx, quem ad modum accomodatam fatis animam revocavit. Septimia Dom[ina (?) (*or* Domna) . . .]

Haverfield suggests that in the curious phrase beginning *quem* . . . *'revocare'* means 'give up'. The same usage appears in the *Gestae purgationis Felicis* of A.D. 314 cited by Haverfield in EE, IX. The phrase will then mean 'at which limit he gave up his soul resigned to its destiny'.

The phrase 'plus minus' strongly suggests that we are here dealing with a Christian inscription. Even if this is not so, it is probable that it should be dated to the fourth century.

PSAN (I), V, 231; *PSAL*, XIV, 262; *CW* (I), XII, 370; XIII, 165 ff. (EE, IX, 1222).

21. *Carlisle* (Carlisle, Tullie House Cat. no. 88)

Tombstone of a girl, found at the Bowling Green, Lowther Street, in 1885. The stone is broken at the top. It is a crude example of the type in which the deceased stands in a niche with a hemispherical head. Height 54 in., breadth 28 in. The stone is at present in the garden at Tullie House.

The inscription is on an ansate panel.

D * I * S | VACIA INF | ANS AN IIII

D(is) I(nferis) s(acrum). Vacia infans an(norum) iiii

I am inclined to believe that DIS stands for *Dis Inferis sacrum*. Haverfield suggests that *Manibus* may have been omitted accidentally. However, DIS is in large letters spaced out to fill the whole line. With so small a panel (13 by 8½ in.), the sculptor would have to be very stupid indeed not to realize that *Manibus* would not fit at the same scale. In fact, if *Manibus* were then added, it and the rest of the inscription would have to be in lettering very much smaller indeed.

Haverfield reproduces a woodcut in the Tullie House Catalogue.

CW (I), VIII, 317 (EE, VII, 1083).

22. *Carlisle* (Carlisle, Tullie House Cat. no. 103). See pl. II

Uninscribed tombstone of a woman, found at Murrell Hill, in the western part of Carlisle. The deceased sits in a chair with a very high back (see J. Liversidge, *Furniture in Roman Britain*, 1955, 18, etc.). In her right hand she holds an open circular fan; her left arm is round the shoulders of a small boy. The figures are seated in a niche. The sides of this are formed by pilasters which support the shell-shaped canopy. In the centre, above the canopy, is a winged sphinx holding a human head. At each side of the sphinx is a lion devouring a human head.

The feet of the figures are missing and it is clear that the lower section of the monument is lost. This must have held a panel for the inscription. The present height of the monument is 50½ in., the breadth 34½ in.

The dating of this stone is uncertain. The motif of a sphinx flanked by two lions, presumably as a symbol of the mysterious and destructive powers of death, is strongly reminiscent of first-century military tombstones, especially that of Longinus at Colchester. Although Longinus' stone has no human heads before the sphinx and lion, the existence of the idea at Colchester is attested by the Colchester Sphinx, a free-standing sculpture of a winged sphinx grasping a human head.

This evidence would suggest a first-century date for the Carlisle monument. But across the river, at Stanwix (110), the motif appears on a stone of Hadrianic or later date. Moreover, the most striking feature of the design is the fan. As far as I know the only parallel to this object in this country is the ivory fan from the inhumation cemetery near the railway station at York (*AJ*, CIII, 78 ff.; [*Roman York*, pl. 71]).

The head is badly damaged. It is therefore impossible to be sure of all the details of hair-style. However, there seems to be no sign of the elaborate coiffure which might be expected on a Flavian lady of some wealth.

We are therefore left with the difficulty that we do not know how late the lion–sphinx–human head motif might appear (and it had had a long history in Gaul) or how early the circular fan came into use.

CW (1), IV, 325 ff.

23. *Carrawburgh* (Durham, Dean and Chapter Library)

Altar from Carrawburgh, now in the undercroft beneath the Refectory at Durham (where all the stones in the possession of the Dean and Chapter have been stored). Dedicated by a woman. The stone is 37 in. in height and 16½ in. in breadth.

D * M * D̤ | T͡RANQV͡IL[. | A * SEVERA | P͡RO * SE * E͡T * SVI | S *
V * S * L * M * *

D(eae) M(agnae) d(edicatum (?)) Tranquil(l)[i]a Severa pro se et
suis v(otum) s(olvit) l(ibens) m(erito).

The third letter of the first line is uncertain. Hübner thought there
was a suggestion of a ligatured ID on the stone and therefore read Deae
Magnae Ideae (?). This is feasible but it is now quite impossible to detect
an I.

Gordon, 94, pl. 41, fig. 2; Horsley, 218 f. (CIL, VII, 618; LS, 154).

24. *Carrawburgh* (Chesters Museum Cat. no. 120)

Tombstone of a woman, found in 1874 by John Clayton re-used
as a flooring slab in the bath-house. Three military tombstones
were also found 'lying promiscuously amongst a mass of rubbish
in another of the apartments'. Two of these record soldiers of the
cohors I Batavorum, the third- and fourth-century garrison. The
stone is decorated with a small relief depicting a table, presumably
a reference in very simple form to the funerary banquet. The stone
is damaged at the edges and the bottom is set in modern concrete
(possibly obscuring the text at the bottom right-hand corner). The
size as now visible is: breadth 32½ in., height 40 in.

D M | AEL COM͡NDO | AN͡NO̤RVM XXXI̤I̤ * | NOBI̤LI̤ANVS DEC * |
CONI͡VGI CAR[.]M |

D(is) M(anibus). Ael(iae) Com(i (?))ndo annorum xxxii Nobilianus dec(urio), coniugi car[i](ssi)m[ae . . . . .]

Hübner gives a P ligatured to the M at the end of line 5. If this existed
it was obliterated when the stone was repaired with concrete. The *-us*
ending to Aelia's name suggests a native origin. Similar names occur on
tombstones at Caerleon (*Caerleon Catalogue*, nos. 24, 58). Nobilianus'
rank indicates the commander of a cavalry troop. His unit is uncertain, but may well have been *cohors I Batavorum*, a *cohors equitata*. The
date of re-use of these stones in a reconstruction of the bath-house is
unknown.

(EE, III, 108; LS, 926.)

25. *Carrawburgh* (Chesters Museum)

Two fragments of a tombstone found in 1876 by John Clayton.

| PAVDI REGVLO VIXIT |]S XXXIIII ET ATEA͡NCTI |] IVGI PIE
VIX [.]NNIS XXXI |]MIE FIL [.]ORVM VIXIT D |]
ILIO EORVM |]VDIVAITIFIL |]ṂỊ̣A HIC E |

[. . . .]paudi Regulo, vixit [anni]s xxxiiii, et Ateancti, [con]iugi
pie, vix(it) [a]nnis xxxi, (et) [. . .]mie, fil(iae) [e]orum, vixit d[iebus
.. et . . . . f]ilio eorum, [ ] . . . . [ ] mia hic [

This is clearly a family tombstone, recording a man and wife, a daughter who lived only a few days, and a son. The reading of the last two lines is extremely uncertain but seems to record the erection of the monument by another child of the parents, possibly (if the last line begins with a feminine name) a daughter.

The beginning of the woman's name *Ate-* is found in a number of Celtic names (Holder, 253), suggesting that this name is also Celtic.

(EE, III, 201; EE, IX, p. 587.)

26. *Carriden* (Edinburgh, National Museum of Antiquities)

Altar to Iuppiter Optimus Maximus, discovered during farming operations at Carriden in 1956. This was found 150 yards east of the fort, at NT 027837. There has been some wear on the face down the right-hand edge but the stone is otherwise intact and in a splendid state of preservation. Height 36 in., breadth 15 in.

I O M | VICANI CONSI[. | TE͡NTE͡S CASTEL[. . | VELVNIATE͡ CV[. . . |
AGENTE͡ AEL * MAN | SVETO * V * S * L * L * M

I(ovi) O(ptimo) M(aximo) vicani consi[s]tentes Castel[lo]
Veluniate(nsi (?)), cu[ram] agente Ael(io) Mansueto, v(otum)
s(olverunt) l(aeti) l(ibentes) m(erito).

This inscription is of the first importance for the study both of the civil history of the frontier region and of the geography of Roman Scotland. It will be considered in detail elsewhere. For the present occasion a few notes may be made.

The closest parallel to the phrase *vicani consistentes castel* . . . is on ILS,

7085 (*vicanis veteribus castel. Mattiac.*). There the last two words have been expanded *castelli Mattiacorum*. However, on the analogy of ILS, 7180 (*consistentes vico Ulmeto*) and others, I am inclined to think that both should be ablative in case. ILS, 7180, is dated to A.D. 140, and therefore probably within half a century of the Carriden inscription whose outside dates are probably A.D. 140 and 212.

The name of the fort agrees with the Ravenna Cosmography, which gives *Velunia* as the first place in its Antonine Wall list. This means that the list runs from east to west, and that *Credigone*, recently placed tentatively at Carriden, must lie somewhere at the other end of the Wall. *Veluniate* is perhaps an abbreviated adjective and not the name itself. However the opposite view is taken by Mr R. P. Wright. If it is not an adjective, I think it must be an ablative of place, from a nominative *Velunias*. The *s* could easily drop out from the Ravenna text.

JRS, XLVII, 229 f., no. 18; *PSAS*, XC, 1 ff.

27. *Carvoran* (Newcastle Museum, Black Gate Cat. no. 158)
Tombstone of the wife of a soldier, found 'in or near Carvoran'.

D * M | AVR * T F AIAE | D * SALONAS | AVR * MARCVS | 7 *
OBSEQ * CON | IVGI * SANCTIS | SIMAE * QVAE * VI | XIT *
ANNIS XXXIII | SINE VLLA MACVLA

D(is) M(anibus) Aur(eliae) T(iti) f(iliae) Aiae, d(omo) Salonas, Aur(elius) Marcus, c(enturiae) Obseq(uentis), coniugi sanctissimae quae vixit annis xxxiii sine ulla macula (posuit).

The style and abbreviations of names suggest a third-century date. The final phrase *may*, as Professor Birley has suggested, indicate a Christian or a Jew.

(CIL, VII, 793; LS, 321.)

28. *Carvoran* (?) (Blenkinsopp Castle)
Tombstone of a woman, erected by her uncle. Found at Blenkinsopp Castle in 1880 in the course of repairs, and probably brought there from Carvoran. Seen in 1940 built into the east face of the garden wall abutting the south-west angle of Blenkinsopp Castle.

D M | LIFANA * B[| CI * FILIA * V[| IT * ANN[| L *
SENO | LVS AV[| CVLVS [| CIT [

D(is) M(anibus). Lifana, B[.]ci filia, v[ix]it ann[os] l (?). Senolus, av[un]culus, [fe]cit . . . .

Since neither the deceased nor her father seems to have more than one name I strongly suspect that L in line 5 is not L(ucius) but is the woman's age.

AJ, XXXVIII, 278 (EE, VII, 1061).

29. *Carvoran* (?) (Carlisle, Tullie House Museum Cat. no. 37)
Small altar to the nymphs dedicated by a mother and daughter; from Blenkinsopp Castle and probably taken there from Carvoran. Its presence at Blenkinsopp was first reported by Horsley.

DEABVS N[. . | PHIS VETT[. . | MANSVETA E[. | CLAVDIA
TVRI[. | NILLA * FIL * V * S * L [.

Deabus N[ym]phis Vett[ia] Mansueta e[t] Claudia Turi[a]nilla fil(ia) (eius) v(otum) s(olverunt) l(ibentes) [m(erito)]

Holder (1998) accepts Turianilla as a Celtic name, but quotes no parallels.
Thoresby (from Cay) *Philos. Trans.* XIX, 663 (= *Philos. Trans. Abridg'd*, III, 425); Horsley, 213 (CIL, VII, 757; LS, 307).

30. *Carvoran* (?)
Tombstone of a woman, attributed to Carvoran by B. Peile in a letter of November 1757.

] XXI | AVRIL[| MATIRL[| RISSIME P[
[. . . annorum] xxi, Aur⟨e⟩l[ia . . . . . .], mat⟨e⟩r, ⟨f⟩(ilie)(?) [ca]rissime (?) p[osuit]

Since the I in line 2 is clearly a misreading for an E, it is probable that the same has happened in the third line. If this is true, then this is a memorial by a mother to her daughter. The L in line 3 may well represent a ligatured group of FIL. In the last line the adjective might alternatively be *rarissime*.

Lukis, *Surtees Society*, LXXX, 137 (EE, VII, 1066).

31. *Carvoran* (?)

Tombstone of a woman and (apparently) a second person, found used as a paving-stone in 1599 by Bainbrigg 'at the Wall-towne'. It is probably to be associated with Carvoran.

SOPH[| ONIVGI SA[| AE ET [

Soph[iae (?), c]oniugi sa[nct]ae, et [. . . . .

Bainbrigg's reading is perhaps inaccurate, but the name Sophe, Sophias or Sophia is found (in various forms) in the Empire, for example in the apparently philhellene but eminently Roman family of L. Aemilius Pertinax Acceianus, knight, decurion of the colony of Misenum (ILS, 6335). It occurs in the form suggested above in Bithynia (ILS, 1539).

The last surviving word probably indicates a second person remembered (e.g. a child) rather than a further epithet.

Bainbrigg, BM Cotton Iulius F. VI, 340 (CIL, VII, 909).

32. *Chesterholm* (Chesters Museum)

Altar to Vulcan, found close to the fort in July 1914.

PRO * DOM͡V | DIVINA ET * NV | MINIBVS * AVG | VSTOR͡VM *
VOL | CANO * SACR͡VM | VICANI VINDOL | ANDESSES CV[. | AGENTE
[| V S L M

Pro domu divina et numinibus Augustorum, Volcano sacrum; vicani Vindolandesses, cu[r(am)] agente [. . . . .], v(otum) s(olverunt) l(ibentes) m(erito)

This inscription attests an association of *vicani* at Chesterholm. It confirms the Ravenna Cosmographer's spelling of the name against the *Vindolana* of the *Notitia*, and, by proving the name, gives a fixed geographical point in both these documents. It is feasible that there was a change in spelling in the time between the original sources from which the map-books drew. If the presence of the Antonine Wall names in the *Ravenna Cosmography* indicates a second-century source for some of the northern British material and if the *Notitia* is relying on a third-century (or later) document then this is quite possible. This would also be consistent with Haverfield's dating of this inscription to the late-second or early-third centuries on the strength of the dedication '*pro domu divina et numinibus Augustorum*'.

Brit. Acad. Supplemental Papers, III (1915), 31 f.

33. *Chesterholm* (Housesteads Museum)

Tombstone of a woman, found by A. Hedley in the fort in
1830. Above the inscription is a rounded niche containing the bust
of a woman.

D M | FLA EMERI | T * FIINIIA | N[

> D(is) M(anibus). Fla(via) Emerit(a), F⟨lavius In⟩(?)[. . . .]

The suggestion is that of R. G. Collingwood. The rest seems hopeless.
Richardson, *Local Historian's Table Book, Historical Division,* IV, 65;
JRS, XVII, 213.

34. *Chesterholm* (Chesters Museum Cat. no. 246)

From 'Littlechesters' (=Chesterholm) in 1818, the tombstone
of a *singularis consularis*. Breadth 26½ in., height 19½ in. It was apparently re-used in the east wall of the fort.

D M | CORN VICTOR * S C | MIL * ANN XXVI CIVES | PANN * FIL *
SATVRNI | NI PP VIX AN LV D XI | CONIVX PROCVRAVI

> D(is) M(anibus). Corn(elius) Victor, s(ingularis) c(onsularis),
> mil(itavit) ann(os) xxvi, cives Pann(onius), fil(ius) Saturnini p(rimi)
> p(ilaris), vix(it) an(nos) lv d(ies) xi. coniux procuravi

For the present purpose the last line is the most important. The stone
is complete and it is clear that the wife did not include her own name.
The phrasing of the last sentence is odd. I should not be surprised if a
final T has disappeared.

AA (1), I, 210 (CIL, VII, 723; LS, 258).

35. *Chesterholm* (Chesters Museum)

Fragment of the tombstone of a woman.

] AVREL [| LA * VIXIT [| NOS XX FILI[|
AVR[|

> [. . . .] Aurel[ia . . . . .]la vixit [an]nos xx fili[e] Aur[elius (?) . . . .]

Except that this is the tombstone of a woman of twenty, probably
erected by her father, little can be deduced.

EE, VII, 1048.

36. *Chesters* (Durham, Dean and Chapter Library)

Tombstone of the daughter of a tribune commanding the first cohort of Vangiones, the second-century garrison of Benwell and third-century of Risingham. The stone is 32½ in. high and 15¼ in. wide. From Walwick Grange, according to Warburton—later taken to Hexham.

D M S | FABIE HONOR | ATE FABIVS HON | ORATVS | TRIBVN |
COH * I * VANGION | ET AVRELIA ECLEC |] IANE FECER | VNT FILIE
D | VLCISSIME

D(is) M(anibus) s(acrum) Fabie Honorate. Fabius Honoratus, tribun(us) coh(ortis) I Vangion(um), et Aurelia Eclec[t]iane fecerunt filie dulcissime

It is rather strange to find the daughter of this tribune buried at Chesters. If she were married to someone stationed at or living in the *vicus* of Chesters, one would expect a mention of the husband. Possibly the father and his family were away from his unit when she died. It is possible that the stone came from Risingham, not Chesters, as Professor Birley suggests.

Horsley, 217 (CIL, VII, 588; LS, 117).

37. *Chesters* (Newcastle Museum)

Tombstone, apparently of three people. It appears from the fact that there is a bust of a single woman that the stone was originally intended for one burial. The stone was at Chesters in Horsley's time, having been found in the 'Oxclose', a field later included in the park and lying between Chesters and Walwick Grange.

D M | VRSE SORORI | IVLIE CONIVGI | CANIONI FILIO | .]VRIO
GERM |

D(is) M(anibus). Urse sorori, Iulie coniugi, Canioni filio, [L]urio (?) Germ[anus f(aciendum) c(uravit) (?)]

Hübner suggests *Lurio* on the basis of a German *Lurio* recorded on CIL, VII, 322.

Horsley, 215 f. (CIL, VII, 616; LS, 119).

Q

38. *Chesters*

Dedication by a veteran, reported by Hutchinson as at Chesters 'in a wall of the barn' and since lost. The object of the dedication is unknown. The text is uncertain, but has tentatively and reasonably been restored by Birley from the two sources, Pococke and Hutchinson, as follows:

| M AVR[| IANVARIVS | EMERITVS PRO SE | ET
SVIS OMNIBVS | V S L L M

[deo . . . . . .] M(arcus) Aur[elius] Ianuarius, emeritus, pro se et suis omnibus v(otum) s(olvit) l(aetus) l(ibens) m(erito).

Other veterans at Chesters are attested by the diplomas.

Pococke, *Surtees Society*, CXXIV, 234; Hutchinson, *Northumberland*, I, 83; *AA* (4), XVI, 248.

39. *Corbridge* (British Museum)

Altar to the Tyrian Hercules, dedicated by a 'high priestess'. The altar is 16 in. deep, 40 in. high and 21½ in. broad. On the left side is a bull's head and a knife, on the right a wreath. On the top is a deep focus. A metal dowel has been let into the top at the right-hand rear corner. It was first noted in Corbridge churchyard by Hunter who reported that it had been there a long time in his day.

ΗΡΑΚΛΕΙ | ✷ ΤΥΡΙѠ ✷ | ΔΙΟΔѠΡΑ | ΑΡΧΙΕΡΕΙΑ

Ἡρακλεῖ Τυρίῳ Διοδώρα ἀρχιερεία.

Philos. Trans. XXIII, 1129 (=*Philos. Trans. Abridg'd*, V, II, 46). Mattaire, *Marm. Oxon.*, 579 (CIL, VII, p. 97 b; CIG, 6806).

While there are other Greek inscriptions in the north, including another at Corbridge (CIL, VII, p. 97a), this is the only mention of a priestess.

40. *Corbridge* (?)

Funerary urn of a woman. Lost. [Mr R. P. Wright points out that Haverfield (*NCH*, x, 504, no. 36a) thought that this urn was

Italian, not Romano-British, and concurs in this opinion. Mackenzie is the only report of its discovery. If it is in fact a modern import it should be deleted from the number of civilian inscriptions of the frontier region.]

D * M * AVRELIAE ACHAICES

D(is) M(anibus) Aureliae Achaices

This woman seems to be a Greek and may be compared with Diodora on (40). It is interesting to note that the Greek form of the genitive is used in her second name.

Mackenzie, *History of Northumberland* (2), I, 453 (EE, III, 96).

41. *Corbridge* (Newcastle Museum, Black Gate Cat. no. 170)
Tombstone of a six-year-old girl, set up by her father.

IVLIA MATE[. | NA * AN * VI * IVL | MARCELLINVS | FILIAE |
CARISSIMAE

Iulia Mate[r]na, an(norum) vi. Iul(ius) Marcellinus filiae carissimae (posuit)

AA (2), VI, 18 f. (CIL, VII, 478; LS, 640).

42. *Corbridge* (Newcastle Museum, Black Gate Cat. no. 168)
Tombstone found in 1895 at Trinity Terrace, Corbridge (outside and east of the Roman town). Height 43 in., breadth 24 in. It is at present set in concrete.

D * M | IVL * PR[. .]VE | CO[. . .]GI C | P C

D(is) M(anibus). Iul(iae) Pr[. .]ve co[niu]gi c(oniux) p(onendum) c(uravit) (?)

The lettering is faint but the name certainly is *not* Iulius Priscus but one (presumably female) starting in *Pr* and ending in *ve*. The expansion of the last three letters is suggested to me by Professor Birley and has the advantage of providing a much-needed subject for the sentence. *Pr . . ve* is then a contracted form of a genitive or dative *Pr . . vae*. If *Iul Pr . . ve* were nominative (i.e. the name of the dedicator), the name of the deceased would be strangely missing.

PSAN (2), VII, 50; *AA* (2), XVIII, xiv (EE, IX, 1153).

43. *Corbridge* (Corbridge Museum)

Tombstone found in the 1911 excavation re-used as a paving-stone on site XXVII (in the western part of the town, south of the Stanegate). The top, and the bottom right-hand corner, are damaged. The style is very simple.

] M |]RATHES ∗ PAL | MORENVS ∗ VEXILA | VIXIT ∗ ANOS ∗ LXVIII

[D(is)] M(anibus). [Ba]rathes Palmorenus, vexila(rius), vixit an(n)os lxviii

There is every reason to believe that this is the same man as the Barates Palmyrenus who erected a magnificent tombstone to his wife at South Shields (107). It is obvious that Barates' heir could not, or did not wish to, spend anything approaching the amount Barates himself spent on a monument. I am wholly convinced by Professor Birley's argument (*Roman Britain and the Roman Army*, 81 f.) that Barates was a *negotiator vexillarius* and not a retired standard-bearer.

AA (3), VIII, 188 ff. (EE, IX, 1153a).

44. *Corbridge* (Corbridge Museum)

Found in 1937 by the Ministry of Works, re-used in a late repair of the Stanegate between sites XI and XXXIX (west end of East Compound); it is the tombstone of a small girl. At the top is an elongated or house-shaped gable, a crude attempt at a niche, containing a bust.

D ∗ M | AHTEHE | FIL ∗ NOBILIS | VIXIT ANIS | V

D(is) M(anibus) Ahtehe fil(iae) Nobilis, vixit an(n)is v.

In a long note in the primary publication Professor Gutenbrunner argues that the affinities of the girl's name are with the Rhineland and that it is a diminutive form. The fact that this diminutive is formed on Germanic and not Latin principles suggested to Professor Gutenbrunner that the family spoke German at home.

AA (4), XV, 290 ff.; *JRS*, XXVIII, 202.

45. *Corbridge* (Corbridge Museum)

Tombstone, found as 44. This tombstone apparently records two deaths of children. The niche shows a very crude relief of a child (?) holding a ball between its hands. However, Mr R. P. Wright has shown that the present inscription, recording the death of a boy, is secondary. The original inscription was in an ansate panel in the space now covered by lines 2–4.

D M | SVDRENVS | ERTOLE NOMINE | VELLIBIA | FELICISSI | ME VIXIT
ANIS IIII | DIEBVS LX

D(is) M(anibus). Sudrenus, Ertole nomine, Vellibia (posuit(?)) felicissime vixit an(n)is iiii diebus lx

Mr Wright points out that line 3 means that Sudrenus' nickname was Ertole (or, less probably, Eriole). Vellibia must be a female relative who erected the memorial.

AA (4), xv, 289 f.; *JRS*, xxviii, 203; xxix, 226 f.

46. *Greatchesters* (Durham, Dean and Chapter Library)

Fragment from Greatchesters, dedicated by a woman and at least one other person. Above the inscription is an urn (?) and an animal of uncertain species. The stone is now 18 in. high and 14 in. wide.

] O M D * |] SABINI FIL * |]INA * REGVLVS |
      ]DVIII [

[I(ovi)] O(ptimo) M(aximo) D(olicheno) [. . . . .] Sabini fil(ia) [. . . .]ina, Regulus [. . . . .] dviii(?)[

Hübner's reading (I) O M D is given as a possibility by Horsley. Otherwise the general reading was D M D.

Horsley, 228 (CIL, vii, 725; LS, 24 f.).

47. *Greatchesters* (Newcastle Museum, Black Gate Cat. no. 57)

Altar to the Veteres (Vitiris), dedicated by a woman.

DIB[| VETERI | BVS POS | VIT ROMA | NA

Dib[us] Veteribus posuit Romana

A number of dedications to this deity or deities (which range from *deo*

Huitri through *dis Veteribus* to our present form) are known from the North, especially from Housesteads and Carvoran (indicating a cult local to this region).

AA (2), I, 249 (CIL, VII, 728; LS, 277).

48. *Greatchesters*

Tombstone, now lost, formerly used as a gate-post at the Wall Mill where it was originally found. The ruins of the Wall Mill, which stand on a tributary of the Haltwhistle Burn, are about 400 yards from the group of Roman tombs (?) lying south of the Vallum. It is assumed that this mill is Horsley's 'Walton Mill', though he places that on the Haltwhistle Burn. Hutchinson puts the stone at Wall Mill.

Above the inscription was the bust of a man.

D M | AEL * MERCV | RIALI * CORNICVL | VACIA * SOROR | FECIT

D(is) M(anibus). Ael(io) Mercuriali, cornicul(ario), Vacia, soror, fecit.

The name Vacia occurs also on (21), above, from Carlisle, and may be local. The presence of the sister of a soldier in a *vicus* suggests local recruiting of troops.

Horsley, 229 f.; Hutchinson, I, 57 (CIL, VII, 739).

49. *Greatchesters* (Newcastle Museum, Black Gate Cat. no. 171)

Found in 1897 together with EE, IX, 1192, 1194 and 1199 reused in an interior building of the fort.

Gabled tombstone. The monument was erected by the deceased's daughter. Height 65 in., breadth 24½ in.

DIS MANIB | L * NOVEL * LLAN | VCCVS * C * R * AN LX | NOVEL *
IVSTINA | FIL |] C

Dis Manib(us). L(ucius) Novell(ius) Lanuccus, c(ivis) R(omanus), ann(orum) lx. Novel(lia) Iustina, fil(ia), [f(aciendum)] c(uravit)

The punctuation in line 2 is certain. While it is just possible that the Welsh *ll* had already appeared, I am inclined in the absence of other evidence to take the *LL* here as a simple case of dittography or of misplacing the stop.

The opening formula suggests a comparatively early date, which would accord with Haverfield's tentative ascription of the monument to the second century on the style of lettering.

AA (2), XIX, 270 (EE, IX, 1198).

50. *Greatchesters*

Tombstone found 'right in front of the station, in a stone wall of a field'. The fragments were joined by Bruce. It appears to be the memorial of a woman. It has since been lost.

D M S | AV[.]E[. . | E AF[. . | V[.]X ✳ A XXXX Y P̣ ✳ CASITTO |
7 [. . .]C | P I̧ [

Hübner restores:

D(is) M(anibus) s(acrum), Au[r]e[li]e Af[re], v[i]x(it) a(nnos) XXXX; [A]u⟨r⟩(elius) (*or* U[l]p(ius)) Casitto c(enturio) [leg(ionis) vi vi]c(tricis) p(iae) f(idelis) [

Considering the poor condition of the stone this was a clever restoration. It is impossible to suggest any amendments. It is at least clear that the stone records the death of a woman of forty. D M S might suggest an African.

(CIL, VII, 740; LS, 283.)

51. *Greatchesters* (Newcastle Museum, Black Gate Cat. no. 172)

Tombstone of a girl, found with (49) (Horsley); 'Near a mile south of the station, at Walltown Mill, in the immediate vicinity of the graveyard of the station' (Hutchinson).

Above the inscription is a representation of the deceased, a very crude frontal figure, whose face is reminiscent of native sculpture. Height 62½ in., breadth 26¾ in.

DIS M | PERVICAE FILIAE

Dis M(anibus) Pervicae filiae

Bruce thought he could read D ✳ M SALVTE | FILIAE | S T T I, but Collingwood had no doubt that the above is the correct reading. The lettering is faint, but the reading does not seem in doubt.

Horsley, 230; Hutchinson, I, 47 (CIL, VII, 743).

52. *Greatchesters* (Newcastle Museum, Black Gate Cat. no. 157)

Tombstone of a woman, found in the excavations of 1897, in the same building as (49) above. According to Haverfield the lettering is perhaps of second-century date. The building may be early third-century.

D M | AVRELIAE | CAVLI [| AVR[. .]IA | S[. . .]ILIA | SORORI
[| RISSIME | VIXIT * AN * | XV M IIII

D(is) M(anibus) Aureliae Cauli[fil(ia) (?)]. Aur[el]is S[. . .]illa (?) sorori [ca]rissime; vixit an(nos) xv m(enses) iiii.

This is the memorial of a girl of fifteen, erected by her sister. The M (for *menses*) has an additional central stroke. This is paralleled on (103) (Risingham). The names of the deceased may also be compared with those on (103). In each case the stone has been re-used in a military reconstruction.

AA (2), XIX, 268 (EE, IX, 1199).

53. *Greatchesters* (?) (Chesters Museum Cat. no. 268)

Tombstone of a man, erected by a female relative, found by John Clayton in excavating Cawfields milecastle. Together with another (from which the inscription had disappeared) it had been re-used in the interior. The stone has been roughly hacked into a circular shape, perhaps for use as a hearth. It probably came from the cemetery of Greatchesters. The lettering is crude.

D M |] * DAGVALDVS MI[|] * PAN * VIXIT * AN
[| PVSINNA [|]X TITVLV[

D(is) M(anibus). [. . . .] Dagualdus, mi[les coh(ortis) I (?)] Pan(noniorum), vixit an(nos) [. . . .] Pusinna [coniu]x (?) titulu[m posuit] (?)

The reading is that suggested to me by Professor Birley. If the stone is in fact late second- or third-century, his suggestion is convincing that there should be an abbreviated *nomen*, perhaps most probably Aur(elius). The man's name seems to be Germanic. Pusinna's name is perhaps Raetian (cf. (78)), maybe a result of the presence of the *cohors VI Raetorum* and the *Raeti Gaesati* at Greatchesters.

AA (1), IV, 54 ff. (LS, 198).

54. *Greta Bridge*

Altar to a Nymph by a man or woman and daughter, found near Greta Bridge in 1702. It is now lost.

DEAE NYMPHA[| NEINEBRICA * ET | IANVARIA * FIL | LIBENTES
EX VO | TO SOLVERVNT

Deae Nympha[e] Neinebrica (?) et Ianuaria, fil(ia) (eius), libentes ex voto solverunt.

The name in line 2 is uncertain and may not be complete. The phrasing is an odd mixture of the common *votum solverunt* and formulae containing *ex voto*, but the meaning is obvious. The single Nymph is probably a local water goddess.

Gale, *Ant. It.* 42; Horsley, 305 f. (CIL, VII, 278).

55. *Greta Bridge*

Tombstone, found at Greta Bridge. The exact find-spot is unknown. It is now lost. Hübner, following Gough, gives:

AVRELIA [ ] F ROM[| SABIN[ ] FILIE PATRI PI | ENTISSIMO
FRARISSI | MO FACVNDVM CVRSRMR | CAS [ ] MGRFMPM

The last line seems hopelessly confused. The order of the rest seems unsual but it is clearly a memorial set up by a woman to her father. It presumably is to be read as something like:

Aurelia, [. . .] f(ilia), Rom(ana) (?), Sabin(o): filie (=a ?) patri pientissimo et (?) rarissimo facundum (=faciendum) cur⟨avit⟩ . . . . .

Gough, *Camden* (2), III, pl. 17, fig. 7 (CIL, VII, 283).

56. *Greta Bridge* (?)

Tombstone of a girl reported at Mortham Hall, near Rokeby, by Bruce. It is now lost.

D M | SALVIA DONA [| VIXSIT AN VIII | M I

D(is) M(anibus). Salvia Dona[ta] vixsit an(nos) viii m(ensem) i

We cannot be sure from which of the Roman sites in the neighbourhood this stone came, but it is reasonable to list it under Greta Bridge, the nearest *vicus*. Possibly it came from the site at Mortham (the provenance of CIL, VII, 280).

(CIL, VII, 283 b.)

57. *Greta Bridge* (?)

Tombstone, bearing a bust of a woman, found in 1703 'at Greens inn'. It is probably to be associated with Greta Bridge.

D M | AVREL[| IS EMERIT[|

D(is) M(anibus) Aurel[i . . . .]is emerit[i . . . . .]

It is impossible to be sure of the correct interpretation. I suggest tentatively that *-is emerit . .* is part of the name of the father or husband (a genitive in *-is*) and his status as a veteran, presumably followed by *filia* or *uxor* and the name of the deceased.

Gough, *Camden* (2), III, 339 (CIL, VII, 282).

58. *Halton Chesters* (Newcastle Museum, Black Gate Cat. no. 161)

Tombstone of a woman, erected by her father. Found near Halton Chesters. The stone is in two fragments of which Hodgson gives the first only. The latter is 18 in. high, 16 in. broad, the whole being reported as 18 in. by 22 in. in the catalogue.

D M | AVRELIA | VICTOR[.]NA * | AVREL[   ]TŌR | P[|
FE[

D(is) M(anibus). Aurelia Victor[i]na. Aurel[ius Vic]tor p[ater] fe[cit]

It seems reasonable to restore the name of the second person as Victor, especially if the fifth line contains *pater*. Both Hübner and Collingwood accept this restoration.

Hodgson, II, iii, 284 (CIL, VII, 573; LS, 89).

59. *Halton Chesters* (Newcastle Museum, Black Gate cat. no. 167)

Found at Halton Castle in 1868 'in lowering the stable yard'. It is presumably a tombstone, from which the top has been broken.

| HARDALIO | NIS * COLLEGIVM | CONSER * | B * M * P

[Dis Manibus] Hardalionis. collegium conser(vorum) b(ene) m(erenti) p(osuit)

The particular interest of this stone is its record of a servile club, presumably a burial society, the first known in the frontier region. It indicates a considerable number of slaves in the district and of sufficient prosperity to be able to join a society which would require subscriptions. It is just possible that the headquarters of the club was not at Halton but down the hill in the town of Corbridge where there must have been slaves both in private service and in industry.

Bruce, *Newcastle Journal*, 4 Feb. 1868; *Gent. Mag.* (4), v (1868), 370 (CIL, VII, 572; LS, 91).

60. *High Rochester* (Durham, Dean and Chapter Library)

Altar to Silvanus Pantheus, found in 1729 near the north-west corner of the fort. It is dedicated by a freedman and his family for the health of the commander of the garrison and his wife. The left-hand edge has been damaged since it was first discovered, and the letters at the beginning of the lines are supplied from Horsley. It is 36¾ in. high and 13¾ in. broad.

SILVANO * | .]ANTHEO | .]RO SAL[... | . .]FINI TRIB * ET |
.]VCILLAE * EIVS | EVTYCHVS | LIB * C * S | V * S * L * M *

Silvano [Pa]ntheo [p]ro sa[lute Ru]fini trib(uni) et [L]ucillae eius Eutychus lib(ertus) c(um) s(uis) v(otum) s(olvit) l(ibens) m(erito).

Professor Richmond's reading of line 7 carries conviction against the *lib(rarius) consularis* (?) of Hübner. Another dedication by a freedman to a fort-commandant is found on (8) above. It seems probable that both the commandant and the freedman had their families at High Rochester. The occasion is perhaps the safe return of the commandant and his wife from a journey or escape from some danger.

Horsley, 243; Hutchinson, *Northumberland*, I, 202; *NCH*, xv, 150, no. 26 (CIL, VII, 1038; LS, 550).

61. *High Rochester* (Elsdon, St Cuthbert's Church)

Tombstone of the commandant of the fort, clearly the officer mentioned on (60), the name of the wife being the same. This stone was found, with another, in 1809 'in a field opposite to the north-east corner of the station and on the north side of the rivulet' (Hodgson). Professor Richmond suggests that there was a cemetery near the turn in Dere Street. The inscription has lost several lines at the top. The stone is now 39 in. high and 32 in. broad.

] COH * I * VARDVL |] COH I AVG | LVSITANOR
ITEM COH II | BREVCOR SVBCVR VIAE | FLAMINIAE ET ALIMENT |
SVBCVRA OPERVM PVBL | IVLIA LVCILLA C F MARITO | B M VIXIT
AN XLVIII | M VI D[. .]B XXV

. . . . . [trib(uno)] coh(ortis) I Vardul[lor(um), praef(ecto)] coh(ortis) I Aug(ustae) Lusitanor(um), item coh(ortis) II Breucor(um), subcur(atori) viae Flaminiae et aliment(orum), subcura(tori) operum publ(icorum), Iulia Lucilla c(larissima) f(emina) marito b(ene) m(erenti) (qui) vixit an(nis) xlviii m(ensibus) vi d[ie]b(us) xxv

This career emphasizes the width of experience the commander of an auxiliary unit could possess, for this officer had already held two posts in the civil administration of Italy. It further underlines that the military and civil administrations were considered as part of the same system of government and not as distinct and rigidly separate organizations. Iulia Lucilla is unusually distinguished, for she is a member of the senatorial class. Professor Birley points out that her title indicates a third-century date, since it is not *epigraphically* common until then. This fits with the presence of the *cohors I Vardullorum* at High Rochester in that century.

Hodgson II, i, 90; *JRS*, XVII, 219; *AA* (4), XII, 200 ff.; *NCH*, XV, 152, no. 31 (CIL, VII, 1054; LS, 560).

62. *High Rochester* (Newcastle Museum)

Tombstone of a woman: a female bust in a niche. The hair-style is dated by Professor Richmond to the early-third century. The inscription was at Campville in Hodgson's time.

D M | R[| M[   ] VIXIT ANN | XXXVIII

D(is) M(anibus). R[. . . . .] M[. . . . .] vixit ann(os) xxxviii

Hodgson's reading *Rhodus Midus* seems quite improbable, especially in view of the female bust. No suggestion can be made as to the true names.

Hodgson, II, i, 144; *NCH*, XV, 152, no. 34 (CIL, VII, 1059; LS, 563).

63. *High Rochester* (Newcastle Museum, Black Gate Cat. no. 166)
Tombstone of a freedman, discovered near High Rochester in
1876. The top is gabled and contains a rosette. The borders are
decorated with chip-carved ornament.

D * M | FELICIO * LIBERTI | VIXIT * ANNIS | XX

D(is) M(anibus) Felicio(nis) liberti; vixit annis xx

AJ, xxxvi, 155; *NCH*, xv, 152, no. 33 (EE, iv, 689).

64. *High Rochester* (?) (Hallington Demesne, 'in the garden-house')
Uninscribed tombstone of a woman. The place of discovery is
unknown, but Professor Richmond points out that the stone is
typical Redesdale sandstone. Bruce in the *Lapidarium* states that it
is from High Rochester. The deceased is shown dressed in what
Professor Richmond describes as a 'long skirted tunic'.

NCH, xv, 153, no. 38 (see under LS, 566).

65. *Housesteads* (Housesteads Museum)
Fragment of an inscription recording work done by order of the
vicani. It was found in the excavations of 1931, in trench E in the
Vallum, unstratified (in top soil). It is from the lower left-hand
corner of a stone.

IVL * S[| D * VICA[

Iul(ius) S[. . . . .] d(ecreto) vica[norum]

The importance of this stone is that it places Housesteads in the group
of four northern *vici* known to have had an organization of *vicani* for
communal action. It is the only inscription to mention action *decreto*.
The man mentioned may have been a *magister vicanorum*, as at Old Carlisle (80), or *curam agens* like Aelius Mansuetus at Carriden (26). Just
possibly he was a person for whose health the stone was dedicated, but
the position of the name, apparently low on the stone, makes this unlikely.

AA (4), ix, 232.

66. *Housesteads* (Housesteads Museum)

Relief depicting three Genii Cucullati, from a domestic shrine in the back yard of site IX in the *vicus*. Votive offerings of coins date from A.D. 220 to 229, the last coin apparently being new when deposited. It seems probable that the active life of the shrine was confined to the second decade of the third century.

JRS, XXIV, 190; *AA* (4), XI, 190 f.; *AA* (4), XII, 187; *Latomus*, XXVIII, 460.

67. *Housesteads* (Newcastle Museum, Black Gate Cat. no. 178)

Tombstone, first noticed by Hunter lying against a hedge a quarter of a mile from Housesteads. It records the deaths of a number of people and was erected by their heir. A woman, *Pervince*, is recorded in line 9. Height 35½ in.; breadth 29¼ in.

] M |]S[|]N[   ]PṚ[|]NTONIS
VENOCARI |]NI OFERSIONIS | ROMVLO ALIMAHI | . .]MILI DALLI |
MANSVETIO SENECIONIS | PERVINCE QVARTIONIS | HERES PROCVRAVIT
DELF | .]NVS RAVTIONIS EX G S

[D(is)] M(anibus) [. . . . . Fro]ntonis Venocari, [. . . . .]ni Ofersionis, Romulo Alimahi, [Si]mili Dalli, Mansuetio Senecionis, Pervince Quartionis, heres procvravit Delf[i]nus Rautionis ex G(ermania) s(uperiori)

It is not clear whether all these people died at one time or whether this is a dedication by the surviving member of a burial club. The woman's name may be compared with that of Pervica, the girl recorded on (52). The names suggest a German origin, and it may be that all are fellow-countrymen of the dedicator.

Philos. Trans, XXIII, 1131 (=*Philos. Trans. Abridg'd*, v, ii, 46) (CIL, VII, 693; LS, 197).

68. *Kirkby Thore*

Altar to Fortuna, erected by a woman, found in 1687 in the garden wall of the clergy house. It is now lost.

FORTVNAE |]SERVATRICI | ANTON[.]A | STRATONI |] V * S

Fortunae [Con]servatrici Anton[i]a Stratoni[ce] v(otum) s(olvit)

The name of the lady suggests an origin in the Greek world—unless she had a connexion with the *equites Stratoniciani* at Brougham. Could she be of servile origin?

Pococke, BM Add. Ms. 15800, f. 34 (CIL, VII, 296).

69. *Kirbky Thore* (Lowther Castle)

Tombstone of a woman, a crude attempt at a monument of the funerary banquet type. The deceased reclines on a couch attended by another figure and, like Victor at South Shields, she holds the customary cup, here two-handled. The couch has recently been studied in detail (Liversidge, *Furniture in Roman Britain*, 4, etc.). To the right, outside the main scene, is a pine cone, and under it a human head and neck. Another head beneath the central panel may be similarly disembodied. Such objects are strongly reminiscent of the severed heads common in pre-Roman Celtic religious monuments in Gaul.

The execution of the work is too poor to make a dating on style possible.

In a small panel to the right:

FILIA | CRESC | IMAG | NIFR

[. . . .]filia Cresc(entis) imag(i)nif(e)r(i)

The woman's name must have been in a similar panel, now lost, to the left of the banqueting scene. She was clearly the daughter of a military standard-bearer. The details of the stone suggest an interesting mixture of Celtic and Roman thought and a striving after Roman design.

(CIL, VII, 303a (primary reference); EE, III, p. 127.)

70. *Maryport* (Maryport, Netherhall Cat. no. 10)

Altar to Virtus Augusta set up by a woman. Found near Maryport. The same woman appears on 71.

VIRTVTI | AVGVSTAE | . . . .]ANA | QVINTI FILIA | HERMIONAE | V S L L M

Virtuti Augustae [Hisp]ana (?), Quinti filia, Hermionae, v(otum) s(olvit) l(aeta) l(ibens) m(erito)

If the name in (70) is correctly restored as Hispana it must surely be so restored here. *Hermionae* is rightly seen to be nominative by Hübner. It represents the Greek long E, and is written E on the next inscription.

The dedications to Virtus Augusta and I O M (71) are most unusual from a woman. This has suggested that she is the wife or daughter of the commandant, a most reasonable conjecture.

Hutchinson, *Cumberland*, 284; Lysons, *Cumberland*, 155, no. 69; Jarrett, Durham B.A. thesis, no. 31 (CIL, VII, 397; LS, 868).

71. *Maryport* (Maryport, Netherhall Cat. p. 148, no. 52)

Altar to Iuppiter Optimus Maximus, erected by the same woman as 70. This inscription is badly damaged but the dedication is certain.

I O M | N[|]AM |]SPANA * Q * F * |
HERMIONE

I(ovi) O(ptimo) M(aximo) . . . . [Hi]spana, Q(uinti) f(ilia),
Hermione

Haverfield's original reading of line 4 was . . . . IANA * Q * F * as was Hübner's on (70). However, Dr Michael Jarrett has recently examined the stone and accepts the reading of SP.

CW (1), V, 239; Jarrett, no. 30 (EE, VII, 971).

72. *Maryport* (Maryport, Netherhall Cat. p. 144, no. 34)

Tombstone of a woman, placed at 'Elenfoot' by Pococke.

]IL SER | QVINA NAT | GALATIA DEC | BVIT GALAT[| XIT
ANN[| MORITV[| DESIDER[| RIS INT |
NON VA[|

[. . . f]il(ia) Serquina, nat(a) Galatia, dec(u)buit (?) Galat[ia, vi]xit ann[os . . .] moritu[ra] desider[avit pat]ris (?) [. . . . . . .

Apart from the fact that this is the memorial of a woman little else is certain of the meaning. *Decumbo* occurs in literature of the 'fall' of a defeated gladiator and may here be a colloquial phrase for 'died'. It would then appear that she died in Galatia, presumably on a visit to her home. Roach Smith's suggestion *desider[avit pat]ris in t⟨umulo sepeliri⟩* may well be at least partly correct, indicating some special arrangement, possibly the shipping of the body to Britain but more likely burial in Galatia with the present tomb a cenotaph. The meaning *desideravit* may, on the other hand, be: 'felt the need of, lacked' her father (?), again referring to some special arrangement.

Pococke, BM Add. MS. 15800, f. 32., Gordon, 99 and pl. 45, 3; C. Roach Smith (cited in LS); (CIL, VII, 405; LS, 880).

73. *Maryport* (Maryport, Netherhall Cat. p. 157, no. 76)

Tombstone of a centurion erected by his wife. See (10) above for a discussion of his rank. The stone is very badly damaged, but most of the inscription seems to have survived.

DIS MA |]L MARINVS ORDIN | VIXIT ANIS XXXX MII |
  ] XX MARITI |] POSVIT

Dis Ma[nibus. Iu]l(ius) (?) Marinus ordin(atus) vixit an(n)is, xxxx, mi⟨l⟩[itavit] xx. Marit⟨a⟩ (*or* marit⟨o⟩) [   ] posuit.

Dr Michael Jarrett's suggestion of MIL in line 3 is surely correct. I have some doubts about his suggestion MARITA in line 4. Bailey's [*Iu*]*l(ius)* in line 2 is convincing. *Ordinatus* is a chiefly third-century title, meaning a centurion, and probably indicates one actually serving in a unit rather than on specialist duty.

CIL, VII, 404 (primary publication); (LS, 884 a).

74. *Maryport*

Tombstone of a man or woman of seventy, reported at Ellenborough by Camden but lost before Horsley's time.

D * M | MORI * REGIS | FILII * ET * HEREDES EIVS * SVBSTITVE |
RVNT * VIX A * LXX

D(is) M(anibus) Mori Regis filii et heredes eius substituerunt: vix(it) a(nnos) lxx

It is quite uncertain whether there are two names or one in line 2. The verb in 3–4 is odd but probably colloquial for *instituerunt*, unless there is an echo of the legal use of the word in connexion with testatory arrangements.

Camden (5), 697; Horsley, 284 f. (CIL, VII, 409; LS, 882).

75. *Maryport*

Tombstone of a boy, reported by Camden but apparently now lost.

D * M | INGENVI * AN * X | IVL * SIMPLEX * PATER | F * C

D(is) M(anibus) Ingenui, an(norum) x, Iul(ius) Simplex pater f(aciendum) c(uravit)

Camden (5), 697; Horsley, 284 (CIL, VII, 407; LS, 881).

76. *Maryport* (Maryport, Netherhall Cat. p. 139, no. 2)

Tombstone of a girl, aged ten.

D M | IVL MARTIN | A VIX AN | X M III D XXII

D(is) M(anibus) Iul(ia) Mar(i)ti⟨m⟩a vix(it) an(nos) x m(enses) iii d(ies) xxii

Iul Martin is the reading of the LS illustration, but Professor Birley's suggestion *Iul(ia) Mar(i)ti⟨m⟩a* seems convincing.

Camden (5), 697; Gordon, 99 and pl. 45, 2 (CIL, VII, 408; LS, 879).

77. *Maryport*

Tombstone seen by Camden and Cotton in 1599, position unspecified. It appears to record the death of a young woman.

D M | LVCA VIX | ANN | IS XX

D(is) M(anibus). Luc(i)a (?) vix(it) annis xx

Camden's illustration shows no gap for the missing I, but it seems not unreasonable to suppose that the name should be Lucia. If there is an error, it may be the lettering mason's and not Camden's.

Camden (5), 697; (6), 636 (CIL, VII, 410; LS, 883).

78. *Netherby* (Carlisle, Tullie House Cat. no. 86)

Tombstone of a woman, found at Netherby in 1788. At the top is a gable containing a crescent.

✱ D ✱ M | TITVLLINIA PVSSITTA ✱ | CIS ✱ RAETA | VIXSIT ✱ |
ANNOS ✱ XXXV | MENSES VIII | DIES ✱ XV ✱

D(is) M(anibus). Titullinia Pussitta, ci(vi)s Raeta, vixsit annos
xxxv menses viii dies xv

Two letters, TV, are cut on the margin at the bottom of the face of the
stone on the border. These are unlike the rest of the lettering in style and
have been added *after* the border had been damaged. They are almost certainly modern.

Professor Birley has suggested that the elaborate stone and the distance
the lady is from home may indicate that she was the wife of an officer or
N.C.O. However, Regina's tomb at South Shields shows how elaborately the wife of a civilian foreigner could be buried. The details of age
perhaps suggest the third century (*CW* (2), LIII, 23); the fact that the
body was cremated (*Archaeologia*, IX, 222) makes it unlikely that it was
any later.

Archaeologia, IX, 222 (CIL, VII, 972; LS, 771).

79. *Netherby* (Carlisle, Tullie House Cat. no. 8)

Altar bearing a very faint inscription, apparently dedicated by
a woman.

D ✱ S ✱ E̱ | IA̱V̱O̱I̱E̱ṈA̱ | MONIME | PR[. . .]VNICI | . . . .] VERISTS
[. . . . | PL[| RIVS POSVIT

D(eae) S(anctae) F(ortunae) (?) Iavo⟨l⟩ena Monime . . . . posuit

The reading is very uncertain. Haverfield thought that in line 1 E
might be a badly cut F, and Professor Birley has suggested *Fortunae* convincingly. *Iavolena*, if correct, is a rare name. However, at least one
Iavolenus is known to have been in Britain, Iavolenus Priscus the jurist,
a Flavian *iuridicus* of the province.

Hutchinson, *Cumberland*, II, 537; *CW* (2), LIII, 24 (CIL, VII, 955; LS,
769).

80. *Old Carlisle* (Carlisle, Tullie House)

Altar to Iuppiter Optimus Maximus and Vulcan, dedicated for
the health of Gordian III. The altar has now been transferred to the
Tullie House Museum, replacing the cast (Tullie House Cat. no.
24). Height 47½ in., breadth 18¼ in.

I O M E̅T̅ | VLK PRO SA | LV̅T̅E D N M A̅N̅T̅O | GO̅R̅DIANI P | F A̅V̅G VIK |
MAG ARAM | ÇOḶ A V D

I(ovi) O(ptimo) M(aximo) et V(o)lk(ano) pro salute d(omini)
n(ostri) M(arci) Anto(ni) Gordiani p(ii) f(elicis) Aug(usti), vi-
k(anorum) mag(istri) aram (aere ?) col(lato) a v(ikanis) d(ono)
(dederunt) (?)

This is the most closely dated of the *vicani* altars from the frontier region (A.D. 238–44); it is the only evidence for *magistri vicanorum*; it mentions the cult of Vulcan whose worship so frequently appears on communal dedications by *vicani*; and there is a hint of financial organization.
I reproduce Haverfield's most ingenious suggestion for the last line.
    Gent. Mag. (2), XVIII (1842), 598 f. (CIL, VII, 346; LS, 829).

81. *Old Carlisle* (Greenhill House, Wigton)
Altar to Belatucadrus, erected by a veteran, found near Old
Carlisle. It was seen in 1944 built into a garden wall at Greenhill
House.

DEO | BELATUCA | DRO * SANCTO | AVR * TASVLVS | VET * V * S *
L * [

Deo Belatucadro sancto, Aur(elius) Tasulus, vet(eranus), v(otum)
s(olvit) l(ibens) [m](erito)

The name of the veteran is probably Celtic (see Holder, 1751).
LS, 831 (primary publication); *CW* (2), XXVIII, 113 (EE, III, 92).

82. *Old Carlisle* (Wigton)
Inscription erected by a veteran, found in 1908 about one hundred paces from the fort. It records the payment of tithes due to
Hercules by the veteran out of his own pocket. In 1944 it was in
the entrance hall of the County Court Registry Office, Wigton.

| HERCVLI | SORTES * SIGI | LIVS * EMERIT | D * D * S * P

[...] Herculi sortes Sigilius emerit(us) d(ono) d(edit) s(ua) p(ecunia)
(*or possibly* d(ono) d(e) s(ua) p(ecunia) (dedit))

CW (2), XI, 472; *CW* (2), XXVIII, 114 (EE, IX, 1128).

83. *Old Carlisle* (Carlisle, Tullie House Cat. no. 87)

Tombstone of a woman, found near Old Carlisle. The top of the inscribed panel is lost but the inscription is probably complete. The fragment measures 19½ in. in height, 25 in. in width.

TANCORIX | MVLIER | VIGSIT ANNOS | SEGSAGINTA

Tancorix, mulier, vigsit annos segsaginta

The spelling of *x* as *gs* is interesting, suggesting a dialect form (possibly a further stage following on the *xs* spelling fairly common in the area). The lettering suggests a comparatively late date, unless it be simply the product of an incompetent workman.

Lysons, *Cumberland*, 159 and 183 (CIL, VII, 355; LS, 837).

84. *Old Carlisle*

Tombstone found in about 1788 under Wigton church tower and re-used then in the re-building of the church. Hutchinson is the only authority for the text, which is in an almost hopeless state of confusion. Only the age of the deceased and the fact that it was erected by someone and a wife (either of the deceased or of the erector) can be elicited.

| ANOS XXXXIV * BOVON | FILIAEIML NIMLIXISAVR |
SEITVMILITMAVRI CO | NIVX PONENDVM | [ ]VRAVERVNT

[vixit] an(n)os xxxxiv . . . . . fil⟨i⟩(o) ⟨L⟩(ucius) Ae⟨mil⟩ (?) . . . . (et) . . . . coniux ponendum [c]uraverunt.

The text above is based on that suggested by Collingwood.
Hutchinson, *Cumberland*, II, pl. facing p.410; *CW* (2), XXVIII, 118 (CIL, VII, 356).

85. *Old Carlisle* (Carlisle, Tullie House Cat. no. 92)

Fragment of a tombstone, set up by the husband or wife.

] AN[| COIVX EIVS [| VRAVIT

[vixit] an(nos) (*or* an(n)orum) [ ] co(n)iux eius [(faciendum *or* ponendum) c]uravit (*or* [proc]uravit)

Lysons, *Cumberland*, 160; *CW* (2), XXVIII, 119 (CIL, VII, 358; LS, 838).

86. *Old Penrith*

Tombstone, noted by Camden but lost before Horsley's time.

D * M | FL * MARTIO * SEN | IN C * CARVETIOR | QVESTORIO |
VIXIT AN XXXXV | MARTIOLA FILIA ET | HERES PONEN | CVRAVIT

D(is) M(anibus). Fl(avio) Martio Sen(iori) (?), in c(ivitate) (?)
Carvetior(um) questorio—vixit an(nos) xxxxv—Martiola, filia et
heres, ponen(dum) curavit

A much disputed interpretation. The mention of the deceased's daughter Martiola qualifies the inscription for a place in this collection, even if
the status of the deceased himself is uncertain. Both were citizens, if
Martiola was correct in describing herself as *heres*. Birley, in the latest
publication of this inscription (*CW* (2), XLVII, 178 f.) has interpreted
the deceased's position as military (*senatori in cohorte Carvetiorum questorio*) and date as fourth century. *Senator* is indeed a rank in the army of
that period (notably in *numeri*, cf. ILS, 2796), but *quaestor* is difficult. The
example cited by Birley is, as he mentions, not fourth-century but late
Antonine (ILS, 2630, A.D. 186) and occurs (once again) in a *numerus*, not
a *cohors*. Of the other examples I have noted, ILS, 2466 and 2469 are both
specifically *quaestores veteranorum*, a post as much civil as military, and
the function of 2381 (even if *q.* is rightly expanded to *quaestor*) is uncertain.

In civil life on the other hand quaestors are found in every sort of organization, down to the humblest (e.g. ILS, 7291, 7353). On the analogy
of *consularis* and *praetorius* a *quaestorius* is clearly a person who has been a
quaestor (or been granted equivalent rank), which is indeed the conno-
tation the word has in literature (e.g. Cic. *Brut.* 76, 263; Suet. *Oth.* 3;
etc.). It could apply not only to those who had held a quaestorship at
Rome but also to those who had served in local government (ILS, 6815,
Carthage).

Birley rightly points out that *senator* cannot refer to membership of a
local *ordo* and there there is no reason for thinking the man was a member
of the Senate. But cannot SEN be part of the *cognomen* Senior (cf. ILS,
7001)? Examination of the text suggests most strongly that there has
been damage on the right-hand side of the stone, resulting in loss of the
ends of lines 2, 3 and 7. The name was probably not abbreviated.

In general it is true that 'it is easier to fit a new tribe into the Roman
army list than a new state into the map of Roman units of local self-
government' (Birley, *op. cit.* 179, n. 38) but not in regions where that

map has large tracts marked 'unexplored'. The interpretation *c(ivitate) Carvetiorum*, is adopted by Hübner (CIL), Haverfield (*CW* (2), XIII, 189), and Holder (820).

Camden (5), 702; Horsley, 273 (CIL, VII, 325; LS, 796).

87. *Old Penrith*

Tombstone of a veteran of the *ala Petriana*, noted by Camden but lost before Horsley.

] A | CADVNO | VLP * TRAI | EM * AL * PETR |
MARTIVS | F * P * C

[Dis Manibus]acaduno, Ulp(ia) Trai(ana), em(erito) al(ae) Petr(ianae), Martius f(ilius) p(onendum) c(uravit)

It is interesting to note a citizen of a *colonia* serving in an auxiliary unit, albeit the *ala Petriana*, the most important auxiliary unit in the British provinces. This *ala* seems to have been in garrison at Stanwix throughout the occupation of that fort. The deceased presumably had retired to the civil settlement at Old Penrith. Since the foundation of the colony of Vetera (if it *is* Vetera) lies between A.D. 98 and 107 (*Bonn. Jhb.* 152, 51), his discharge (and therefore this inscription) cannot be much earlier than 120. For the name Martius compare (85). It may well have been local.

Camden (5), 702; Horsley, 273 (CIL, VII, 323; LS, 794).

88. *Old Penrith*

Tombstone of a man and a small girl, probably his daughter, erected by the man's brother as it seems. Just possibly they are two brothers and a sister. Lost.

D * M * CROTILO GERMANVS VIX | ANIS * XXVI * GRECA VIX
ANIS IIII | VINDICIAVS FRA[ ] TITVLVM POS

D(is) M(anibus). Crotilo Germanus vix(it) an(n)is xxvi; Greca vix(it) an(n)is iiii; Vindicia(n)us, fra[ter], titulum pos(uit)

The primary source omits D M C in line 1, ANIS XXVI in line 2 and VINDICIAVS in line 3. It is therefore uncertain whether the original observer omitted some letters or Camden restored the inscription. However, the name and age of the girl are certain.

BM Cotton Iulius F.VI, f. 322, Camden (5), 702; Horsley, 273; *CW* (2), XIII, 189 f. (CIL, VII, 326; LS, 802).

89. *Old Penrith*

Tombstone of a woman and her daughter, erected by the husband. The stone was found a little before 1586 at Old Penrith. Lost before Horsley's visit.

D M | AICETVOS MATER | VIXIT * A * XXXXV | ET LATTIO FILIA VIX | A * XII LIMISTVS | CONIV ET FILIAE | PIENTISSI | POSVIT

D(is) M(anibus). Aicetuos, mater, vixit a(nnos) xxxxv; et Lattio filia vix(it) a(nnos) xii. Limistus coniu(gi) et filiae pientissi(mis) posuit

In line 5 the T should perhaps be read as I. The origin of the name is uncertain. A certain L. Limisius Rogatianus occurs on CIL, VIII, 12041.

BM Cotton Iulius F.VI, f. 305 ff.; Camden (5), 702; Horsley, 274; *CW* (2), XIII, 190 f. (CIL, VII, 327; LS, 800).

90. *Old Penrith* (Lowther Castle)

Tombstone of a small boy, found in 1829 about 200 yards north of the fort on the east side of the present main road.

DIS | MANIB * M * COCCEI * | NONNI * ANNOR * VI | * HIC * SITVS * EST

Dis Manib(us) M(arci) Coccei Nonni, annor(um) vi; hic situs est

Haverfield pointed out that *hic situs est, dis manib(us)* almost in full, and the long I's in DIS and HIC indicate an early date. This cannot be later than the first years of the second century. Whether this is the earliest proof of an extra-mural settlement in the region turns on the significance of the boy's name. If his family was enfranchised under Nerva (as argued by Birley, *CW* (2), XLVII, 175 f.), his father can hardly have been an officer, and the child and whoever looked after him must have dwelt in an extra-mural settlement. But while there is a strong presumption that the citizenship was granted by Nerva, it is not proven. The Celtic *cognomen* (Holder, 759) makes it certain that the family was not a branch of the Roman house of the Coccei itself but had obtained the franchise through that house. But the emperor was not the first eminent Cocceius Nerva. The tradition of public service went at least as far back as the suffect consul of 39 B.C. (whose freedmen, recorded on ILS, 7731, acquired the name of L. Cocceius Auctus) and the M. Cocceius Nerva, consul in 36 B.C., who was great-great-grandfather of the emperor. An almost unbroken succession of Coccei Nervae in the high offices of the state from Augustus to Domitian makes it probable that more than one family owed its citizenship to that house before the principate of Nerva. Nor is it impossible that the descendant of a Celt enfranchised early in the Principate should have commanded a unit at the end of the first century. It cannot therefore be ruled out that the erector of this large and comparatively expensive tombstone was in fact the commandant, and the deceased an inhabitant not of a *vicus* but the *praetorium.*

AA (1), II, 265; *CW* (2), XIII, 191 (CIL, VII, 328; LS, 795).

91. *Old Penrith* (Lowther Castle)

Tombstone of a boy of thirteen, foster-son of a *tribunus militum.* The lettering is faint, but Haverfield was fairly certain of the following reading (stops and ligature added):

D * M | HYLAE * ALV̂M | NI * KARIS | SIMI * VIXI[|]N * XIII * CL
S | EVERVS * TRIB | MILIT[

D(is) M(anibus) Hylae, alumni karissimi—vixi[t a]n(nos) xiii—Cl(audius) Severus, trib(unus) milit[um, posuit (?)]

The erector's title indicates a legionary tribune.

CIL, VII, 328a; *CW* (2), XIII, 191 (LS, 801).

92. *Old Penrith*

Tombstone of a boy of eleven, erected by his father, found in about 1860 near Plumpton Wall.

D M * ÂVRELIVS * VIXIT ANNIS | XI * ÂVO * PATE * PIENTISSIMVS |
TAM * SIBI * QV̂AM * ET * FILIO SVO * POSVIT

D(is) M(anibus). Aurelius vixit annis xi. Avo, pate(r) pientissimus tam sibi quam et filio suo posuit

Avo is certainly the name of the father and not the ablative of *avus.* It also occurs in Gaul.

(CIL, VII, 1344; LS, 798.)

93. *Overborough* (*Burrow-in-Lonsdale*)

Tombstone of a man and wife, erected by another member of the family. The inscription, now lost, was reported by Thomas Machell (died 1698), quoted by Watkin (*Roman Lancashire*, 194) as at Tunstall Vicarage, having been brought there from 'Burrow upon Lewin in the said Parish'. Machell's drawing is reproduced from Watkin by Birley (*CW* (2), XLVI, 137 f. and fig. 2) whose reading is followed here, with slight alterations.

D | M S | ET PERPETVE SEC | VRITATI AVR PVS[| NNI CIV[| |
AN * LIIII M III [| AVR EVBIAE CON[| |]
XXXVII * AVR PR[|

D(is) M(anibus) s(acrum) et perpetue securitati Aur(eli) Pus[i]nni civ[is (qui) vixit] an(nos) liiii m(enses) iii [d(ies)   , et] Aur(eliae) Eubiae con[iugis (eius, quae) vixit an(nos)] xxxvii, Aur(elius) Pr[ ]

If Machell's drawing was not utterly inaccurate, Professor Birley's reading cannot be very far from the original. The husband is probably but not certainly civilian, and, as Birley points out, if civilian his name Aurelius indicates a date during or after the reign of Caracalla, if military, not earlier than Marcus Aurelius.

The name Pusinnus may be compared with Pusitta (78) and Pusinna (53). Both these ladies may have had Danubian connexions and the same may be true of this Pusinnus. Probably *civis Pannonius* or *civis Raetus* should be read in line 5. The suggestion of Africa in D M S cannot safely be emphasized, but it is interesting to note that Eubia's Greek name is analogous to that of the dedicator of another D M S inscription (102), where evidence for African origin is rather stronger. It is worth remembering that much of the North African coast was Greek, especially the cities of Cyrenaica which had passed from the Ptolemaic kingdom to Rome in 96 B.C. Greek culture was, moreover, extremely popular in North Africa under the empire. The possibility that Eubia or her family originated in Africa cannot be ruled out.

Machell MSS (Watkin, *op. cit.*; Birley, *op. cit.*) in the Dean and Chapter Library, Carlisle (EE, VII, 947).

[93a. *Papcastle* (Tullie House Museum)

Tombstone of a man, a woman (?) and a girl, found in excavation in 1962, re-used as a floor-slab in the commandant's baths at

Papcastle. From curved abrasions on one edge of the stone it has been conjectured that it had been previously re-used as the side of a water tank (cf. Corbridge). The slab is of buff sandstone, 37 in. by 32 in. by 3 in.

D I M | APVLLIO * VIX A | N XXXV SABINA | V AN XVII * HVCTIA | V AN XLII

D(is) I(nferis) M(anibus). Apullio vix(it) an(nos) xxxv, Sabina v(ixit) an(nos) xvii, Huctia v(ixit) an(nos) xlii

The last A's in line 2 and in line 4 are blind.
JRS, LIII, 160 f., no. 6.]

94. *Piercebridge* (Piercebridge, Cliffe Hall)

Tombstone of an *ordinatus*, erected by his wife. The stone was found in 1844 on Dere Street south of the river at the point where the present drive to Cliffe Hall leaves the main road.

.] M | . .]R ACILIO |]INATO [. . .]MAN SVPER | . . . .]XXII
AVRELIA [. . .]ILLA CON | . . .]I FACIEND | VM CVRAVIT

[D(is)] M(anibus). [Au]r(elio) Acilio, [ord]inato, [Ger]man(iae) super(ioris), [—v(ixit) a(nnos) xx]xxii (?)—Aurelia [Fad]illa (?) con[iug]i faciendum curavit

I am not wholly satisfied with Dr Steer's suggestion STIP(endiorum) XXII in line 4. The lack of any statement of age is most unusual. Admittedly, the age of twenty-two would be surprisingly young for an *ordinatus*. I therefore tentatively suggest reading [V AN X]XXII or [V A XX]XXII or something similar. The rank may suggest a third-century date (see 10, above).

Gent. Mag. (2), XXII (1844), 24 (CIL, VII, 421; LS, pp. 3 ff.; EE, IX, 1132).

95. *Risingham*

Altar to Fortuna, Augusta, dedicated by a woman. The stone is lost. Hunter omits the stop in line 5 and reads AET in line 3.

FORTVNAE | AVG | AEL | PROCVLINA | V * S

Fortunae Aug(ustae) Ael(ia) Proculina v(otum) s(olvit)

This dedication may be compared with that dedicated *Virtuti Augustae* at Maryport (69). Here again the woman in question may have had some connexion with official circles.

Warburton, *Map of Northumberland*; Hunter, *Philos. Trans.* XLIII, 160 (=*Philos. Trans. Abridg'd*, X, iv, 1272); *NCH*, XV, 134, no. 15.

96. *Risingham* (Newcastle Museum)

A gabled altar, dedicated to the Nymphs by a soldier. The inscription is in a sort of verse. The stone was noted in 1825 'in the back of a hedge, near a spring, and close to the east side of Watling Street, where that ancient way is crossed by a bridle road' (the road from Ridsdale to Broomhope Mill (Richmond)).

SOMNIO PRAE | MONITVS | MILES HANC | PONERE IVS | SIT | ARAM
QVAE | FABIO NVP | TA EST NYM | PHIS VENE | RANDIS

Somnio praemonitus miles hanc ponere iussit aram (eam) quae Fabio nupta est Nymphis venerandis

The Nymphs are most probably local, perhaps associated with the spring. It is not clear who Fabius or his wife are—they may be the soldier and his own wife. The versifying makes the sense rather difficult to make out.

Hodgson, II, i, 90; *NCH*, XV, 138, no. 26 (CIL, VII, 998; LS, 607).

97. *Risingham* (Newcastle Museum, Black Gate Cat. no. 74)

Altar to an unknown deity erected by a freedman for the safety of one Arrius Paulinus. The first part of the inscription has been cut away. Breadth $18\frac{1}{2}$ in., present height $13\frac{1}{2}$ in.

|]RO SALVTE | ARR * PAVLINI | THEODOTVS | LIB

.... p]ro salute Arr(i) Paulini Theodotus lib(ertus)

Professor Richmond points out that Theodotus is to be compared with Eutychus (60) and Celer (9). Paulinus was probably the commandant.

AA (2), I, 234; Richmond, *NCH*, XV, 138, no. 27 (CIL, VII, 1000; LS, 610).

98. *Risingham* (Newcastle Museum, Black Gate Cat. no. 185)
Fragment of a tombstone, found 'in the possession of one of the villagers' in 1877. Height 14½ in., breadth 16¼ in.

]s | v[ ]s * DVL |]NTIBVS SVIS |
        ] ETVDINEM SIT |] ORD * FILIO |
        ] SVBSTITVTVS

]s | v[. .]s dul[cissimis pare]ntibus suis [cum per val]etudinem sit [impeditus nat(urae)] ord(ine) filio [. . . . .] substitutus

It appears that this records the erection of a memorial to his parents by a man through the agency of another, he himself being unable to order the work satisfactorily owing to illness.

AJ, xxxv, 65; *NCH*, xv, 141, no. 41 (EE, IV, 668).

99. *Risingham* (Cambridge, Trinity College)
Tombstone of a small girl, erected by her father. This stone was in the collection of Sir Robert Cotton and is now permanently fixed to the wall in the well of the staircase to the Library. It is of the gabled variety, containing a very crude bust, probably female. The stone is 27¾ in. high, 15¼ in. wide and 3 in. thick.

D * M | BLESCIVS | DIOVICVS | FILIAE | SVAE P | VIXSIT ANVM |
* I * ET DIE | XXI

D(is) M(anibus). Blescius Diovicus filiae suae p(osuit). Vixsit an(n)um i et die(s) xxi

The names are Celtic (Holder, 452; 1285). P in line 5 seems to be an afterthought.

Bainbrigg, BM Cotton Iulius F.VI, f. 309, *NCH*, xv, 140, no. 35 (CIL, VII, 1017; LS, 612).

100. *Risingham* (West Woodburn)
Tombstone of a young woman, first recorded in 1910 and rediscovered by Mr R. P. Wright fixed in the east gable of the Yellow House, ¼ mile north-east of the bridge at West Woodburn.

]FILIA CO[. . | ERANI * VI[. . . | ANNO[. | XVII[| * S * T * T * [.

. . . .] filia Co[. .]erani, vi[xit] anno[s] xvii[i], s(it) t(ibi) t(erra) [l(evis)]

Cf. (102) for the closing formula.
PSAN (3), IV, 287; NCH, XV, 142, no. 44.

101. *Risingham* (Newcastle Museum)
Tombstone of a boy, found at Chesterhope, near Risingham. It is gabled, containing three rosettes in the pediment.

D M | AEMILIANVS | ANNORVM | X

D(is) M(anibus). Aemilianus annorum x

Hodgson, II, i, 144; Hutchinson, *Northumberland*, I, 185; *NCH*, XV, 140, no. 34 (CIL, VII, 1013; LS, 619).

102. *Risingham* (Newcastle Museum, Black Gate Cat. no. 159)
Found re-used in the fort wall, 20 ft south of the north-east corner. Both the top and bottom ends have been cut away, but the inscription is clearly complete. The stone is the tombstone of a woman, erected by her son. Height 29½ in., breadth 21 in. The last two lines are enclosed in a circle.

D M S | AVR * LVPV | LE MATRI | PIISSIME | DIONYSIVS |
FORTVNA | TVS FILIVS | S T | T L

D(is) M(anibus) s(acrum). Aur(elie) Lupule, matri piissime, Dionysius Fortunatus, filius. S(it) t(ibi) t(erra) l(evis)

Professor Richmond points out that the son's name suggests that the lady's husband was of eastern Mediterranean origin (or at least from an area under Greek influence). The formula at the end is not common on civil tombstones in this area but occurs on (103) from this site. The opening formula and the name Fortunatus may indicate an African origin (a point I owe to Professor Birley) (cf. 93).

Gent. Mag. (2), XVII (1842), 536 f.; *NCH*, XV, 139, 31 (CIL, VII, 1014; LS, 616).

103. *Risingham* (Newcastle Museum, Black Gate Cat. no. 160)
Tombstone of a girl, found with (102). Height 34¼ in., breadth 26¾ in.

D M * S | AVR * QVARTĪL | LA * VIX * AN | NIS * XIII * M * IV |
D * X̂XII * AVR * | QVARTINVS | POSVIT * FILI | AE * SVAE

D(is) M(anibus) s(acrum). Aur(elia) Quartilla vix(it) annis xiii m(ensibus) iv d(iebus) xxii. Aur(elius) Quartinus posuit filiae suae

The form of M (for *mensibus*) with vertical stroke is paralleled on (52). (See the commentary on (52) for further points of similarity.)
Gent. Mag. (2) (1842), XVII, 536; *NCH*, XV, 140, no. 32 (CIL, VII, 1015; LS, 620).

104. *Risingham* (Newcastle Museum, Black Gate Cat. no. 162)
Tombstone of a woman.

] AV[|]MENI | FILIAE |]NI CONI[|
M * AVREL C[| VICSIT A | XXXVII

[Dis Manibus] Au[reliae . .]meni filiae, [. . . .]ni coni[ugi], M(arcus) Aurel(ius) C[. . . .]—vicsit annos xxxviii—(posuit ?)

The exact meaning is uncertain. The name of the dedicator and the fact that the deceased seems to be recorded as .... *coniugi* suggests that the stone has perhaps been erected by her son.
AA (2), I, 253 (CIL, VII, 1016).

105. *Risingham* (Newcastle Museum, Black Gate Cat. no. 173)
Tombstone of a small boy, found in the same place as (102) and (103). Broken at the top: present height 39 in., breadth 21½ in.

D * M | SATRIVS HONORATVS | VIXIT AN | NIS * V * ME | SIBVS VIII

D(is) M(anibus). Satrius Honoratus, vixit annis v mesibus viii

Collingwood pointed out that the omission of N in *mesibus* is an example of the change in pronunciation which occurred under the Middle Empire. Professor Birley (cited by Professor Richmond, *NCH*, xv) stated that Satrius is an Italian name of Etruscan origin.
Gent. Mag. (2), XVII (1842), 536; *NCH*, XV, 139, 30 (CIL, VII, 1019; LS, 617).

106. *Risingham*

Found at Chesterhope, near Risingham. Tombstone of a young woman. Now lost.

D [| IVLIONA |]NI FILIA VIXIT | ANN[.]S XVI M * XI | DI[
XIIII

D(is) [M(anibus)]. Iuliona [. . . .]ni filia, vixit ann[o]s xvi, m(enses) xi, di[es] xiiii

Professor Richmond draws attention to the form of the deceased's name. The ending *-iona* is typically Gallic.

Hutchinson, *Northumberland*, i, 184 f.; *NCH*, xv, 140, no. 36 (CIL, VII, 1018; LS, 615).

107. *South Shields* (South Shields, Roman Fort Museum)

Tombstone of a woman (pl. III a), found in 1878 'a little to the south of Bath Street' in an area close to the main road to the fort and where other burials have been discovered. Above the inscribed panel is an elaborate architectural niche with vaulted head, flanked by pilasters. The arched front of the vault breaks into the pediment which surmounts the whole. The lady is shown seated. At her left side is her work-basket, and in her lap she holds what appear to be a piece of material, a needle and a ball of wool. With her right hand she lifts the lid of a box fitted with a heavy lock, probably her jewel case. Below the lock is a crescent-shaped fitting, surely a handle and not a 'lunar ornament . . . an indication of her chastity' (Bruce). The stone is 48 in. high and 30 in. broad.

D M * REGINA * LIBERTA * ET * CONIVGE * | BARATES *
PALMYRENVS * NATIONE * | CATVALLAVNA * AN * XXX *

(in Palmyrene characters, right to left):

RGYN' BRTIN BT HRY' HBL

D(is) M(anibus). Regina, liberta et coniuge, Barates Palmyrenus, natione Catuallauna, an(norum) xxx

The last line translates 'Regina, freedwoman of Barates (*literally* 'daughter of freedom'), alas!(?)'.

The transcription and the translation of the Palmyrene were kindly provided by Dr David Smith.

Hübner considered the Latin lettering to be late-second or early-third century though Bruce (while conceding that the lack of ligatures suggested no very late date) was inclined to place it later than Hübner. Professor Wright thought the style of the last line would, at Palmyra, be third to fourth century, or possibly earlier. Professor Toynbee confirms my impression that the sculpture stylistically could be late second or early third, where I would tend to place the stone on general grounds (including the construction here of a new and special supply depot for sea transport of stores under Severus). I am strongly inclined to think that Barates (who surely is the same man as on (44)) was engaged in army contracting.

AA (2), x, 239 ff.; (4), xxxvii, 203 ff.

108. *South Shields* (South Shields, Roman Fort Museum)

Tombstone of a freedman (pl. III, b). The top fragment (the pediment) which had been burnt after separation from the lower section, was found in about 1882 approximately half way between the intersection of Cleveland Street with James Mather Street and the east end of Cleveland Street.

The lower part was found in 1885 at the intersection. The deceased is represented in a banqueting scene, flanked by pilasters and topped by a pediment. In the centre of the pediment is a lion-head with a ring through its mouth. Busts, now too damaged to recognize, project from the background above the two lower corners of the pediment. The deceased lies on an elaborate couch supporting himself on a bolster. A cup is held in his left hand, while a bunch of grapes (?) dangles from his right. A boy hands up a cup, presumably filled from the large, probably metal, crater on the floor. The background is filled with an elegant design of tendrils. Artistically and technically this is first-class provincial work by a sculptor trained in an eastern school. Damage to the stone is confined to loss of the faces of the boy and of the right-hand bust and part of those of the deceased himself and of the left-hand bust, and slight damage to the edges of the inscribed panel and the pediment.

S

D M VICTORIS * NATIONE MAVRVM |]NNORVM * XX * LIBERTVS *
NVMERIANI |]QITIS ALA * I * ASTVRVM * QVI * | PIANTISSIME
PR[. . .]QVTVS EST

D(is) M(anibus) Victoris, natione Maurum, [a]nnorum xx,
libertus Numeriani [e]q(u)itis ala(e) I Asturum qui piantissime
pr[ose]qutus est

The master was a trooper in the unit known to have been in garrison
at Benwell in the third century. The general style of the lettering suggests
the latter half of the second or the first half of the third century, and the
sculptural style is not inconsistent with that dating. The occurrence of
single names only is probably not significant as it is clear that the sign-
writer had considerable difficulty in squeezing in the whole inscription.
These two stones are among the finest from Britain, let alone the
frontier region. They imply a wealthy community here, most probably
in the late second or early third century, almost certainly to be associated
with the extraordinary shipping activity of that time.

AA (2), x, 311 ff.; (4), xxxvii, 203 ff. (EE, vii, 1002).

109. *South Shields* (South Shields, Roman Fort Museum)
Tombstone of a boy, erected by his father. The stone is a rectangular panel and may have formed part of a tomb. A rough incised border surrounds the inscription. The name of the father is
Italian, but there is no indication of his occupation. At some period
this stone has been heavily burnt, like (108) from the same site.

D M S * | AV[ ]DVS | VIX[.]T ANNO | VIIII MENSES * VIIII |
L * ARRVNTIVS SAL | VIANVS * FILIO | B M * PIISSIMO *

D(is) M(anibus) s(acrum). Au[gen]dus vix[i]t anno(s) viiii,
menses viiii. L(ucius) Arruntius Salvianus filio b(ene) m(erenti)
piissimo.

The suggestion *Au[gen]dus* I owe to Professor Birley.
AA (2), x, 244.

110. *Stanwix* (Stanwix, Drawdikes Castle)
Found 'in Stanwiggs feild nere unto the picts wall'. Like (22) this
tombstone bears lions devouring humans on either side at the top.
The stone was erected by the deceased's wife.

DIS MANIBV | S * MARCI TROIANI | AVGVSTINI IITVM *
FA | CIENDVM * CVRAVI | T * AEL * AMMILVSIMA | CONIVX KARISS

Dis Manibus Marci Troiani Augustini ⟨t⟩itu(lu)m (?) faciendum curavit Ael(ia) Ammilusima coniux cariss(ima).

The combination of the lion motif, the writing of *Dis Manibus* in full and the use of the genitive for the deceased's name combine to suggest a fairly early date for this stone. A drawing of the stone is reproduced by Richmond (*RW* (11), 205).

Bainbrigg, BM Cotton Iulius F.VI, f. 339; Camden (5) (1600), 706 (EE, VII, 920).

111. *Watercrook* (British Museum)

Tombstone of a former legionary centurion erected by the freedmen he had made his heirs. This stone appears to have formed part of a masonry tomb. The right-hand edge is damaged and Mr R. P. Wright has conjectured from the fact that only parts of the first letters of lines 3 and 4 are present that a second slab on the left held about 5 letters for each line. However, it is equally possible that the truncated letters merely overlapped the border, and that the opening formula (which must be postulated) came on the upper part of the tomb. Height 16 in., present breadth 20 in.

| P * AEL * P * F * SERG * BASS[| Q * D 7 LEG *
XX * V V * VIX * AN[| S ET * PRIVATVS * LIBB * ET *
HER [| VM * 7 LEG * VI * VIC * F C * C * SI Q[
| SEPVLC * ALIVM * MORT[| ERIT * INFER *
F * D * D * NN * [| INS * AEL * SVRINO

[D(is) M(anibus)]. P(ublius) Ael(ius), P(ubli), f(ilius), Serg(ia), Bass[   ] q(uon)d(am) c(enturio) leg(ionis) xx V(aleriae) V(ictricis), vix(it) an(nos) [   ]s et Privatus, lib(erti) et her(edes), [per (?)   ]um, c(enturionem) leg(ionis) vi V(ictricis) f(a)c(iendum) c(uraverunt). Si q[uis in hoc] sepulc(ro) alium mort[uum intul]erit, infer(at) f(isco) d(ominorum) n(ostrorum) [sestertium   ] ins(tante) Ael(io) Surino

The restoration of this text has accumulated a considerable literature, but since most of the points do not affect the present subject I have not felt it necessary to go into them in detail or to incorporate in my text more than can with reasonable certainty be inferred from the surviving portion. It is certain that the deceased is a retired centurion and it seems probable, since the two freedmen act through an agent, that he was at Watercrook only temporarily and had not brought his establishment with him into permanent residence. Since the erection of the monument is carried out by a serving centurion (possibly a *praepositus* in charge of the station), it is perhaps more likely that Bassus was residing in an official building at the time of his death than in a *vicus* whose existence has yet to be proved [cf. p. 124, n. 1]. This inscription is probably to be assigned to the third century.

Horsley, 300; *CW* (2), xxx, 99, 106; *CW* (2), lv, 46; *JRS*, xlvii, 228 (CIL, vii, 292; EE, ix, p. 565).

[112. *Westerwood* (Dollar Park Museum, Falkirk)

Altar erected by the wife of a legionary centurion, found in 1963 either inside or just without the fort.

SILVANIS [. . | QVADRVIS CA[.]LESTIB SACR | VIBIA PACATA | FL *
VERECV[. .]I | C LEG * VI * VIC | CVM SVIS | V * S * L M

Silvanis [et] Quadruis Ca[e]lestib(us) sacr(um): Vibia Pacata, Fl(avi) Verecu[nd]i c(enturionis) leg(ionis) vi vic(tricis) (uxor), cum suis v(otum) s(olvit) l(ibens) m(eritis).

JRS, liv, 178, no. 7.   Addendum, Jan. 1965.]

BIBLIOGRAPHY

I. GENERAL

ALFÖLDI, A. Epigraphica. *Arch. Ért.* (3), 1 (1940), 214 ff.

BARADEZ, J. *Vue-aérienne de l'organisation romaine dans le sud-algérien 'Fossatum Africae'.* Paris, 1949.

BARKÓCSY, L. Beiträge zum Rang der Lagerstädte am Ende des II., Anfang des III. Jahrhunderts. *Acta Arch. Acad. Scient. Hung.* III (1953), 201 ff.

BEHRENS, G. Verschwundene Mainzer Römerbauten. *Mz. Zeitschr.* 48/9 (1954), 70 ff.

BELL, H. I. A Latin Registration of Birth. *JRS*, XXVII (1937), 30 ff.

BIRLEY, E. An introduction to the excavation of Chesterholm-Vindolanda. *AA* (4), VIII (1931), 182 ff.

—— Excavations at Chesterholm-Vindolanda, 1931. *AA* (4), IX (1932), 216 ff.

—— A New Inscription from Chesterholm. *AA* (4), XI (1934), 127 ff.

—— Fourth Report on Excavations at Housesteads. II. Civil Settlements. *AA* (4), XII (1935), 205 ff.

—— Marcus Cocceius Firmus: An Epigraphic Study. *PSAS*, LXX (1936), 363 ff.

—— A Modern Building at Housesteads. *PSAN* (4), VIII (1938), 191 ff.

—— The Brigantian Problem and the First Roman Contact with Scotland. *Dumfr. & Gall.* XXIX (1950–1), 46 ff.

—— *Roman Britain and the Roman Army.* Kendal, 1953.

—— The Roman Milestone at Middleton in Lonsdale. *CW* (2), LIII (1953 (1954)), 52 ff.

—— The Hinterland of Hadrian's Wall (unpublished paper to R.A.I., 1954).

BIRLEY, E. (ed.) *The Congress of Roman Frontier Studies,* 1949. Durham, 1952.

BOHN, O. Rheinische 'Lagerstädte'. *Germania,* 10 (1926), 25 ff.

BOSANQUET, R. C. Excavations on the line of the Roman Wall in Northumberland; the Roman Camp at Housesteads. *AA* (2), XXV (1904), 193 ff.

BROGAN, O. Trade between the Roman Empire and Free Germans. *JRS*, XXVI (1936), 195 ff.

BRUCE, J. C. *The Roman Wall,* (3), London, 1867.

BUCKLAND, W. W. *A Textbook of Roman Law from Augustus to Justinian.* Cambridge, (1), 1921; (2), 1950.

CHEESMAN, G. L. *The Auxilia of the Roman Imperial Army.* Oxford, 1914.

CICHORIUS, C. *Die Reliefs der Traianssäule.* Berlin, 1896–1900.

CLARKE, J. Excavations at Milton (Tassiesholm) in Season 1950. *Dumfr. & Gall.* (3), XXVIII (1950), 199 ff.

COLLINGWOOD, R. G. Romano-Celtic Art in Northumbria. *Archaeologia* LXXX (1930), 37 ff.

—— An Introduction to the Prehistory of Cumberland, Westmorland and Lancashire North of the Sands. *CW* (2), XXXIII (1933), 163 ff.

COLLINGWOOD, R. G. Prehistoric Settlements near Crosby Ravensworth. *CW* (2), XXXIII, 201 ff.

—— The Middleton Milestone. *CW* (2), XXXVIII (1938), 296.

COLLINGWOOD, R. G., and MYRES, J. N. L. *Roman Britain and the English Settlements* (2). Oxford, 1937.

CORDER, P. The Reorganization of the Defences of Romano-British Towns in the Fourth Century. *AJ*, CXII (1955 (1956)), 20 ff.

CORDER, P., and RICHMOND, I. A. Petuaria, *JBAA* (3), VII (1942), 1 ff.

CURLE, J. An Inventory of Objects of Roman and Provincial Roman Origin found on Sites in Scotland not definitely associated with Roman Constructions. *PSAS*, LXVI (1932), 277 ff.

DOMASZEWSKI, A. VON. *Die Rangordnung des römischen Heeres*. Bonn, 1908.

EGGER, R. Bemerkungen zum Territorium pannonischer Festungen. *Anz. öst. Akad. Wiss.* LXXXVIII (1951 (1952)), 206 ff.

EGGERS, H. J. *Die römische Import im freien Germanien*. Hamburg, 1951.

FAIR, M. C. Roman and Briton. A Theory for future establishment of facts. *CW* (2), XLIII (1943), 82 ff.

GILLAM, J. P. Calpurnius Agricola and the northern frontier. *DN*, X, iv (1953), 359 ff.

—— Roman and Native, A.D. 122–197, in Richmond, I. A. (ed.). *Roman and Native in North Britain*, 60 ff.

HAVERFIELD, F. *The Romanization of Roman Britain* (3). Oxford, 1915.

—— On Julius Verus, a Roman Governor of Britain. *PSAS*, XXXVIII, (1903–4 (1905)), 54 ff.

HAWKES, C. F. C. Britons, Romans and Saxons round Salisbury and in Cranborne Chase. *AJ*, CIV (1947 (1948)), 27 ff.

HOGG, A. H. A. The Votadini, in *Aspects of Archaeology in Britain and Beyond*. London, 1951.

HOLDER, A. *Alt-Celtischer Sprachschatz*. Leipzig, 1896–1907.

JACOBI, L. *Das Römerkastell Saalburg bei Homburg vor der Höhe*. Homburg v.d. H., 1897.

JOBEY, G. Some rectilinear settlements of the Roman period in Northumberland. Part I. *AA* (4), XXXVIII (1960), 1 ff.

JOLIFFE, N. Dea Brigantia. *AJ*, XCVII (1940 (1941)), 36 ff.

JOLOWICZ, H. F. *Historical Introduction to the Study of Roman Law*. Cambridge, 1952.

JORNS, W. Die Ausgrabungen am Zugmantel im Herbst 1935. *Saalb.-Jhb.* X (1951), 50 ff.

JORNS, W. and SCHLEIERMACHER, W. Das Lagerdorf der Kastells Butzbach. *Saalb.-Jhb.* XIV (1955), 12 ff.

KUNKEL, W. (ed.) Jörs, P. *Römisches Privatrecht*. Berlin, 1949.

LAUR-BELART, R. *Vindonissa, Lager und Vicus*. Berlin, 1935.

MERRIX, J. *The Buildings of Roman Extramural Settlements and Their Occupants* (n.d., unpublished B.A. dissertation, Durham).

BIBLIOGRAPHY

Mócsy, A. Das territorium legionis und die canabae in Pannonien. *Acta Arch. Acad. Scient. Hung.* III (1953), 179 ff.

Mommsen, T. Römische Lagerstädte, *Gesammelte Schriften* (Berlin, 1910) (1905–1913) VI, 176 ff. (=*Hermes*, VII, 301 ff.).

Morris, J. The Vallum again. *CW* (2), L (1950 (1951)), 43 ff.

Nash-Williams, V. E. *The Roman Frontier in Wales.* Cardiff, 1954.

Nash-Williams, V. E. and Nash-Williams, A. H. *Catalogue of the Roman Inscribed and Sculptured Stones found at Caerleon, Monmouthshire.* Cardiff, 1935.

Newstead, R. The Roman Station, Prestatyn. First Interim Report. *Arch. Camb.* XCII (1937), 208 ff.

Petrikovits, H. von. Die Ausgrabungen in der Colonia Traiana bei Xanten. *Bonn. Jhb.* CLII (1952), 41 ff.

—— Ein Ziegelstempel der Cohors II. Varcianorum aus Gelduba-Gellep. *Bonn. Jhb.* CLIV (1954), 137 ff.

—— Vetera, *Paulys Realencyclopädie der klassischen Altertumswissenschaft* col. 1801 ff. (1958).

Royal Commission on Ancient Monuments (Scotland). *Roxburghshire,* I. Edinburgh, 1956.

Richmond, I. A. Excavations on Hadrian's Wall in the Birdoswald-Pike Hill Sector, 1929. I. Birdoswald Fort. *CW* (2), XXX (1930), 169 ff.

—— The Roman fort at South Shields. *AA* (4), XI (1934), 83 ff.

—— The Sarmatae, *Bremetennacum Veteranorum* and the *Regio Bremetennacensis. JRS,* XXXV (1945), 15 ff.

—— Roman Settlement, in *Scientific Survey of North-eastern England* (British Association, 1949), 61 ff.

—— *The Roman Fort at South Shields: A Guide* (n.d. (? 1953)), South Shields.

—— Queen Cartimandua. *JRS,* XLIV (1954), 43 ff.

—— *Roman Britain.* London, 1955.

Richmond, I. A. (ed.) *Roman and Native in North Britain.* Edinburgh, 1958 (including Richmond, 'Roman and Native in the Fourth Century A.D. and After,' 112 ff.).

Richmond, I. A. and Crawford, O. G. S. The British Section of the Ravenna Cosmography. *Archaeologia,* XCIII (1949), 1 ff. (cf. *Roman and Native in North Britain,* 131 ff. and 150 ff.).

Robertson, A. S. *An Antonine Fort: Golden Hill, Duntocher.* Edinburgh, 1957.

St Joseph, J. K. Air Reconnaissance of North Britain. *JRS,* XLI (1951), 52 ff.

Schauer, W. Doctoral dissertation, Vienna (unpublished).

Schönberger, H. Plan zu den Ausgrabungen am Kastell Zugmantel bis zum Jahre 1950, *Saalb.-Jhb.* X (1951), 55 ff.

Schulten, A. Das territorium legionis. *Hermes,* XXIX (1894), 481 ff.

Schulz, F. Roman Registers of Births and Birth Certificates. Part I. *JRS,* XXXII (1942), 78 ff.; Part II. *JRS,* XXXIII (1943), 55 ff.

Seeck, O. *Notitia Dignitatum,* Berlin, 1876.

Sherwin-White, A. N. *The Roman Citizenship,* Oxford, 1939.

STEER, K. A. Roman and Native in North Britain: The Severan Reorganisation, in *Roman and Native in North Britain.* 91 ff.

—— The Antonine Wall, 1934–59, *JRS*, L (1960), 84 ff.

STEVENSON, G. H. *Roman provincial administration till the age of the Antonines.* Oxford, 1939.

STRAUB, A. *Les canabenses et l'origine de Strasbourg.* . . . Paris, 1886.

SWINBANK, B. *The Vallum reconsidered* (unpublished Ph.D. dissertation, Durham, 1954).

SWOBODA, E. *Carnuntum, seine Geschichte und seine Denkmäler.* Vienna, 1953.

SZILAGYI, J. *Aquincum.* Budapest, 1956.

VAN GIFFEN, A. E. Drie Romeinse Terpen. *Jaarverslag van de Vereeiniging voor Terpenonderzoek,* XXIX–XXXII (1948), 9 ff.

VORBECK, E. *Militärinschriften aus Carnuntum.* Vienna, 1954.

WHEELER, R. E. M. (Sir Mortimer). The Roman Fort near Brecon. *YC,* XXXVII (1926), 1 ff.

WILMANNS, G. Die Römische Lagerstadt Afrikas, in *Commentationes philologae in honorem Theodori Mommseni.* Berlin, 1877.

WLASSAK, M. Zum römischen Provinzialprozess. *Akad. d. Wiss. in Wien, phil.-hist. Klasse, Sitzungsberichte,* 190, iv Abhandlung (1919).

WOELCKE, K. Die neue Stadtplan von Nida-Heddernheim. *Germania,* XXII (1938), 161 ff.

WRIGHT, R. P. The establishment of the fort at Chester-le-Street in A.D. 216. *AA* (4), XXII (1944), 83 ff.

II. BIBLIOGRAPHY TO THE DETAILED DESCRIPTIONS OF SITES, INSCRIPTIONS AND SCULPTURES

BAILEY, J. B. Maryport and the Tenth Iter, with further notes on Roman Antiquities. *CW* (2), XXIII (1923), 142 ff.

BAILEY, J. B. and HAVERFIELD, F. Catalogue of Roman Inscribed and Sculptured Stones, Coins, Earthenware etc., discovered in and near the Roman Fort at Maryport, and preserved at Netherhall. *CW* (2), XV (1915), 135 ff.

BAINBRIGG, R. (see Abbreviations, *BM Cotton Iulius F.VI*).

BELL, JOHN Account of Risingham. *AA* (1), III (1844), 156 ff.

BELL, Jos. (and FERGUSON, R. S.). Roman Station at Plumpton Wall. *CW* (1), XV (1899), 46 f.

BELLHOUSE, R. L. Roman sites on the Cumberland Coast, 1954. *CW* (2), LIV (1954 (1955)), 28 ff.

—— Some Roman roads in Cumberland. *CW* (2), LVI (1956 (1957)), 37 ff.

BELLHOUSE, R. L. and MOFFAT, I. Further Roman finds in the Beckfoot cemetery area. *CW* (2), LVIII (1958 (1959)), 57 ff.

BIRLEY, E. Three Notes on Roman Cumberland: Bewcastle, Bowness-on-Solway, Petrianae. *CW* (2), XXXI (1931), 137 ff.

—— Materials for the History of Roman Brougham. *CW* (2), XXXII, (1932) 124 ff.

BIRLEY, E. Excavations at Chesterholm-Vindolanda, 1931. *AA* (4), IX (1932), 216 ff.

—— Old Penrith-Voreda. *CW* (2), XXXIV (1934), 217 f.

—— Three Roman inscriptions. *AA* (4), XII (1935), 195 ff.

—— Fifth report on excavations at Housesteads. *AA* (4), XIV (1937), 172 ff.

—— Roman inscriptions from Chesters (*Cilurnum*). *AA* (4), XVI (1939), 237 ff.

—— The Roman Site at Burrow in Lonsdale. *CW* (2), XLVI (1946 (1947)), 126 ff.

—— Figured samian from Benwell, 1938. *AA* (4), XXV (1947), 52 ff.

—— Old Penrith and its Problems. *CW* (2), XLVII (1947 (1948)), 166 ff.

—— The Roman fort at Moresby. *CW* (2), XLVIII (1948 (1949)), 42 ff.

—— *The Centenary Pilgrimage of Hadrian's Wall.* Durham, 1949.

—— Discoveries at Old Penrith in 1812. *CW* (2), L (1950 (1951)), 202 ff.

—— The Roman fort and settlement at Old Carlisle. *CW* (2), LI (1951 (1952)), 16 ff.

—— *Roman Britain and the Roman Army.* Kendal, 1953.

—— The Roman fort at Netherby. *CW* (2), LIII (1953 (1954)), 6 ff.

—— The Roman fort at Brough-under-Stainmore. *CW* (2), LVIII (1958 (1959)), 31 ff.

—— The Roman fort at Ravenglass. *CW* (2), LVIII (1958 (1959)), 1 ff. (and see under *JRS* (Roman Britain: Inscriptions) below).

BIRLEY, E., CHARLTON, J. and HEDLEY, W. P. Excavations at Housesteads in 1931. *AA* (4), IX (1932), 222 ff.

—— Excavations at Housesteads in 1932. *AA* (4), X (1933), 82 ff.

BIRLEY, E., BREWIS, P. and CHARLTON, J. Report for 1932 of the North of England Excavation Committee. II. Excavations at Benwell (Condercum). *AA* (4), X (1933), 101.

—— Report for 1933 of the North of England Excavation Committee. *AA* (4), XI (1934), 176 ff.

BIRLEY, E. and CHARLTON, J. Third report on excavations at Housesteads. *AA* (4), XI (1934), 185 ff.

BIRLEY, E. and KEENEY, G. S. Fourth report on excavations at Housesteads. *AA* (4), XII (1935), 204 ff.

BIRLEY, E., RICHMOND, I. A. and STANFIELD, J. A. Excavations at Chesterholm-Vindolanda: Third Report. *AA* (4), XIII (1936), 218 ff.

BIRLEY, E., RICHMOND, I. A. and GUTENBRUNNER, S. Excavations at Corbridge, 1936–1938. *AA* (4), XV (1938), 243 ff.

BLAIR, R. (see Abbreviations, *RW* (6)).

BLAKE, B. Crop-marks near the Roman fort at Ambleside. *CW* (2), LV (1955 (1956)), 318 f.

BOSANQUET, R. C. The Roman Camp at Housesteads (see Bibliography to Part I).

—— The Roman Tombs near High Rochester. *PSAN* (4), VI (1935), 246 ff. (cf. Richmond, I. A. quoted *ibid.* 272).

BRAILSFORD, J. W. *Guide to the Antiquities of Roman Britain.* British Museum, London, (2), 1958.

BRAND, J. *The history and antiquities of the town and county of the town of Newcastle upon Tyne.* London, 1789.

BRITTON, J. and BRAYLEY, E. W. *The Beauties of England and Wales,* III. London, 1802.

BRUCE, J. C. *The Roman Wall.* London and Newcastle, (1), 1851; (2), 1853; (3), 1867.

—— *Handbook to the Roman Wall* (see Abbreviations, under *RW*).

—— Catalogue of the Inscribed and Sculptured Roman Stones in the possession of the Society of Antiquaries of Newcastle-upon-Tyne. *AA* (2), I (1857), 221 ff.

—— Roman Chester-le-Street. *PSAN* (1), I (1858), 121 f.

—— (on Corbridge). *Gent. Mag.* (3), x (1861), 669 f.

—— Excavations at Corbridge. *AA* (2), VI (1865), 18 f.

—— Roman Carlisle. *AA* (2), VI (1865), 52.

—— Altars to Antenociticus discovered at Condercum. *AA* (2), VI (1865), 153 ff.

—— (on Halton Chesters). *Gent. Mag.* (4), v (1868), 370.

—— *The Wall of Hadrian: with especial reference to recent discoveries.* Newcastle upon Tyne, 1874 (two lectures, 1873).

—— *Lapidarium Septentrionale* (see Abbreviations, under *LS*).

BRUCE, J. C. The fountain of Coventina at Procolitia, on Hadrian's Wall, England, in *Commentationes philologae in honorem Theodori Mommseni.* Berlin, 1877.

—— On the Recent Discoveries in the Roman Camp on the Lawe, South Shields. *AA* (2), x (1885), 239 ff.

—— Later Discoveries at the Lawe, South Shields. *AA* (2), x (1885), 311 ff.

BUDGE, E. A. W. *An Account of the Roman Antiquities preserved in the Museum at Chesters, Northumberland.* London, 1903.

CAMDEN, W. *Britannia sive florentissimorum regnorum, Angliae, Scotiae, Hiberniae, et insularum adjacentium descriptio.* (1), London, 1586. Other editions used: (5), 1600; (6), 1607 (see also Gibson, Gough, Holland, below).

CHADWICK, H. M. *Early Scotland.* Cambridge, 1949.

CHRISTISON, D. Account of the Excavation of Birrens, a Roman Station in Annandale. *PSAS,* xxx (1896), 81 ff.

CLARK, E. C. and others. (Report of a discussion at the meeting of the Cambridge Antiquarian Society, 23 February 1885.) *Cambridge University Reporter,* no. 575 (1885), 495 ff.

CLAYTON, J. Account of Excavations at the Mile Castle of Cawfields, on the Roman Wall. *AA* (1), IV (1855), 54 ff.

—— Description of Roman Remains discovered near to Procolitia, a Station on the Wall of Hadrian. *AA* (2), VIII (1866), I ff.

CLAYTON, J., WATKIN, W. T., HÜBNER, E. and STEPHENS, G. On the Discovery of Roman Inscribed Altars, etc., at Housesteads, November 1883. *AA* (2), x (1885), 148 ff.

COLLINGWOOD, R. G. Report of the Excavations at Papcastle 1912. *CW* (2), XIII (1913), 131 ff.

—— Explorations in the Roman Fort at Ambleside (fourth year, 1920) and at other sites on the Tenth Iter. *CW* (2), XXI (1921), 1 ff.

—— The Last Years of Roman Cumberland. *CW* (2), XXIV (1924), 247 ff.

—— Roman Inscriptions and Sculptures belonging to the Society of Antiquaries of Newcastle upon Tyne. *AA* (4), II (1926), 52 ff.

—— Old Carlisle. *CW* (2), XXVIII (1928), 103 ff.

—— Roman Ravenglass. *CW* (2), XXVIII (1928), 353 ff.

—— *Roman Eskdale.* Whitehaven, 1929.

—— The Roman Fort at Watercrook, Kendal. *CW* (2), XXX (1930), 96 ff.

—— Roman Objects from Stanwix. *CW* (2), XXXI (1931), 69 ff.

—— Objects from Brough-under-Stainmore in the Craven Museum, Skipton. *CW* (2), XXXI (1931), 81 ff.

—— (see also *RW* (9) and below under *JRS* (Roman Britain: Inscriptions).

COWPER, H. S. Roman-British Fibulae and other Objects from Brough. *CW* (2), III (1903), 70 ff.

CURLE, J. *A Roman frontier Post and its People.* Glasgow, 1911.

FAIR, M. C. (A report on Ravenglass), notes: *CW* (2), XXV (1925), 374 ff.

FERGUSON, R. S. On the Remains of a Stockade recently found in Carlisle. *CW* (1), III (1878), 134 ff.

—— Some recent Roman Finds. *CW* (1), IV (1880), 324 ff.

—— Earthworks in Cumberland. *CW* (1), VI (1883), 190 ff.

—— Recent Roman Finds. *CW* (1), VIII (1886), 317 ff.

—— *A history of Cumberland.* London, 1890.

—— On a massive Timber Platform of early date recovered at Carlisle: and on sundry relics found in connection therewith. *CW* (1), XII (1893), 344 ff.

—— On the Roman Cemeteries of Luguvallium, and on a Sepulchral Slab of Roman date found recently. *CW* (1), XII (1893), 365 ff.

—— A Fourth Century Tombstone from Carlisle. *CW* (1), XIII (1895), 165 ff.

FORSTER, R. H. and KNOWLES, W. H. CORSTOPITUM: Report on the Excavations in 1909. *AA* (3), VI (1910), 205 ff.

FORSTER, R. H. and others. CORSTOPITUM: Report of the Excavations in 1907. *AA* (3), IV (1908), 205 ff.

—— CORSTOPITUM: Report on the Excavations in 1910. *AA* (3), VII (1911), 143 ff.

—— CORSTOPITUM: Report on the Excavations in 1913. *AA* (3), XI (1914), 279 ff.

—— CORSTOPITUM: Report on the Excavations in 1914. *AA* (3), XII (1915), 227 ff.

GALE, T. (ed. Gale, R.) *Antonini Iter Britanniarum.* London, 1709.

GIBSON, E. (ed.). W. Camden, *Britannia.* London, (1), 1695; (2), 1708.

GIBSON, J. P. Excavations on the line of the Roman Wall: Great Chesters (AESICA). *AA* (2), XXIV (1903), 19 ff.

GILLAM, J. P. Types of Roman coarse pottery vessels in northern Britain. *AA* (4), XXXV (1957), 180 ff.

GORDON, A. *Itinerarium Septentrionale.* London, 1726.

GOUGH, R. (ed.). W. Camden, *Britannia*. London, (2), 1806.

HAFEMANN, D. Beiträge zur Siedlungsgeographie des römischen Britannien. I. Die militärischen Siedlungen. *Akad. d. Wiss. u. d. Lit. (Mainz), Abhandlungen d. Math.-Naturwiss, Klasse* (1956), iii, Wiesbaden, 1956.

HARKNESS, R. On a Roman Gravestone, recently found at Brocavum (Brougham). *CW* (1), II (1876), 147 ff.

HAVERFIELD, F. Newly discovered Roman Inscriptions. I. Roman Altars, etc., at *Aesica* (Great Chesters). *AA* (2), XIX (1898), 268 ff.

—— Report of the Cumberland Excavation Committee, 1897. *CW* (1), XV (1899), 172 ff.

—— Report of the Cumberland Excavation Committee for 1902. *CW* (2), III, (1903), 328 ff.

—— CORSTOPITUM: 1911—Inscriptions. *AA* (3), VIII (1912), 186 ff.

—— Voreda, the Roman fort at Plumpton Wall. *CW* (2), XIII (1913), 177 ff.

—— Roman Britain in 1914. *British Academy Supplemental Papers*, III (1915), London.

—— *A Catalogue of the Roman Inscribed and Sculptured Stones in the Museum, Tullie House, Carlisle*. Carlisle, (2), 1922 (posthumous publication, edited by R. G. Collingwood).

HEDLEY, A. An Account of a Sepulchral Inscription, discovered at Little Chesters, in the county of Northumberland. *AA* (1), I (1822), 208 ff.

—— An Account of some Roman Shoes lately discovered at Whitley Castle, Northumberland. *AA* (1), II (1832), 205 f.

HEDLEY, W. P. The last days of Corstopitum and the Roman Wall—the coin evidence. *AA* (4), XIV (1937), 95 ff.

HEELIS, A. J. A Find of Roman Coins near Brougham Castle. *CW* (2), XI (1911), 209 ff.

HEICHELHEIM, F. M. Genii Cucullati. *AA* (4), XII (1935), 187 ff.

HILDYARD, E. J. W. Excavations at Burrow in Lonsdale, 1952–3. *CW* (2), LIV (1954 (1955)), 66 ff.

HODGKIN, J. E. Notes on the Roman bridge and station at Piercebridge. *PSAN* (4), VI (1935), 235 ff.

HODGSON, C. Account of a Roman Inscription found at Old Penrith. *AA* (1), II (1832), 265 f.

—— Account of an ancient Pitcher, found in digging the Foundations for a New Gaol, at Carlisle. *AA* (1), II (1832), 313 f.

—— Account of two Roman Inscriptions. *AA* (1), II (1832), 419 f.

HODGSON, J. Observations on the Roman Station of Housesteads, and on some Mithraic Antiquities discovered there. *AA* (1), I (1822), 263 ff.

—— *History of Northumberland*, II, iii. Newcastle, 1840.

—— Roman Gravestones at Habitancum in Northumberland. *Gent. Mag.* (2), XVII (1842), 536 f.

HODGSON, J. and MATTHEWS, R. Roman Altar found at Old Carlisle. *Gent. Mag.* (2), XVIII (1842), 598 f.

BIBLIOGRAPHY

HOGG, R. A Roman cemetery site at Beckfoot, Cumberland. *CW* (2), XLIX (1949 (1950)), 32 ff.

HOGG, R. and GILLAM, J. P. Excavations in Carlisle, 1953. *CW* (2), LV (1955 (1956)), 59 ff.

HOLDER, A. (see General Bibliography).

HOLLAND, P. *Translation and revision of* BRITAIN, *W. Camden*. London, 1637.

HOOPPELL, R. E. On the Discovery and Exploration of Roman Remains at South Shields in the years 1875–6. *Nat. Hist. Trans.* VII (1880), 126 ff.

—— Vinovia. *JBAA* (1), XLIII (1887), 111 ff., 299 ff., XLVI (1890), 253 ff.

HORSLEY, J. *Britannia Romana: or the Roman Antiquities of Britain*. London, 1732.

HUDDLESTON, C. R. A Roman cremation-burial at Old Penrith. *CW* (2), LII (1952 (1953)), 183 ff.

HUDDLESTON, C. R. and BIRLEY, E. Recent discoveries at Kirkby Thore. *CW* (2), LIII (1953 (1954)), 214 f.

HUNTER, C. *Roman* Inscriptions and Antiquities in *Yorkshire*. *Philos. Trans. Abridg'd,* v, ii, 46 ff. (1721) (=*Philos. Trans.* XXIII, 1129, 1702).

—— An antient *Roman* inscription at *Rochester* in *Northumberland*, and two others at *Risingham*. *Philos. Trans. Abridg'd,* x, iv, 1271 f. (1756) (=*Philos. Trans.* XLIII, 159, 1744).

HUTCHINSON, W. *A View of Northumberland*, Newcastle upon Tyne, 1778.

—— *The History and Antiquities of the County Palatine of Durham*. Newcastle upon Tyne, 1785–94.

—— *The History of the county of Cumberland, and some places adjacent*. Carlisle. 1794.

JACKSON, W. The Camp at Muncaster and certain Roman Discoveries there. *CW* (1), III (1878), 17 ff.

JARRETT, M. G. *Roman Maryport* (unpublished B.A. dissertation, Durham, 1954).

JEFFERSON, S. *The History and Antiquities of Cumberland. I. Leath Ward*. Carlisle, 1840; II. *Allerdale Ward*. Carlisle, 1842.

JRS (Roman Britain in . . .). *JRS*, XI–, 1921–.

JRS (Roman Britain: Inscriptions). R. G. Collingwood, *JRS*, XI (1921), XXVII (1937); E. Birley, XXVIII (1938); R. P. Wright, XXIX (1939).

KEENEY, G. S. Corstopitum as a civil centre. *AA* (4), XI (1934), 158 ff.

—— Excavations at the Roman Fort of Piercebridge in 1939. *DN*, IX, ii (1941), 127 ff.

KILBRIDE-JONES, H. E. and others. The Excavation of a Native Settlement at Milking Gap, High Shield, Northumberland. *AA* (4), XV (1938), 303 ff.

LELAND, J. T. Hearne (ed.), *The Itinerary of John Leland*, London, (2), 1744–5; (3) 1768–9.

—— T. Hearne (ed.), *De rebus Britannicis collectanea*. London, (2), 1770.

LINGARD, J. R. C. Bosanquet (ed.), *Enquiries Sept.* 4, 1800 (First Notebook). *AA* (4), VI (1929), 133 ff.

—— *Mural Tourification, Aug. 24th*, 1807 (Second Notebook). *AA* (4), VI (1929), 139 ff. (editorial introduction *ibid.* 130 ff.).

LIVERSIDGE, J. *Furniture in Roman Britain,* London, 1955.

LOSH, J. Antiquities found at Plumpton in Cumberland in 1812 *(drawings)*. *AA* (1), I, Donations, 2, pl. IX (1822).

LUKIS, W. C. (ed.). *Family Memoirs of W. Stukeley, Roger and Samuel Gale, &c.* *(Surtees Society,* LXXIII, LXXVI, LXXX). Durham, 1882–7.

LYSONS, D. and LYSONS, S. *Magna Britannia.* IV (Cumberland). London, 1816.

MACDONALD, SIR GEORGE. The Roman Forts on the Bar Hill, Dunbartonshire, excavated by Mr Alexander Whitaker of Earlstone, F.S.A. Scot. *PSAS,* XL (1906), 403 ff.

—— The Roman Fort at Mumrills, near Falkirk. *PSAS,* LXIII (1929), 396 ff.

—— The bath-house at the fort of Chesters (Cilurnum). *AA* (4), VIII (1931), 219 ff.

—— Birrens Reconsidered. *PSAS,* LXXXIII (1939), 254 ff.

—— (and see Abbreviations, under *RWS* (2) for *The Roman Wall in Scotland*).

MACDONALD, J. Account of the Excavation of Birrens, a Roman Station in Annandale: The Inscribed Stones. *PSAS,* XXX (1896), 112 ff.

MACHEL, T. A Strange *Well* and some *Antiquities* found at *Kirkbythore* (1687). *Philos. Trans. Abridg'd,* III (1716), 430 ff.

MACKENZIE, E. *An historical, topographical, and descriptive view of the County of Northumberland, and of those parts of the County of Durham situated north of the Tyne, with Berwick on Tweed* Newcastle upon Tyne, 1825.

MACLAUCHLAN, H. Memoir on the Roman Roads, Camps, and Earthworks, between the Tees and the Swale, Yorkshire. *AJ,* VI (1849), 213 ff.

—— *The Watling Street.* London, 1852 (survey).

——*Memoir written during a Survey of the Watling Street from the Tees to the Scotch border.* London, 1852.

—— *A Survey of the Roman Wall.* London, 1858.

—— *Memoir written during a Survey of the Roman Wall.* London, 1858.

MAITTAIRE, M. *Marmorum, Arundellianorum, Seldenianorum, aliorumque, Academiae Oxoniensi donatorum* (2). London, 1732–3.

McKIE, H. U. Remarks and Memoranda as to the Subsoil, Debris, and Ancient Remains discovered in cutting the Sewers in the City of Carlisle. *CW* (1), IV (1880), 337 ff.

NORTH, O. H. A Roman Cremated Burial found near Voreda. *CW* (2), XLII (1942), 232.

NORTH, O. H. and HILDYARD, E. J. W. Trial trenching at Burrow in Lonsdale, 1947. *CW* (2), XLVIII (1948 (1949)), 23 ff.

PENNANT, T. *A Tour in Scotland* (3), II. Warrington, London, 1774.

PETCH, J. A. Excavations at Benwell *(Condercum). AA* (4), IV, (1927), 135 ff. (report for 1926).

—— Excavations at Benwell *(Condercum). AA* (4), V (1928), 46 ff. (report for 1927 and 1928).

POCOCKE, R. (documents on the northern journey of Bishop Pococke) in *Surtees Society,* CXXIV. Durham, 1914.

POWELL, T. G. E. *The Celts.* London, 1958.

RENDAL, G. W. The Benwell Discoveries. *AA* (2), VI (1865), 169 ff.

RICHARDSON, G. H. Excavations at the Roman fort of Piercebridge, 1933–1934. *DN*, VII, ii (1936), 235 ff.

RICHARDSON, M. A. *The local historian's table book of remarkable occurrences . . . connected with the counties of Newcastle-upon-Tyne, Northumberland and Durham.* Historical Division, IV. London, 1844.

—— Certaine verie rare Observations of Cumberland, Northumberland, &c. . . . *Reprints of Rare Tracts and Imprints of Antient Manuscripts, &c.* VII. Newcastle upon Tyne, 1849 (Harleian MSS, no. 473).

RICHMOND, I. A. Excavations on Hadrian's Wall in the Gilsland–Birdoswald–Pike Hill Sector, 1928. *CW* (2), XXIX (1929), 303 ff.

—— The Roman fort at South Shields. (see Bibliography to Part I).

—— Roman Leaden Sealings from Brough-under-Stainmore. *CW* (2), XXXVI (1936), 104 ff.

—— The Romans in Redesdale. *NCH*, XV (1940), 63 ff.

—— Roman legionaries at Corbridge, their supply-base, temples and religious cults. *AA* (4), XXI (1943), 127 ff.

—— The Four *Coloniae* of Roman Britain. *AJ*, CIII (1946 (1947)), 57 ff.

—— Excavations at the Roman Fort of Newstead, 1947. *PSAS*, LXXXIV (1950), 1 ff.

—— *The Roman Fort at South Shields: A Guide* (see Bibliography to Part I).

—— Excavation at Milecastle 49 (Harrows Scar). *CW* (2), LIII (1953 (1954)), 212 f.

—— *Roman Britain.* London, 1955.

—— Excavations at Milecastle 49 (Harrow's Scar). *CW* (2), LVI (1956 (1957)), 18 ff.

RICHMOND, I. A. (ed.) (see Abbreviations (*RW*) and Bibliography to Part I).

RICHMOND, I. A. and BIRLEY, E. Excavations at Corbridge 1938–9. *AA* (4), XVII (1940), 116 ff.

RICHMOND, I. A., ROMANS, T. and WRIGHT, R. P. A civilian bath-house of the Roman period at Old Durham. *AA* (4), XXII (1944), 1 ff.

RICHMOND, I. A., GILLAM, J. P. and BIRLEY, E. The Temple of Mithras at Carrawburgh. *AA* (4), XXIX (1951), 1 ff.

RICHMOND, I. A. and GILLAM, J. P. Further exploration of the Antonine fort at Corbridge. *AA* (4), XXX (1952), 239 ff.

—— (and SIMPSON, G.). Buildings of the first and second centuries north of the granaries at Corbridge. *AA* (4), XXXI (1953), 205 ff.

—— Some excavations at Corbridge, 1952–54. *AA* (4), XXXIII (1955), 242 ff.

RICHMOND, I. A. and STEER, K. A. *Castellum Veluniate* and Civilians on a Roman Frontier. *PSAS*, XC (1956–7), 1 ff.

ROBERTSON, A. S. The Numismatic Evidence of Romano-British Coin Hoards, *Essays in Roman Coinage presented to Harold Mattingly* (ed. R. A. G. Carson and C. H. V. Sutherland). Oxford, 1956, 262 ff.

ROBINSON, J. The Roman Camp at Beckfoot (Mowbray) Cumberland. *CW* (1), v (1881), 136 ff.

Notes on the Excavations near the Roman Camp, Maryport, during the year 1880. *CW* (1), v (1881), 237 ff.

ROOKE, H. *Antiquities in Cumberland and Westmorland. Archaeologia*, IX (1789), 219 ff.

ROY, W. *Military Antiquities of the Romans in Britain*. London, 1793.

ROYAL COMMISSION ON HISTORICAL MONUMENTS (ENGLAND). *An Inventory of the Historical Monuments in Westmorland*. London, 1936.

SHAW, R. C. Romano-British Carlisle: its Structural Remains. *CW* (2), XXIV (1924), 94 ff.

SIMPSON, F. G. Report of the Cumberland Excavation Committee for 1931. 3. Stanwix. *CW* (2), XXXII (1932), 147 ff.

SIMPSON, F. G. and RICHMOND, I. A. Report of the Cumberland Excavation Committee for 1931. 1. Birdoswald. *CW* (2), XXXII (1932), 141 ff.

—— Report of the Cumberland Excavation Committee for 1933. 1. Birdoswald. *CW* (2), XXXIV (1934), 120 ff.

—— The Roman fort on Hadrian's Wall at Benwell. *AA* (4), XIX (1941), 1 ff.

SIMPSON, J. Brougham Castle. *CW* (1), I (1874), 60 ff.

SIMPSON, W. D. Brocavum, Ninekirks, Brougham: a Study in Continuity. *CW* (2), LVIII (1959), 68 ff.

SMITH, D. A Palmyrene sculptor at South Sheilds? *AA* (4), XXXVII (1959), 203 ff.

SMITH, H. Draught of an Antient *Roman* Sweating-Stove. *Gent. Mag.* (1), XX (1750), 27.

STEER, K. A. *The Archaeology of Roman Durham* (unpublished Ph.D. dissertation, Durham, 1938).

STEPHENS, T. (note on a Roman inscription at Woodburn), *PSAN* (3), IV (1910), 287.

STEVENS, C. E. A Roman inscription from Beltingham. *AA* (4), XI (1934), 138 ff.

STEVENSON, J. *Vita Sancti Cuthberti*. London, 1887.

STUKELEY, W. *Itinerarium Curiosum*. I, London, 1724; II (including the *Iter Boreale*), London, 1776.

SWINBANK, B. Pottery from levels of the second and third century, covering the Vallum at Benwell. *AA* (4), XXXIII (1955), 142 ff.

THORESBY, R. Two *Roman* Altars in *Northumberland*. *Philos. Trans. Abridg'd*, III (1716), 425 f.

TOYNBEE, J. M. C. A Roman (?) Head at Dumfries. *JRS*, XLII (1952), 63 ff.

—— Genii Cucullati in Roman Britain. *Latomus*, XXVIII (1957), 456 ff.

URBAN, S. (ed.). Roman Sepulchral Inscription found near Piercebridge. *Gent. Mag.* (2), XXII (1844), 24.

WARBURTON, J. *Vallum Romanum; or the history and antiquities of the Roman Wall, commonly called the Picts' Wall, in Cumberland and Northumberland....* London, 1753.

BIBLIOGRAPHY

WATKIN, W. T. On Britanno Roman Inscriptions, found in 1877. *AJ*, XXXV (1878), 63 ff.

—— Roman Inscriptions found in Britain in 1878. *AJ*, XXXVI (1879), 154 ff.

—— Roman Inscriptions discovered in Britain in 1880. *AJ*, XXXVIII (1881), 277 ff.

—— Roman Inscriptions found in Britain in 1882. *AJ*, XL (1883), 135 ff.

—— *Roman Lancashire.* Liverpool, 1883.

WHEELER, SIR MORTIMER. *Rome Beyond the Imperial Frontiers.* (2), London, 1955.

WHELLAN, W. *The history and topography of the counties of Cumberland and Westmoreland.* Pontefract, 1860.

WHITAKER, T. D. *The history of Richmondshire, in the North Riding of the county of York....* London, 1823.

WILSON, J. The Medieval Name of Old Carlisle. *The Antiquary*, XLI (1905), 409 ff.

WOOLLEY, C. L. CORSTOPITUM: Provisional Report of the Excavations in 1906. *AA* (3), III (1907), 161 ff.

WOOLER, E. *The Roman Fort at Piercebridge, County Durham.* Frome and London, 1917.

WRIGHT, R. P. The Stanegate at Corbridge. *AA* (4), XIX (1941), 194 ff.

—— The establishment of the fort at Chester-le-Street ... (see General Bibliography).

—— (and see under *JRS* (Roman Britain: Inscriptions) above).

WRIGHT, R. P. and GILLAM, J. P. Third report on the Roman site at Old Durham. *AA* (4), XXXI (1953), 116 ff.

ADDENDA

Since the completion of this book the following reports have been published in *Archaeologia Aeliana* (4), XL, 1962:

Carrawburgh. SMITH, D. J. 'The shrine of the nymphs and the *genius loci* at Carrawburgh'. 59 ff. *Severan altar, secondary third-century screen-wall and (after demolition of nymphaeum), fourth-century well.*

Chesterholm. BIRLEY, R. E. 'Some excavations at Chesterholm-Vindolanda'. 97 ff. *Outside south-west angle of the fort—workshop, occupied from mid-third century to mid-fourth, and another building of better masonry.*

Housesteads. BIRLEY, R. E. 'Housesteads *Vicus*, 1961'. 117 ff. *South of the Vallum —Hadrianic rubbish pit, mid-second century workshop (leather and woodworking) lying under early third century temple (Mars Thincsus ?), and two other mid-second century stone buildings; possible Hadrianic timber structure (see also AA (4), XXXIX, 1961, 301 ff.)*

DANIELS, C. 'Mithras *Saecularis*, the Housesteads mithraeum and a fragment from Carrawburgh'. 105 ff. *Discussion of sculptures—in particular providing further evidence for the predominance of officers in Mithraic worship.*

273

The following have also appeared since the compilation of the Bibliography:

BLAKE, B. Excavations of Native (Iron Age) Sites in Cumberland. *CW* (2), LIX (1959 (1960)), 1 ff.

BELLHOUSE, R. L. Excavations at Old Carlisle, 1956. *CW* (2), LIX (1959 (1960)), 15 ff.

—— Excavation in Eskdale, the Muncaster Roman kilns. *CW* (2), LX (1960), 1 ff.

—— Excavation in Eskdale: the Muncaster Roman Kilns. *CW* (2), LXI (1961), 47 ff.

BIRLEY, E. *Research on Hadrian's Wall.* Kendal, 1961.

—— Sir John Clerk's Visit to the North of England in 1724. *DN*, XI (1962), 221 ff.

—— Roman Papcastle. *CW* (2), LXIII (1963), 96 ff.

PREVOST, W. A. J. and BIRLEY, E. Sir John Clerk's Journey to Carlisle and Penrith, August, 1731. *Dumfr. & Gall.* (3), XXXVIII (1959–60 (1961)), 128 ff.

RICHARDSON, G. H. Recent Roman Discoveries at Piercebridge. *DN*, XI (1962), 165 ff.

Note: MACMULLEN, R. *Soldier and Civilian in the Later Roman Empire.* Cambridge, Mass., 1963, arrived too late to be taken into account in the present book.

INDEX I
GAZETTEER OF SITES

The English names are those at present in general use. Roman place-names, where known, are as on the Ordnance Survey Map of Roman Britain (Third Edition), except for VELVNIA (Carriden), the conclusive evidence for which is inscription (26), discovered after the map was compiled. Four-figure National Grid references are appended. Page references (in heavy type) are to the main site descriptions.

275

INDEX II

GENERAL

References to the main descriptions of sites are in heavy type

Aballava, see Burgh-by-Sands
Aelia Ammilusima, 259
Aelia Comindo, 219
Aelia Proculina, 251
P. Aelius Bassus, 259
Aelius Mansuetus, 220, 237
Aelius Mercurialis, 230
Aelius Surinus, 259
Aemilianus, 254
Aemilius Macer, 33
L. Aemilius Pertinax Acceianus, 223
Aesica, see Greatchesters
Afutanius, 211
Agricola, 1, 5, 47
Agriculture, in the frontier region, 114
Ahtehe, 27, 60, 228
Aicetuos, 134, 248
Alaisiagae, 90
ala I Asturum, 62, 258
    Petriana, 46, 100, 133, 247
    II Pannoniorum, 28
Alauna, see Maryport and Watercrook
Aldborough (*Isurium Brigantum*) 182f
Alexander Severus, 33f
Alföldi, A., 32
Allectus, 3, 197, 198
Alston, 95
Amandus, 107
Ambleside, **124f,** 151, 204, inscr. 208
Anicia Lucilia, 215
Annamoris, 18, 136, 214
Annexes, in Scotland, 156f
Antenociticus, 70, 76
Antonia Stratonice, 140, 238
Antoninus Pius, 184f
Apollonius, 91

Apullio, 251
Apulum, 10n, 179n
Aquincum, 10n, 12, 25, 181
Arbeia, see South Shields
Architecture, in the frontier region, 165f
Arrian, 28, 157
Arrius Paulinus, 252
L. Arruntius Salvianus, 62, 258
Astarte, 19n, 21, 60n
Ateanctis, 220
Athens, votive capitals, 133
Auchendavy, 24, 156, **159f,** inscr. 208
Audagus, 136
Augendus, 258
Augst, Römerhaus, 169
Aurelia Achaice, 227
Aurelia Aia, 221
Aurelia Afra, 22n, 231
Aurelia Aureliana, 216
Aurelia Eclectiana, 225
Aurelia Eubia, 280
Aurelia Fadilla, 145, 251
Aurelia Lupule, 111, 254
Aurelia Quartilla, 111, 255
Aurelia Senecita, 215
Aurelia Victorina, 77, 234
Aurelius, 18, 134, 249
Aurelius Acilius, 144n, 145f, 251
Aurelius Concordus, 210
M. Aurelius Ianuaris, 226
Aurelius Iulianus, 210
Aurelius Marcus, 221
Aurelius Pusinnus, 137, 138, 250
Aurelius Quartinus, 255
Aurelius Severus, 211
Aurelius Tasulus, 244

Suetonius, 246
Swinbank, Dr B., 13, 73
Swinbow, F., 210
Swoboda, 169n

Tacitus, 23n, 29n, 181n, 188n, 195
Tancorix, 245
Taunenses, 13n
Taylor, J., 215
territorium, 151, 188f
testatio, 32
Theodosius, 4, 63
Theodotus, 111, 159, 211, 252
Thoresby, R., 222
Thrace, 171
Threlkeld, 131
Titullinia Pussitta, 32, 109, 243, 250
Trade, 24f
Trajan, 2
Tranquilla Severa, 219
Traprain Law, 184
Trimontium, see Newstead
Towns, 41f
Toynbee, Professor J. M. C., 257
Troesmis, 10n
M. Troianus Augustinus, 259
Tunnocelum, see Moresby

Ulmetum, 221
Ulpia Traiana, see Xanten
Ulpian, 177n, 180
Ulpius Apolinaris, 216
Ulpius Marcellus, 186
Unseni Fersomari, 133
Ursa, 225
Uxellodunum, see Castlesteads

Vacia, 217, 230
Valerius Maximus, 25n
Vallum, 68f, *et passim*
van Berchem, 188n
Vechten, 169n
Vegetius, 24n
Vellibia, 229

Velunia, see Carriden
Venicones, 182
Venus, 118
Venutius, 37, 182, 184
Vercovicium, see Housesteads
Verecunda, 159, 208
Verterae, see Brough-under-Stainmore
Vetera, see Xanten
Veterans, 27f, 29, 38, 81
Veteres, 19, 94, 229
Vettia Mansueta, 222
Vibia Pacata, 260
vicani, 177f, *et passim*
vicus, 9f, 179f, 180f, 190f, *et passim*
Victor, 24, 27, 61, 62, 64, 239, 258
Victory, 43, 85
Villy, 137
Viminacium, 10n
Vindicianus, 247
Vindolanda, see Chesterholm
Vindomora, see Ebchester
Vindonissa, 11, 24
Vinovia, see Binchester
Virunum, 10n
Voreda, see Old Penrith
Vortigern, 119
Votadini, 16, 182, 184
Vrocata, 209
Vulcan, 19, 21, 25f, 223, 243

Wall, Antonine, 4, 66, 155f, 221, 223
Wall, Hadrian's 66f, *et passim*
Wallis, 91n
Wallsend, 26n, **69f**, 165n
Warburton, 225, 252
Watkin, 250
West Brandon, 142
Watercrook, 7, 124, 126f, 170, inscr. 259f
Watson, Mr and Mrs K., 208
Westerwood, 160, inscr. 260
Wheeler, Sir Mortimer, 132n, 171
Whellan, 131n
Whitaker, 137

PLATE I

Piercebridge *vicus*

Photograph by J. K. S. St Joseph. Crown copyright reserved.

PLATE II

Carlisle: Tombstone of a lady with a fan (22)

PLATE III

(a) South Shields: Tombstone of Regina (107)

(b) South Shields: Tombstone of Victor (108)

PLATE IV

(*a*) Old Carlisle: bronze steelyard weight

(*b*) Carrawburgh: mithraeum and *vicus* west (left) of the fort

PLATE V

Corbridge: Streets and strip-houses as crop marks in the western part of the town, looking east. The Stanegate runs diagonally from bottom to top of the picture and Dere Street emerges to meet it from beneath the aircraft's wing. The granaries and part of the west compound are visible at the top

PLATE VI

Ewe Close: native settlement, probably a village

Photograph by J. K. S. St Joseph. Crown copyright reserved.

PLATE VII

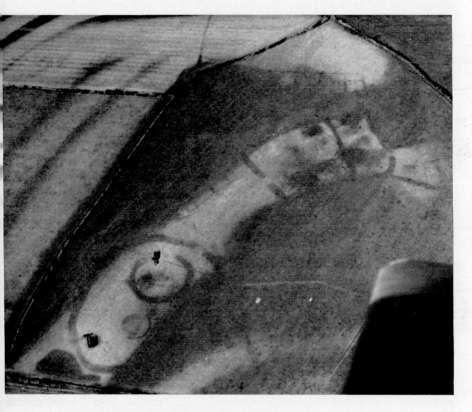

Wolsty Hall: native farms

PLATE VIII

Maryport: strip-houses along the road north of the fort

Photograph by J. K. S. St Joseph. Crown copyright reserved.